'KEEPING THE LAKES' WAY'

Reburial and the Re-creation of a Moral World
among an Invisible People

Paula Pryce

Virtually unknown of First Nations in Canada, the Arrow Lakes or Sinixt Interior Salish of the North American Columbia Plateau have been declared officially extinct. This book investigates why this circumstance came about and how contemporary Sinixt have responded.

Most of the Arrow Lakes people have lived in diaspora for a hundred years or more, due in part to destructive mining activity in their historical territory. Since 1989, many have made pilgrimages to an ancient burial ground and village site at Vallican, British Columbia, where they have worked against many obstacles to protect ancestral remains exhumed by archaeologists and road-builders. Paula Pryce explores this history, showing how time is culturally embedded in the land. Social memory, time perspectives, sense of place, and the act of reburial have enhanced cultural continuity, meaning, and identity among the Lakes people.

While telling a troubling story of dispossession and diaspora, grave sites and reburials, this powerful narrative also looks at the complex process of the construction and reconstruction of identity in a world of constantly shifting boundaries. It is the first book devoted to the story of the Sinixt.

PAULA PRYCE is a writer and anthropologist who grew up in the historical territory of the Sinixt Interior Salish, British Columbia.

'KEEPING THE LAKES' WAY'

Reburial and the Re-creation of a Moral World among an Invisible People

PAULA PRYCE

UNIVERSITY OF TORONTO PRESS
Toronto Buffalo London

© University of Toronto Press Incorporated 1999
Toronto Buffalo London
Printed in Canada

ISBN 0-8020-4419-0 (cloth)
ISBN 0-8020-8223-8 (paper)

Printed on acid-free paper

Canadian Cataloguing in Publication Data

Pryce, Paula
   'Keeping the Lakes' way': reburial and the re-creation of a moral world
   among an invisible people

   Includes bibliographical references and index.
   ISBN 0-8020-4419-0 (bound)   ISBN 0-8020-8223-8 (pbk.)

   1. Sinixt Indians.   2. Sinixt Indians – Funeral customs and rites – British
   Columbia – Vallican.   3. Cemeteries – British Columbia – Vallican.

   E99.S2P79 1999   971.1'62004979   C99-930965-X

University of Toronto Press acknowledges the financial assistance to its publishing program of the Canada Council for the Arts and the Ontario Arts Council.

This book has been published with the help of a grant from the Humanities and Social Sciences Federation of Canada, using funds provided by the Social Sciences and Humanities Research Council of Canada.

University of Toronto Press acknowledges the financial support for its publishing activities of the Government of Canada through the Book Publishing Industry Development Program (BPIDP).

Canadä

In memory of my father, Colin John Pryce

*Remembering his childhood in the Himalayan foothills,
he chose this land for me*

Contents

Acknowledgments

I thank the Sinixt people at the village and burial site at Vallican, British Columbia, for welcoming me. In particular, I acknowledge the help and interest of Robert Watt, Marilyn James, Bob Campbell, Eva Orr, and Jackie Heywood. Robert Watt and Jackie Heywood were especially generous in giving me access to original correspondence and many other important documents, some of which were unavailable elsewhere.

My gratitude goes to University of Toronto Professors Krystyna Sieciechowicz and Stuart B. Philpott, whose encouragement and direction have been important to the development of the ideas in this book.

I acknowledge the financial assistance of the Pisapio Scholarship Trust of Nelson, British Columbia, and Ontario Graduate Scholarships.

Thanks go to my parents, Margaret and Colin Pryce of Castlegar, British Columbia, who gave me both moral and logistical support during my fieldwork in Vallican, and to the other members of my family, each of whom has contributed to my work as a writer and anthropologist.

I greatly appreciate friends and colleagues who have encouraged, assisted, inspired, and guided me, especially Jeanne Iribarne, Alicia Hawkins, Susan Roy, Alan Cairns, Tom Heintzman, Anne Vallely, Mark Mealing, Helen Lee, Bob Galois, and Michael Freisinger.

Very special thanks go to my compatriot Gastón Gordillo for our many provocative and clarifying conversations, his astute suggestions, his willingness to read and reread, and his fearless criticism.

Finally, I thank Tom Pryce-Digby, who has tirelessly offered his keen eye for literary rhythm and logic, his faith in my pursuit of a sometimes taxing profession, as well as his proofreading, patience, cooking, and unyielding support.

While each of these people has made invaluable contributions to the writing of this work, I nevertheless accept full responsibility for any mistakes or misinterpretations herein.

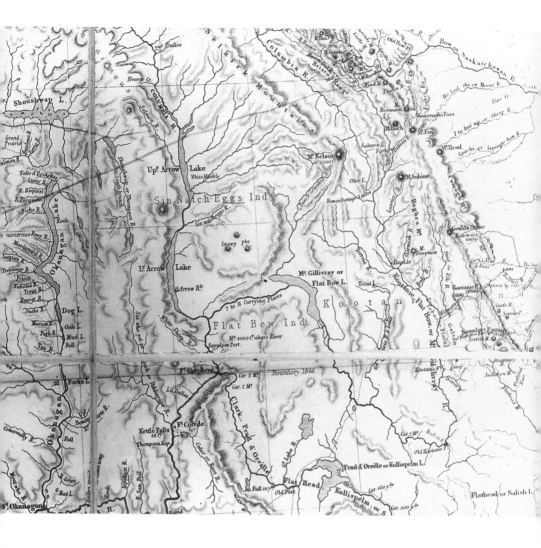

Map 1 Portion of 'The Provinces of British Columbia and Vancouver Island; with portions of the United States and Hudson's Bay Territories, Compiled from Original Documents by John Arrowsmith, 1859.' Note 'Sin Natch Eggs Ind.' and the absence of the Slocan valley, a key portion of their territory. Map from Hudson's Bay Company Archives, Provincial Archives of Manitoba.

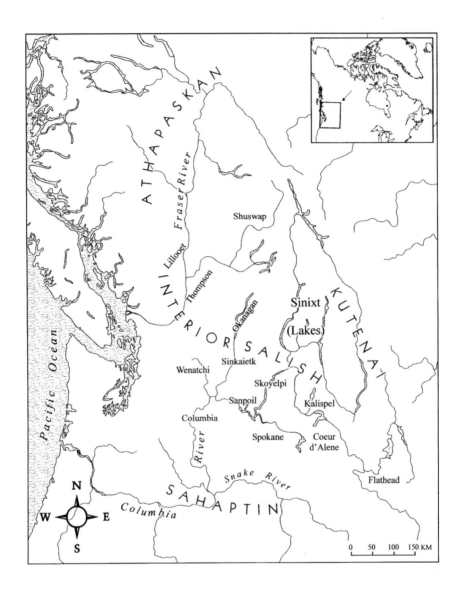

Map 2 Columbia Plateau linguistic families, detailing selected Interior Salish languages.
Map by Hermina A. van Gaalen.

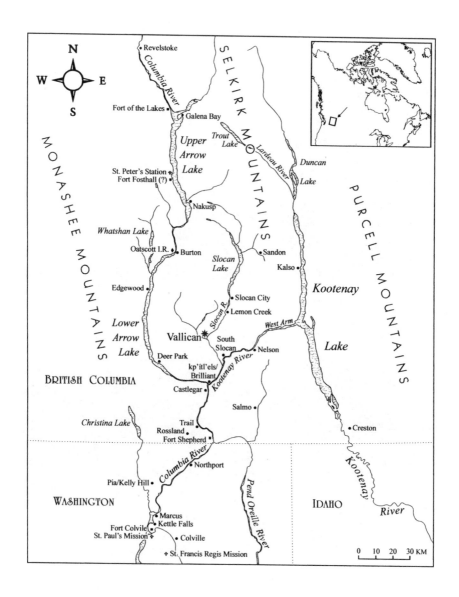

Map 3 Area of discussion, including historical locations of Hudson's Bay Company forts and Jesuit missions. Map by Hermina A. van Gaalen.

Tipis mark the cut line, protesting road building in the vicinity of the Vallican village and burial site. Photo by Cliff Woffenden.

Early days of the Sinixt encampment, showing the Council Fire where most important decisions concerning the Vallican burial site are made. Photo by J. Swan.

Robert Watt frames the roof of the new indoor kitchen, built with the help of non-Sinixt supporters. Photo by J. Heywood.

Eva Orr (right) welcomes Abbot Jangtse Chojey Rinpoche and other visiting Tibetan Buddhist monks to the Vallican burial site. Photo by J. Addington.

Robert Watt (left) and biologist Wayne McCrory hike into the White Grizzly Wilderness Area in the Selkirk Mountains. Photo by J. Heywood.

Gathering wild ginger at Vallican.

Robert Watt and Marilyn James discuss future logging plans for Sinixt territory with provincial forestry officials in Grand Forks, BC. Photo by J. Heywood.

Bob Campbell after a 1998 reburial at Vallican. Photo by P. Pryce.

'KEEPING THE LAKES' WAY'

Introductions:
The Journey Home

By the time I was nine years old, I frequently made my way down the gravel road to the confluence of the Columbia and Kootenay Rivers. I had a habit of sitting among the river stones and comparing them to the veined, precipitous rock cliffs of Mount Sentinel. Before me Tin Cup Rapids varied in fierceness, depending on the whim of engineers at Hugh Keenleyside Dam, and sometimes foamed with effluent discharged at night from the pulp mill upstream.

The Columbia River valley at Castlegar, British Columbia, is a broad seam between mountain ranges, teethed with gravel benches left behind from the meltwaters of the last sweep of glaciation. Great walls circle the valley, in places heavily forested, sheared round from the blanket of moving ice. Some peaks to the north still retain their crags, high enough in altitude to have been above the grinding force, rock islands in the ice.

The striking double-peaked Mount Siwash is further off, up Kootenay River way. Rising above the others on the east side of the valley, its curved face is the last to collect the colour of sunset and the first to disappear into thunder clouds. My father told me that it was named after an Indian word – devil, he thought it meant. I had difficulty forming the concept of 'Indian' in that context, confused partially by my father's stories of growing up in his birth-country, India, and partially by the fact that I had never met a North American 'Indian' nor did I know of any in the West Kootenays, where we lived. In British Columbia, with its large aboriginal population, such vacancy is an oddity, but to me, not having lived anywhere else in the province, it was the unquestioned norm. Hence, my idea of 'Indian' lay somewhere in a blur of hooting movie actors stomping around a campfire, Southeast Asia, and the black and red drawings (strange and frighteningly bold, I thought) of the Northwest Coast. Certainly, Indians had nothing to do with my own place or time.

Siwash and the other mountains, I knew, were immeasurably old. And the smooth striped stones I held in my hand, I was sure, had come from those mountains a very long time ago. People, by contrast, appeared incomparably new. Time, a faint scratch on that imposing landscape, began for us with the oldest house in Castlegar. A log cabin surrounded by horse pasture on the dirt road to the river, it was dwarfed entirely by the aged ranges around it. Not far off sat more evidence of the beginning: a rusting, decrepit rock crusher on which I sometimes played, an abandoned piece of machinery in the eaten-out hollow of a gravel bed. Along with the nineteenth-century Silver Rush ghost towns and Second World War shacks left over from interned Japanese Canadians, these artefacts, these droppings of humanity, were the most ancient of relics in my world.

I was aware of this uncloseable gap between mountain-time and people-time, and had no idea that there might have been a greater depth of history embedded everywhere in the land around me.

It was not until I was twenty years old, when I had gone away to live with Aymara people in Bolivia, that I began to seriously wonder why there were no aboriginal peoples in the valley of my birth. Some years after this, back home in the winter of 1989, I came across a congregation of tipis with my friend Helen. Having lived most of my life in the West Kootenays, I was certain that this was not a usual sight and was thoroughly confused by their presence there. We were on a wooded gravel road near Vallican on the Slocan River close to my friend's cabin, one valley east of the Columbia River. Helen explained to me the circumstances of this unlikely settlement: the mountain road on which we travelled had only recently been built, and during excavation, the bulldozers had turned up human remains. The Indians were here to see that no more burials were disturbed.

Smoke curled from one of the canvas structures into the dingy overcast, indistinct against the grey, but there was little movement otherwise. A few camping trailers, lean-tos, and a pile of firewood were also scattered among the spindly conifers. The scene looked rather dreary to me, and a little foreboding. Tipis were not part of my cultural vocabulary, even though I was then an anthropology student at the University of British Columbia, and they certainly appeared misplaced in this valley. For me, the Slocan Valley was associated with a variety of peoples: hippies and draft-dodgers, Doukhobors, loggers and millworkers. But Indians? Not in my lifetime and not in the time of anyone I knew.

'No cars,' said Helen. 'Maybe they've gone into town.'

'Who are they?' I asked. 'Kutenais?'

The year before, Helen had been my supervisor at the nearby West Kootenay National Exhibition Centre, where I had been hired to write a children's ethnobotany on the Kutenai Indians. I had yet to comprehend that just because this region was called the West Kootenays it was not necessarily the historical territory of Kutenai peoples.

'No, they're Interior Salish,' she explained.

I noticed then a 'No Trespassing' sign posted by the British Columbia Heritage Trust, indicating that this was a recognized archaeological site newly protected by the provincial government.

'They came up from the Colville Reservation in Washington State,' she said. 'They call themselves the Arrow Lakes Band.'

'Arrow Lakes? Never heard of them.' I tried to recall some of the linguistic maps I had studied while at university. 'Oh, you mean the *Lakes*? But I thought they were extinct.'

'Apparently not.'

Another winter afternoon a few years later, a little colder and just as grey, I approached the Vallican camp to inquire about fieldwork. I had left a note tacked to an empty A-frame cabin a day or so before to tell them who I was and when I would return. I knew they would want to know my purpose. Why should they consider working with me? What did I want? Good questions, but since my ideas were then just forming, they were not so easy to answer. Perhaps I hoped to consider the ill-shaped tensions I felt growing up in this monumental land: how do people fit against this bold landscape? What stories are locked in these crevasses of rock? What place do humans have here? And more recent questions: who are you? Where did your people go and why have you come here to seek them?

The Lakes' appointed caretaker of the Vallican burial grounds, Robert Watt, and his partner, Jackie Heywood, were expecting me. In this first meeting with them, the old anthropological classics came to mind, ethnographies which open with a predictable narrative of the fieldworker's journey into a romanticized 'wild' unknown. 'Here's an ironic twist,' I thought. 'This time the "unknown" is coming to me, the anthropologist, and the narrative is about my own home.' But this was my home in a way I had not understood it before.

The difference between our ideas of my home became evident in just one afternoon's discussion. And this difference became even more apparent after I confessed that I had lodged my truck into a snow bank trying to get up an icy gravel road, despite many winters' experience driving in the mountains. Robert Watt and I spent a considerable time shovelling, chaining, and hauling – a good ice-breaker, so to speak. At one point we stopped to rest from our digging and Robert pointed to a mountain on the close horizon. It was one I had always marvelled at when travelling through the Slocan Valley: broad and flat-topped like an anvil. It was unusual and elusive, only visible on certain curves in the road.

'That's Frog Mountain,' Robert said, telling me a little of its story. 'Do you see the frog?'

I looked and looked but couldn't see any frogginess about it. 'No.'

He traced the mountain's shape: 'See? That slope is the back and tail. There's the eye and the nose pointing up at the sky.'

I squinted to see from his perspective. It took a while but I got it: there was definitely a frog in that mountain, and in a moment something so familiar was changed irrevocably. The truck free, I set off for Castlegar, looking with new suspicion at a landscape I had always known. How different from his are those cultural layers I cast onto the land?

Here began my work with the Arrow Lakes people. I returned several months later in the summer of 1994 to learn more of what this land holds for them. I chose to work at the Vallican encampment and the surrounding area rather than travelling to those Lakes people who remained at the Colville Reservation in Washington. The pull of the Slocan brought people from all over, and it became clear that for some Lakes people the journey to the Vallican burial grounds was a kind of pilgrimage. Most came from Colville, but they also came from other reservations and regions – people who trace their matrilineage to the Lakes and their historic territory even though they have lived among other ethnic groups for some generations. I became interested in what drew them to this camp with its modest arrangement of tipis, open-air kitchen, and single one-room cabin. Indeed, it was these Vallican 'pilgrims' – their feeling of connection with the landscape and the ancestors buried therein – who became the focus of my work.

The Arrow Lakes Band, also known as the Sinixt Interior Salish, have occupied the Vallican site in the Slocan Valley of southeastern British Columbia since 1989. They have withstood many bureaucratic and legal struggles to keep their presence in the region. Their goal is to protect the gravesites from further disturbance and to repatriate those remains which have been exhumed from the site during preconstruction archaeological assessments of the area. Neither this endeavour nor their maintenance of a 'security camp' has been easy, however, because this people's traditional territory was bisected by the international border between the United States and British North America in 1846.

Most Sinixt have resided south of the line for several generations and have been considered Americans by others since the mid-nineteenth century. Although they are officially recognized in the United States on the Reservation of the Colville Confederated Tribes, the Canadian government has determined the Arrow Lakes Band to be 'extinct' since 1956. As a result, this people is currently not a legal entity in Canada and has therefore had little credibility with either the institutions which hold their ancestral remains or Canadian immigration authorities. Several deportation orders and governmental surveillance have made life difficult for the Sinixt at Vallican.

One member of the band, Robert Watt, has challenged the government's position in the Federal Court of Canada, basing his case on the fact that the international boundary bisects Sinixt traditional territory. His view is that, whether born in Canada or the United States, his people should be able to travel and reside freely anywhere within their cultural homeland. Contributing to the confusion is the fact that the Sinixt have not dwelled as a cohesive group in the Canadian portion of their territory for several generations because of various historical factors, including heavy silver and gold mining activity which has caused much social disruption since the 1850s. Furthering the quandary, several adjacent First Nations in Canada have chosen to incorporate the West Kootenays into their land claims negotiations with the federal and provincial governments. This people's extinct status in Canada, in conjunction with an ethnographic and historical record which has remained largely unpublished, places the Sinixt at Vallican into a position of political ambiguity.

Despite their obscurity in Canada and the scattered documentation of their presence in the area, both archival and published materials show that the Sinixt Interior Salish resided along the Columbia River, Arrow Lakes, Slocan Valley, and parts of Kootenay Lake in what is now called the West Kootenays of Canada. Chapter 2, 'Presence,' discusses Sinixt ethnography and the larger anthropological classification to which it belongs, the Plateau culture area of North America. In particular, it discusses how anthropologists have made a greater contribution to the obscurity than to the knowledge of the Sinixt. Indeed, although they are recognized, the Sinixt are usually discussed only briefly or as an aside to their cultural neighbours. In addition, much of the more comprehensive writing on this people has been left to moulder unpublished. Anthropologists have failed to offer a clear view of Lakes people. Certainly, such incohesiveness and inaccessibility of data has caused a near vacuum of knowledge, especially in Canada. Here I draw together the dispersed references not so much to describe the ethnographic details of the Sinixt's world as to reveal the cultural distinctiveness of Sinixt identity. Identity is the cultural basis of the relationship of living Sinixt with their ancestors and is therefore a major motivator in their occupation of the Vallican burial site.

Chapter 3, 'The Latent Land,' similarly strings together the Lakes' unvoiced story, this time from disconnected pieces of historical data. Like the ethnographic record, historical documentation on the Sinixt is equally obscured. Much historical data remains unpublished, languishing in various archives or in the private possession of individuals. Published information tends to be hidden deep in the folds of missionary and fur trader diaries. Those scholars who have attempted a comprehensive overview of West Kootenay history have often chosen a starting point that is well after most Sinixt had already been displaced from their land. Some offer brief or skewed information on the aboriginal inhabitants of the area. My aim in this chapter is not to catalogue every historical reference to this people, but to uncover the key factors which led to the Lakes' diaspora and their *latent presence* north of the international boundary.

Because of its rugged terrain, the northern territory was settled late by non-native immigrants. Many Sinixt appear to have taken advantage of their initial isolation and kept a healthy distance from immigrant communities when necessary. Even though the Plateau Indian Wars against the United States government may have made the north safer for the Sinixt in the mid-1800s, the effects of epidemics and the people's involvement with fur traders and missionaries seem to have increased a southerly focus. Nevertheless, it was not until the West Kootenay Silver Rush of the 1880s and 1890s that the refuge-like quality of the north was thoroughly shattered.

Although some Sinixt maintained residence north of the boundary into the twentieth century, most moved either onto the Colville Reservation in Washington State or among other First Nations in British Columbia. Their contact with the area since then has been limited but consistent; over the years some have quietly traversed the boundary to berry-pick, fish, and attend religious sites. Many living Sinixt have never travelled this way, though oral histories have kept alive an awareness of the land upstream.

The Vallican site has recently drawn many Lakes people north to the place of their ancestors. Today, the Sinixt at Vallican hold fast to an ideal of protecting and reburying their ancestral remains, even through innumerable obstacles. Why would they bother with such an effort, one which has brought them poverty and imprisonment, among other difficulties, when most of these people had not even visited the site before road crews began construction? Many Lakes people have a strong sense of cultural identity in spite of the fact that historical circumstances have dispersed them. In particular, they have social memory which attaches them to their land.

This cultural sense of place, passed on in part through oral accounts of specific locations, fuses historical people with those living today; that is, people from different times come together through the memories associated with certain places, thereby fostering a sense of continuous cultural identity. In addition to this association with particular sites in their territory, the Sinixt also seem motivated in their repatriation and reburial by the ideas behind a historical movement which anthropologists have called the Prophet or Ghost Dance. During my fieldwork with the Lakes, I found that ideas of prophecy, the destruction of our present reality, and resurrection exist side by side with discussions about the importance of protecting the graves of their ancestors. For the Lakes, protecting the ancestors is a way of protecting their world from collapse. These ideas, along with the social memory which gives Vallican its significance, make the Sinixt's activity at the gravesite crucial enough to withstand the challenges they face from a number of opponents.

Certainly, the Sinixt see themselves as an ethnic group which has continuous historical identity. Others, however, see them as an anachronism, a people which no longer exists as a cultural, political, or legal entity. In chapter 4, 'Competing Prophecies,' I outline the theoretical basis for some of the conflicting world views of European North Americans and First Nations peoples. The expectations of European North Americans that Indians would inevitably vanish is rooted in nineteenth-century Social Darwinism. Such expectations, or *prophecies* if you like, come from an idea that one cannot be both aboriginal and modern, that Indians are only Indians because they have stood still in time, have been changeless. Aboriginal peoples, on the other hand, seem to be quite comfortable with the fact that they still exist. Unlike those held by some European North Americans, their prophecies have claimed that the ancestors shall rise up to set the universe back in its proper order.

In effect, we have two competing prophecies, one claiming that aboriginal peoples will or have already vanished, the other asserting their enduring cultural and political strength. The 'broken culture' motif of the dominant society claims that social change constitutes a breach in historical consciousness and cultural identity, while aboriginal peoples' position sees no incongruity in the coexistence of change and continuity. To be sure, change and continuity are not opposites; rather, change is an integral part of the continuity of any culture. Ethnic identity does not rest in people being relics of a frozen past, but instead comes from their current understanding of a connection with that past.

The Sinixt's situation at Vallican reflects this ongoing conflict between world views. In the minds of Canadians, the Sinixt have indeed vanished and their late resurrection does nothing but confound authorities and local residents alike. From the Sinixt's perspective, they always have and always will exist as a people. The problem here is that the dominant society's opinion tends to have more political power than the assertions of a small, marginalized ethnic group.

Chapter 5, 'Emergence,' examines how social memory has encouraged the Sinixt to publicly reclaim their territory in Canada despite the obvious obstacles. Vallican is considered important partly because it is a complex archaeological site and one of the very few which have not been destroyed by hydroelectric projects in the West Kootenays. More than this, social memory of both the Slocan Valley region and ancient mortuary practices has motivated the people's desire to protect the gravesites at Vallican. As mentioned, such memory is also accompanied by ideas of prophecy, destruction, and resurrection. Inspired in part by what they consider to be the immoral actions of those who disinterred their ancestors, the Sinixt have recently found a focal point of cultural identity in the Vallican site.

Yet identification with their land does not stop here. These people feel they need to create a viable working community, a moral world away from the fray of the various competing factions which challenge their sense of righteous living. The world is endangered by the selfish practices of such people, they feel; it will fall to pieces with the weight of the immorality of their political, economic, and spiritual behaviour. Like their ancestors' earlier response to the arrival of immigrants, the Sinixt of today hope to create a refuge from the inevitable destruction, one in which they can be free of both native and non-native bureaucracies and one which incorporates their ethical code of reciprocity, egalitarianism, and peace.

In light of this desire 'to keep the Lakes' way,' as one elder puts it, performing reburials at Vallican has become a symbolic act of resurrection. For an ethnic group which seeks its autonomy, it is a way of putting the world back into its proper order. The act of reburial re-establishes the appropriate relationship with the ancestors, with the land in which they are buried, with their continuous identity in space and time. To put ancestral remains back into the earth where they belong is like planting a seed: it is like planting an ideal society, one in which they can assert their ethnicity, their idea of justice, and a life of spiritual, political, and economic morality.

chapter two

Presence:
Sinixt Interior Salish Ethnography,
or the Contribution to Obscurity

Ceremonies and fishing and berry-picking, it all went underground. If you want to maintain that, you got to be quiet about what you do.

Marilyn James, Sinixt

I allowed the Shuswap the territory along Arrow Lakes almost down to Robson. I had not then been in that district, and was misled by some statements of the Shuswaps of Shuswap Lake region, which appeared to be corroborated by white testimony, to the effect that the Arrow Lake country was former Shuswap territory, partly occupied in recent years by Colville Indians chiefly for hunting and trapping purposes. This is not correct ...

James Teit, Columbia Plateau anthropologist, c. 1910[1]

The Vallican archaeological site in southeastern British Columbia tells us only a little of their story. It tells us that some people had a village, and that the Slocan Valley was a good place to live. People stayed there a long time, more than two thousand years. Sometimes they lived as a nuclear family in their own home, and sometimes several families lived together. The site also tells us a little about the food they ate, how they got it and prepared it. Through the burials, it suggests something of their ideas about politics and death. It even suggests cultural affiliations with other peoples around them; the style of housing and burials shows us a cultural link to some of their neighbours. But what the Vallican site cannot tell us for sure is this: what those people called themselves two thousand or even five hundred years ago, or what language they spoke. No archaeological site can tell us something as temporal as that.

For archaeologists, identity is tricky. So is political territoriality. Physical objects are limited in what they say about ethnic identity, something as contemporary and ever-changing as the way people view themselves. They cannot look at an arrowhead and proclaim definitively that the person who put it there was Nubian or French or Haida or Lebanese, even if the style of artefact is considered to be culturally diagnostic. After all, the person who made the object may not be the one who used it. Archaeologists confirm connections between places and peoples through corroborative historical and ethnographic documentation and oral history.

In Canada, identifying the culture of archaeological sites and drawing the boundaries of aboriginal territories are treacherous propositions. Such acts are fraught with difficulties: freezing territoriality to a particular time, forcing it to conform to bounded ideas of the modern nation-state, ignoring the subtleties of interplay between neighbouring peoples. The current state of land claims negotiations magnifies the trials of such a project; there is much to lose when, intentionally or not, a government pits First Nations against each other over territory they may have once shared, or fought for, or traded in, or travelled through.[2]

There is ethnographic and historical evidence to support the Sinixt's claim to the Slocan and other parts of the West Kootenays. I do discuss territory in this chapter, but it is not the important part of the story. Let us focus instead on how these people perceive the land they call their own: what it means to them. Yet to understand some of the cultural meanings at play in Vallican, we must first understand the history of how the Sinixt have been categorized both by themselves and by others.

Significantly, an integral part of the way the Sinixt feel comes from their invisibility. Their invisibility to other peoples has made the Lakes' cultural, political, and economic life unstable. How ethnographers have categorized (and miscategorized) the Sinixt helps us understand not only who this people is today, but also how other peoples' ignorance of them has impacted upon them. It gives us some idea why a place of their own like Vallican – a place where the Sinixt can live as *they* understand themselves – is so crucial to them.

A poor ethnographic record is one of the main reasons the Sinixt are little known today, especially in Canada.[3] Reviewing the ethnographic literature on the Sinixt, I illustrate in this chapter how vague and sometimes contradictory academic renderings have perpetuated confusion about this people. In particular, I examine erroneous or misleading linguistic and cultural classifications as well as the multiple labels by which this group has been named. While exploring their contribution to the

Sinixt's obscurity, I discuss how some ethnographers have proffered a clearer picture of the Sinixt's cultural distinctiveness, particularly in regards to their political systems and spiritual life. In addition, I consider how the ethnographic and historic literature depicts the boundaries of an historical Sinixt homeland before the Lakes people concentrated their community in the southern part of the territory, in what is now the United States of America.

Before comparing ethnographers' lists of cultural attributes, however, I must comment upon their actual worth in giving us a clear understanding of the Sinixt's ethnic identity. As Frederik Barth (1969) points out, ethnicity is not an object to be quantified. We cannot separate out all the parts of a group's way of life, find the differences, and hold these up as icons of a distinct identity. True enough, difference between language, economy, political structure, religious life, territory, and so on may well affect a people's sense of distinction from other peoples. Yet, like archaeological artefacts, such 'objective' cultural traits alone cannot house identity. Identity is more ambiguous than this, residing very much in social memory, in a people's contemporary understanding of their connection to a cultural history. In other words, identity comes from the way individuals currently define their group through time, not from fixed cultural lifeways. If it were dependent upon fixity, no group would have a sense of identity since every culture continually changes. Identity is not found only in ways of behaviour and thought, but also in a view of oneself and one's people.

For years, ethnographers endeavoured to list all the components of objective culture, usually in an 'ethnographic present' which relegates peoples to cultural stasis. They made up these lists in an effort to draw boundaries between dissimilar lifeways and thus define cultural identity. However, divergent political and cultural identities can exist between peoples who, according to their matching ethnographic details, should be of a single unified culture. Gastón Gordillo (1992: 68) describes the confusion that ethnographers can create when they presume that cultural similarity is equivalent to homogenous ethnic identity. In the 1930s, says Gordillo, Alfred Métraux wrote that the Tobas and Pilagás of the Pilcomayo River of the Argentine Chaco were actually a single people (which he called the 'Tobas-Pilagás') even though they themselves made statements to the contrary. The Tobas and Pilagás still *appear* to be culturally similar to outsiders, yet to this day these peoples consider themselves politically and ethnically distinct from one another.

In this chapter on Sinixt Interior Salish ethnography, we will see that anthropologists working among Columbia Plateau peoples have made comparable misidentifications. While the exploration of ethnographic data which follows is important to our understanding of the Sinixt, we must not make the mistake that these descriptions of ways of life – that 'objective' cultural features – are the only factors determining their ethnic identity.

What's in a Name?

Many gaps exist in the ethnographic record, yet that record in conjunction with historic sources offers enough data to round out a partial picture of Sinixt lifeways from the early nineteenth century to the present. Nevertheless, inconsistent and inaccurate scholarly presentation of that data has caused obstacles to a general understanding of the Sinixt. The method by which the Sinixt have been named in the literature as well as the categorization of their language shows a kind of academic chaos. Beginning in the very first written records, an inconsistency of terminology causes disarray not only for anthropologists and historians but also for governments and the public, who both depend upon the accuracy and integrity of scholarly exploration.

As one might expect, the first written names of aboriginal[4] peoples in North America were usually conjured by those Europeans first on the scene, principally fur traders and missionaries. These names do not necessarily reflect the title an ethnic group has used for itself. Written names were chosen by newcomers who often did not speak local languages and who preferred words more sensible to themselves than to the people they attempted to define. Thus, ethnic labels sometimes described physical attributions, as in the case of the Nez Percé's bodily adornment. Or perhaps they made reference to a geographical description of the people's territory or a colonial bureaucratic department with which they were associated. One group often donned several non-native names, and these multiple variations can be bewildering, especially in historical documents which use arbitrary names that are not well contextualized geographically or linguistically. The most frustrating reference of all ignores any specification of ethnicity: generic terms like 'Indian' and 'native' are used liberally in the historic literature. Although a researcher may suspect the ethnicity of the group to which an author refers, such terminology usually defies positive identification. Despite the inaccuracy of these non-native terms, they often stay on historic, ethnographic, and governmental records indefinitely.

As is true of most aboriginal peoples in North America, Interior Salish-speaking peoples like the Sinixt have suffered the inconsistent labelling of outsiders. Along with the English terms Arrow Lakes and Lakes, Sinixt (thus spelled by current band members) is the indigenous term these people use for themselves.[5] As the Sinixt do, I use the terms interchangeably. Verne Ray (1933: 11), an anthropologist who worked extensively in the Columbia River Basin during the first half of this century, noted that 'Sinixt' comes from their word *a'itckst^u*, meaning 'a small speckled fish of the upper Columbia river,' either lake trout or Dolly Varden char (Teit 1930: 199; Bouchard and Kennedy 1985: 6, 99).[6]

Initially, immigrant authors did not often use the term Sinixt to refer to this people. One of the first non-natives in the area, the geographer David Thompson (1971 [1811]: 313) gives us our first known historical reference to people on the Arrow Lakes when they helped him through the lake ice in the autumn of 1811. Unfortunately, Thompson does not name these people. It is possible that fur traders were slow to distinguish the Sinixt because trade missions did not frequent the heart of this people's territory in the Slocan Valley. Indeed, the isolated Slocan, where the most populous Sinixt villages were situated, was one of the last places non-natives 'explored' and does not appear on some maps even as late as 1859 (John Arrowsmith 1859; see Map 1) and 1872 (British Columbia 1872).

Hudson's Bay Company records at Fort Colvile refer to several different ethnic groups generally as the 'Chaudières' by francophone fur traders. Known as the 'Kettles' in English, they were so named for their association with Kettle Falls, where the fort was established on the upper Columbia River in 1825. These various peoples were also called 'Colvilles' for bureaucratic reasons, namely to identify them as peoples who hunted furs for trade at Fort Colvile.[7] These terms confound the literature; it is often difficult to determine to which ethnic group a document refers. If there are no other clues, such as a chief name or village location, it may be impossible to accurately identify ethnicity. Even though 'Kettles' and 'Colvilles' now usually refer to the Skoyelpi Interior Salish,[8] whose territory lies directly south of the Sinixt's, one cannot depend upon historical or even contemporary documents to be accurate in their distinction.

To further the confusion, since the establishment of the Colville Reservation in Washington in 1872, the eleven resident ethnic peoples often use a bureaucratic shorthand for self-identification. They 'speak of themselves as "Colvilles" though they belong to many divergent groups' (Ray 1936b: 111, n. 19).[9] For these reasons, the Colvilles or Kettles which many authors describe may actually include Sinixt Interior Salish and other peoples.

A recent publication on the West Kootenays, *Historic Nelson*, exemplifies the stubbornness of this obfuscation. Despite his reference to documents which thoroughly discuss the distinction between Lakes and Skoyelpi (e.g., Bouchard and Kennedy 1985), author John Norris (1995: 34) considers the two groups to be synonymous 'Colvilles.' Similarly, Ruby and Brown (1986: 36) place a famous Sinixt chief, Aropaghan, under the rubric of 'Colville,' even though the authors themselves warn against mistaking 'the Colvilles proper' (that is, Skoyelpi) for fellow Colville Reservation residents.[10]

Even though they have been lumped into generalized regional categories, the Sinixt were nevertheless recognized for their cultural distinctiveness from the early nineteenth century. Soon after the arrival of nonnative immigrants, this people was named for its area of residence in the large narrow lakes on the upper Columbia River. Francophone fur traders and missionaries called them 'Les Gens du Lac de la Colombie' or simply 'Gens des Lacs' (De Smet c. 1842–8; Québec Mission 1955: 16). In English this became Lake, Lakes, or Arrow Lakes people after their practice of lodging arrows into a certain rock cleft high above the water line (De Smet 1905: 549). Occasionally in the early 1800s they were called Columbia Lake people, as in Dease's 1827 citation (Bouchard and Kennedy 1984: 102).[11]

The spelling of oral languages continues to be divergent, except for professional linguists who use standardized systems like the International Phonetic Alphabet.[12] Speakers of English and French did not have the literary tools to transcribe the unusual sounds they heard when speaking with aboriginal peoples, and thus the spellings differ wildly, even within the writings of a single person. Consider David Thompson's (1971 [c. 1811]: 290, 313; 1994: 334) 'Ilthkoyape' Falls for what is now commonly spelled 'Skoyelpi,' or his 'Teekanoggan' and 'Occhenawaga' for 'Okanagan.'

So too, the word 'Sinixt' is variously spelled, depending upon the ear of the listener. The earliest possible version I have located is difficult to confirm because of its strange spelling: the Arrow Lakes are labelled 'Chatthnoo-nick' on an 1814 map by Aaron Arrowsmith, the information for which came largely from David Thompson (Belyea 1994: xii). Although I have not seen any other application of this spelling, it is a plausible version. Spelled 'Sinachicks,' the earliest fully attributable reference of which I am aware appears in 1824, found among the letters of Hudson's Bay Company Governor George Simpson (1931 [1824]: 169; cf.

Bouchard and Kennedy 1985: 6). After this, many versions of 'Sinixt' appear, offered in the writings of fur traders, missionaries, ethnographers, government officials, as well as Lakes people themselves. Appendix 1 lists a selection of spellings through the nineteenth and twentieth centuries.

As we have seen, designating a group's name is a complicated task which sometimes causes error and ambiguity. Linguistic classification can provide equally puzzling results. The Sinixt language is part of the Interior Salish linguistic family which, according to Jorgenson (1969), has six Interior Salish language groupings. These are the Okanagan/Lakes/Sanpoil, the Thompson/Shuswap, the Lillooet, the Wenatchi/Columbia, the Spokane/Kalispel/Flathead, and the Coeur d'Alene. James Teit (1930: 198) adds 'Colville' to the Okanagan/Lakes/Sanpoil group, as do Bouchard and Kennedy (1984; 1985), although these latter scholars use the aboriginal name Skoyelpi, spelled 'sx̱weyí7lhp.' Teit, Bouchard and Kennedy, and Spier (1936) also include a southern Okanagan dialect, the Sinkaietk. Considering these additions by other anthropologists, it becomes evident that Jorgenson excludes a number of language dialects from his Okanagan/Lakes/Sanpoil linguistic division. All this variation points to ethnographers' collective indecision about how to classify the language group to which the Sinixt belong.

Often foreshortening this linguistic division to 'Okanagon' (Duff 1969; McMillan 1988; Teit 1930) or 'Okanagan-Colville' (Bouchard and Kennedy 1984; 1985), ethnographers imply (or directly state) that the other languages within that grouping are offshoots. In this framework, Sinixt is rendered as a subset of the 'true' Okanagan or Okanagan-Colville language; they become 'an Okanagon-speaking tribe,' a subordinate rather than one of several dialects which make up a larger class (see, for example, Duff 1969: 32; Dyen 1962: 160–1; Turnbull 1977: 16). In some cases, such as in the work of Anastasio (1974), the Lakes are entirely absent. This omission is also true in the publications of Canada's recent Royal Commission on Aboriginal Peoples, or RCAP (1996). While other Interior Salish language groups in Canada – the Lillooet, Shuswap, Thompson, and Okanagan – make a significant appearance, RCAP makes no reference to the Sinixt anywhere in its voluminous studies.

More reliable than RCAP and the others, thorough classifications can be found in the scholarship of Verne Ray (1933: 9–10; 1936b: 107), who avoided this linguistic conundrum by listing each of the subgroups or by employing categories the native peoples use themselves. Using the latter method, he calls the Okanagan/Lakes/Sanpoil linguistic group in question 'nsi'ltxtctn.' Kehoe (1981: 359) has also offered a clearer treatment of linguistic diversity by listing most dialects separately.[13]

Of People and Culture

Despite some of the confusion outlined above, scholars have nevertheless categorized the Sinixt Interior Salish as a unique cultural entity. But, as we found in the linguistic classifications, that entity does not stand alone in the minds of anthropologists. The Sinixt have been placed into a much larger class of ethnicity called the Columbia Plateau culture division of North America. Of course, like any category, the idea of Plateau has its limitations.

Anthropological culture divisions in North America have been largely based on ecological paradigms. Geographically, the Plateau includes the watersheds of the middle and upper Columbia and upper Fraser Rivers. Its reaches thus defined, this culture area incorporates four separate linguistic families: Athapaskan, Sahaptin, Kutenai, and Interior Salish (see Map 2). Before the extensive damming of rivers for flood control and the generation of electricity, salmon was the major staple, and continues to be important in some areas. Roots, particularly bitterroot, were also a key food. The majority of the Plateau constitutes a dry belt, 'sagebrush-juniper and partly bunch-grass steppe, with pine forest on the higher levels' (Kroeber 1963 [1939]: 55–66; Ray 1939).

To those familiar with the geography of the Sinixt's historic territory, this people's placement within the Plateau culture category may seem strange. The West Kootenay region has none of the ecological features which define the classic Plateau: it is neither dry nor flat, it has neither sagebrush nor bitterroot, and there are no vast expanses on which to run large herds of horses. Sinixt territory could hardly be more different. Unlike the arid and open terrain of those peoples to the south, the east, and the west of them, the Sinixt homeland is one of steep, jagged mountain ranges which are either thickly treed to near impenetrability, or barren with rock cliffs. In between these are long narrow lakes, large rivers, small areas of marsh, and the occasional flat bench created by fluvial deposits or glacial meltwaters. A few patches here and there on the eastern side of the Columbia River valley are covered with the balsam root and Ponderosa pine forests indicative of aridity, but the dominant local ecosystem is moist enough to be classified as temperate rainforest, the precipitation being much higher here than anywhere else in the desert-like Plateau.[14]

The terrain of the West Kootenays clearly contrasts with the usual picture of the Columbia Plateau. Why then are the Sinixt part of this cultural division? The key is to remember that ecology is not destiny. Alfred Kroeber (1963 [1939]) has been careful to remind us that ecological formulations are heuristic devices rather than strict laws which define bounded geographical units of rigid, reified culture types. Influenced strongly by the historicism which was introduced to anthropology by his teacher Franz Boas, Kroeber emphasizes that these 'geographical units of culture' simply show how environmental conditions can affect lifestyle choices. More important, he stresses, is the impact of history in creating cultures:

> While it is true that cultures are rooted in nature, and can therefore never be completely understood except with reference to that piece of nature in which they occur, they are no more produced by that nature than a plant is produced or caused by the soil in which it is rooted. The immediate causes of cultural phenomena are other cultural phenomena. (Kroeber 1963: 1)

Cultural areas, then, are more *historical* than they are ecological; they are open to shifts and variation depending on any number of volatile factors, including migration, environmental change, contact with other culture groups, and internal innovation.

Evidently, Alfred Kroeber's conceptual framework does not approve of the frozen-in-time constancy of 'ethnographic present' theories which have been prevalent in anthropology. Kroeber acknowledges the challenge of working in North America where the time-depth of written history is limited. This restriction has required that scholars devise other methods of understanding oral societies, such as spatial classifications rather than temporal ones. However, the temptation has been to go a step too far, to presume that space has been more influential than time. Scholars have pushed theoretical tools to an erroneous extreme, believing that an absence of documentary evidence indicates an absence of history. Kroeber argues vehemently against this perspective of 'timelessness.' Yet as we shall see in forthcoming chapters, even today, some sixty years after Kroeber made his stand and a hundred years after Franz Boas first provoked us to consider an historical approach, many scholars still have difficulty grasping that cultures everywhere are indeed products of history.

The Sinixt have been classified as a Plateau people not because of geography, then, but because of their historical connections to other peoples in the culture area. Culturally, they share certain important features with other groups on the Plateau. Having worked most of his professional life on the Columbia River, anthropologist Verne Ray (1939) was devoted to showing the distinctiveness of the Plateau while still acknowledging the considerable diversity within it. Ray concludes after years of study that Plateau peoples share several prevalent though not uniform cultural traits. Some of these are: an ethic of social egalitarianism and local autonomy, an emphasis on pacifism,[15] and strong concepts of the vision quest, guardian spirits, and shamanism. Ray (1936b: 110) also notes the central importance of salmon in the area as well as a tendency to share and trade resources across cultural groups, especially at salmon fisheries. Despite their ecological distinctiveness, the Sinixt have all of these features to varying degrees. Ethnographers have therefore found it academically useful to include them within the category of the Plateau. While he agrees with this classification, Verne Ray (1936b: 108) nevertheless separates the Sinixt Interior Salish into a distinctive Columbia Plateau subcategory.[16]

Here again arises Kroeber's dilemma: anthropologists' tendency to inadequately consider the sway of history when describing North American aboriginal cultures. While Ray and others consider the Sinixt to be distinctive among Plateau peoples, they also acknowledge their similarity to the Skoyelpi and Sanpoil, those peoples to the south among whom the Sinixt immigrated during the nineteenth century. Considering this recently intensified cultural contact among neighbours, how do we understand who the Sinixt were historically, how they have changed, and as a result, who they are today? There is no simple answer to understanding a people through time. Our aids are ethnography, oral and documentary history, and archaeology. Yet with such confusion in the literature, the task of defining Sinixt identity and history is not easy.

Ethnographers Randy Bouchard and Dorothy Kennedy (1984; 1985; 1997) have attempted to rectify this dilemma by making thorough investigations into the historical and ethnographic documents describing this people. Through these, Bouchard and Kennedy have revealed that the Sinixt do indeed have a particular cultural, linguistic, and geographic past, and while doing fieldwork among Lakes people in Washington State beginning in about 1978, they have also noted a strong contemporary ethnic identity among them. This powerful sense of identity has been similarly noted by other scholars, including myself (cf. Teit 1912; Ray 1936b: 115; Chance 1973: 25; Eldridge 1984: 50). During my fieldwork since 1993, those Sinixt people with whom I worked at Vallican have shown a profound feeling of cultural unity and distinctiveness from other aboriginal peoples. Indeed, they have expressed great frustration at their current state of anonymity or mistaken identity, realizing that they are often dropped by non-Sinixt into various other categories rather than being understood and identified on their own terms.

Having lived in the northern portion of Sinixt territory most of my life, I can confirm that this confusion among academics is shared by most local West Kootenay residents. As far as I am aware, there were very few non-natives in the area who had knowledge of the Sinixt during my child-hood or at the time of my fieldwork; my references to the Arrow Lakes people typically elicit a blank, uncomprehending stare.[17] Given the legal circumstances of deportation cases as well as the official governmental position that the Arrow Lakes people are extinct, the Canadian bureaucracy appears similarly ignorant.

At least part of this confusion has arisen as a result of sporadic and patchy ethnographic fieldwork among Arrow Lakes people. No major work or comprehensive ethnography has been written on the Sinixt. However, James Teit, Verne Ray, William Elmendorf, Randy Bouchard, and Dorothy Kennedy have done limited fieldwork, the latter three without publishing their results.[18]

Significantly, no anthropologist was in the area before the majority of Sinixt began to winter among the Skoyelpi people near Fort Colvile at Kettle Falls, Washington, in the nineteenth century. Often ethnographers have assumed the Sinixt to be ethnically similar to neighbouring peoples, either to the Skoyelpi and Sanpoil, as in Ray's (1939) example, or to the Shuswaps and Okanagans as in Teit's (1909b; 1930). Again, very little of the listed ethnographers' material has been published, the remainder being confined to personal fieldnotes and unpublished manuscripts for bureaucratic agencies. The lack of available data has sometimes caused secondary writers to unwittingly draw faulty conclusions. One notable mistake, the reputable British Columbia anthropologist Wilson Duff (1969: 32) depicts the 'Arrow Lakes Tribe' as 'a small mixed group' affiliated with Shuswap, Okanagan, and Kutenai speakers.[19]

Besides its inaccessibility, another of the ethnographic literature's restrictions is that the small amount of available information focuses overwhelmingly on the Sinixt's political economy. Despite their limitations, these data do offer an illustration of this group's cultural particularity. In *Cultural Relations in the Plateau of Northwestern America*, for example, Verne Ray (1939) has attempted to show how political structures differ from one group to another. He notes that the Lakes were unusual in that, unlike most of their neighbours and allies, their political organization was not focused on local village autonomy, but rather on a more central-ized governing system. After having done fieldwork with the Sinixt, Ray (1939: 11; 1975) concludes that they had developed a 'tribal organiza-tion' distinct from their neighbours. He writes:

> The northern-most group of the Columbia Basin, the Lakes, exhibited quite a different type of political unity. A marked feeling of solidarity seems to have grown out of the uniqueness of their habitat. They occupied a series of interconnecting lakes and rivers over which they travelled in circuits, making for a maximum of social intercourse and demanding considerable coopera-tion. Moreover, they were effectively shut off from adjacent groups on the west and north by high mountain ranges. Though conditions of this nature do not in themselves produce political unity ... they may prove significant factors in such a development. Among the Lakes this development appears to have occurred. (Ray 1936b: 115)

Elmendorf (1935–6) and Bouchard and Kennedy (1985: 41, 62–9) cor-roborate Ray's position with their historical investigation of Sinixt leader-ship. They establish that, quite unlike the village-centred polities around them, this group recognized a single chief for the entire area. Chiefs could be either male or female. In fact, the most favoured chief in mem-ory is a woman, the mother of the long-time nineteenth-century chief, Grégoire.[20] In carrying out their duties, Sinixt chiefs relied on the advice of a council of 'thinkers' appointed from the various local groups, and on the talents of individuals who presided over salmon fisheries or led spe-cific military and hunting excursions. Although these 'sub-chiefs' had influence, decision-making ultimately rested with the main chief. Sinixt chieftainship tended to be loosely hereditary, depending on whether an individual was considered suitable and able to fit the demands of the pre-dominant role, that being one of 'peacekeeper.'

Grégoire certainly took the diplomatic aspect of his position seriously. Ray recounts this chief's part in arresting a violent confrontation between the Spokane and the Lakes in southern Sinixt territory:

> Gregory, the Lakes chief, stripped off his clothing and walked between the two opposing lines. The Spokane shouted for his death, saying that score would thereby be evened. But Gregory spoke: 'You say that nothing but my death will stop you from fighting.' Turning to his own people he continued, 'There is nothing to stop you from fighting except your own will power.' Then to all, 'When I lie dead, the sun will disappear behind the clouds; there

will be no sun. Deep darkness will prevail. No one can know how long it will remain dark. There will be no children, no old crippled folk. I do not wish to frighten you. But if you drop your arms, the trail will be open. We shall have no more bloody days until the end of our time. You can kill me if you will, but if you drop your arms, there will be no more bleeding. We shall have an open trail.' And it is said that the antagonists dispersed. (Ray 1939: 36–7)

Grégoire's speech to the Spokane and Lakes shows a political dependence on rhetoric and diplomacy. While Chief Grégoire used his rhetorical skills to gain 'a wide reputation as a peacemaker among whites and Indians' (Ruby and Brown 1986: 188), historic evidence suggests that 'keeping the peace' sometimes included the use of corporal punishment. Commanding officer of the Hudson's Bay Company's Fort Shepherd, Jason O. Allard (1926) states that Grégoire 'ruled his tribe with an iron hand ... and did not hesitate to have some of his warriors publicly whipped if they broke any of the rules he established for the conduct of his people.' Even so, both David Chance (1973: 32, 96–8) and Bouchard and Kennedy (1985: 63) make note of an earlier source which describes chiefly powers in a different way. John Work, the second manager of the Hudson's Bay Company's Fort Colvile, stated in 1829 that chiefs had little authority in the way of punishment and instead played a role more like that of an arbitrator. Physical discipline was probably instigated by the Hudson's Bay Company and missionaries, who used such control tactics liberally (cf. Whitehead 1988: 16). Whether this is true or not, the degree of authority which Lakes chiefs possessed appears to be distinctive from the more egalitarian forms of political structure found elsewhere in the region.

While revealing some of the contradictions in the ethnographic literature, this examination of political structure also illuminates the distinctiveness of Sinixt culture. Other ethnographic data on the Sinixt, such as local economic strategies and house-building techniques, similarly show some of the ways they differ from neighbouring peoples. We know, for example, that during the fur trade the Sinixt were considered the best beaver trappers in the Fort Colvile region (Heron 1830–1 in Bouchard and Kennedy 1984: 105; Chance 1973: 47). In his 1935–6 fieldnotes, William Elmendorf further describes their seasonal rounds:

The adaptive strategy of the Lakes involved winter occupancy of semi-permanent river villages and temporary summer occupancy of fishing, berrying and root-digging camps. With the arrival of spring, the winter village population would disperse and family groups would move out to a succession of temporary camps where they hunted, fished and gathered for several weeks at a time. Foodstuffs obtained were dried and cached at these temporary camps until enough had been accumulated to last over the winter months. These were collected at the end of the season [and transported] ... to the winter village ... by canoe and packing. (Elmendorf 1935–6 quoted in Eldridge 1984: 5–6)

Unfortunately, this sort of depiction is not overly detailed. It does not offer us too much idea of how the lives of Sinixt people varied from other Plateau peoples, even though we can extrapolate that their unique territory alone must have made some kind of difference to subsistence activities. Yet Elmendorf (in Bouchard and Kennedy 1985: 48) does elaborate. He mentions, for instance, that bitterroot and white camas, on which other Plateau peoples were highly dependent, were unavailable in the wet climate of Lakes territory. Also, fishing and smoking kokanee or 'red fish,' a land-locked salmon found abundantly in West Kootenay waters, were of particular importance to Sinixt subsistence. Interesting to note, Mary Marchand, one of the Sinixt informants of Bouchard and Kennedy (1985: 97), explained that the meaning of *slhu7kín* (Slocan) is 'pierce' or 'strike on head,' most likely in reference to harpooning salmon, which were much more plentiful in the Slocan area before the extensive damming of the Columbia River. Despite this evidence that salmon and other fish were an important staple for this people, Bouchard and Kennedy (1985: 36, 43) claim that 'the Lakes depended more on hunting than on fishing,' unlike most of the Plateau peoples around them.[21]

In regards to their housing, Ray (1939: 137–8) states that the Sinixt erected temporary conical mat lodges when pursuing hunting and gathering activities away from the established winter village. These structures were similar to those of their southern neighbours. However, the Lakes' unusual method of building their circular semisubterranean dwellings – the winter pithouses unique to parts of the Plateau – demonstrate cultural distinctiveness:

The Lakes pit lodge differs considerably from those of the Shuswap and other neighbors. A roof of radiating poles is encountered here, a type of construction dominant to the south. The central posts are likewise absent. The roof is sufficiently steep so that the radiating poles maintain their positions after being anchored in the ground and tied to the hatchway frame. The foundation poles are spaced about four feet at the base. These are

crossed by horizontal purlins or hoops, both inside and out. Then stub
rafters are placed and covering material added. (Ray 1939: 135)

This technique of pithouse construction does show differentiation from
those neighbours who developed other Interior Salish styles (Shuswap,
Okanagan, Sanpoil, Thompson, etc.), and from those who did not have
pithouses at all (Kutenai, Kalispel, Coeur d'Alene, Spokane, Flathead,
etc.).

Like seasonal rounds, however, housing designs do not tell us a great
deal about how the Sinixt felt about their homes, or their winters, or their
neighbours, or in fact themselves. While they can infer ways of thought,
many data on material culture do not offer us specifics the way the
Sinixt viewed the world: their philosophies, their stories, their desires,
their fears. One expects this single-minded collection of economic information from fur traders' journals, but it is surprising that neither missionaries, who were present in the district from about 1836 (Chance 1973:
33), nor anthropologists cared to fully detail Sinixt world view.

As limited as this kind of information is, the record is not entirely
blank. William Elmendorf (1935–6 in Mohs 1982a: 67–8) mentions that
the Sinixt are a matrilineal people who generally followed an endoga-
mous matrilocal marriage pattern. Well into the nineteenth century,
polygyny was relatively common, the practice of which required the establishment of a separate household for each female spouse. Families lived
either as nuclear groups in single lodges or more frequently in multi-
family dwellings. Women had a separate quarter in the village where they
secluded themselves during menstruation, puberty training, and child-
birth. Women, according to Elmendorf's informant, Nancy Wynecoop,
did not take sweatbaths in earlier times, whereas men constructed sweat-
lodges in their own place of retreat a little distance upstream from the
village. As well, women and men were apparently discouraged from
speaking together in public.

Bouchard and Kennedy (1985: 51–2) note that this gender segregation
among the Sinixt was probably less pronounced than Mrs Wynecoop suggested since 'early traders and trappers reported that [temporary] Indian
camps were limited to one or two lodges inhabited by both men and
women together' and that 'such rigid segregation ... seems unlikely in a
society where women could be chiefs and could obtain the right to speak
at assemblies.'

A cycle of ceremonies followed annual subsistence activities. According
to Elmendorf (1935–6 in Mohs 1982a: 61, 71–2), women's plant gather-

ing was celebrated every spring with a 'fruitful season ceremony' during which women sang and danced through the daylight hours while the men provided them with food. The men burnt any leftover food to ensure that the harvest of fruits, nuts, and roots would be plentiful in the gathering season to come. There were also 'first salmon,' 'canoe building,' 'fall hunting,' and 'winter dance' ceremonies.

Lakes people continue to hold the Winter Dance on the Colville Reservation; the first Winter Dance at Vallican took place in December 1998. Furthermore, they had a culturally specific sun ceremony, which has now taken on many Lakota attributes. Bouchard and Kennedy (1985: 5) note also that the Sinixt celebrate 'root feasts' at Kelly Hill, Washington, possibly a current version of Elmendorf's 'fruitful season ceremony.' Another adaptation of this and the first salmon ceremony may be the Thanksgiving celebrations which have taken place at Vallican since 1989; these also feature root, berry, salmon, and wild game harvests.

As part of the Lakes' ceremonial life, Elmendorf (in Mohs 1982a: 69) describes a Lakes 'tribal emblem,' the Mountain Goat, signified by a 'tribal pole' which bears the skull of the symbolic animal. The pole represented Sinixt genealogy since the time of creation and was held in the custody of the chief. Interestingly, the Skoyelpi and the Okanagans had similar forms of insignia, but theirs are Coyote and White Wolf respectively.

In addition to these examples of Sinixt cultural life, William Elmendorf (in Mohs 1982a: 71) also sketches out a death concept and cultural taboos in his fieldnotes, but only briefly. According to him, the Sinixt of an earlier era believed that the spirits of righteous people 'merge with the entire body of nature like a bubble melting or bursting into a stream.' The depiction is painfully bare. Worthy of consideration, Bouchard and Kennedy (1985: 52) suspect that Elmendorf's informant's view had taken on a rather derogatory 'Victorian' tone from having lived with missionaries. The perspective with which she provided Elmendorf contributed a significant amount to the understanding of women's work, for example, but appears to have been somewhat limited in other areas.

Like Elmendorf, Verne Ray (1937; 1939; 1975) must also have inquired about Sinixt conceptual and spiritual life during his fieldwork in 1931 and 1944, since his comparative work offers positions, although limited, on guardian spirit concepts and death practices. Ray claims that the Lakes lived a life dominated by 'power' in which they sought 'a highly specific relationship with a powerful [spiritual] ally available for personal action in any exigency.' Guardian spirit quests and formal training, undertaken before puberty among the Lakes, included taking sweatbaths in an isolated sweatlodge and attempting journeys to 'the land of the dead.' Guardians were usually animal spirits which take human form upon contact. Sinixt youth were required to find their guardian spirits or 'power' as individuals; they did not receive them as an inheritance as did some other Plateau peoples.

Ray claims also that the Lakes received their power through a vision, not a dream as among other peoples. If that power took control over its host, a shaman would attempt to subdue the guardian spirit and bring the person back to the human world. While the spirit quest was open to all, according to Ray, the more rare shaman's power revealed itself to only a few. Either male or female, Sinixt shamans were ritual specialists who hold particular powers as bestowed by a specific shamanic guardian spirit. Such specialization was not considered to be a personal or social choice; rather, the shamanic guardian spirit itself was said to choose its candidate (Ray 1937: 593; 1939: 76, 80–1, 83, 88, 91–5).

Only recently published, a work written by a Plateau woman, Christine Quintasket (Mourning Dove 1990), corroborates some of Ray's and Elmendorf's assertions on the guardian spirit and other aspects of Sinixt world view. Although heavily edited by Jay Miller, *Mourning Dove* nevertheless offers greater insight into the cultural life of Lakes people than the sometimes sketchy notes of ethnographers. Christine Quintasket wrote this autobiography sometime before her death in 1936. The author, who goes by the pen-name Mourning Dove, grew up at Pia (now known as Kelly Hill) which, according to Bouchard and Kennedy (1984: 100, 398–9) and my own field data, is a central location of the Sinixt community in Washington State. In fact, Bouchard and Kennedy (1985: 5) have called Kelly Hill 'the focal area for the "Lakes experience" today.'

Largely set in that locale, Christine Quintasket's important work outlines the female life cycle and spiritual training, as well as political economy and religious institutions like the Winter Dance and shamanism. The information is richly detailed, relayed in personal accounts of family and community life from the late 1880s onward. Quintasket also includes oral histories of earlier times which she had received from her grandmother and other elders. While those peoples which Christine Quintasket describes may not be exclusively Sinixt, she herself is of Sinixt-Skoyelpi descent and many of the incidents of which she writes occur in traditional Lakes territory among Lakes people.[22] Along with certain aspects of Sinixt cultural life, her work allows us to see a portrayal of the complex multiethnic relationships which occur between peoples of the Plateau. Quintasket's material is helpful in understanding some of the activities

among the Sinixt at Vallican today, thus I offer some of the specifics
of her work as required later on, particularly in chapter 5, 'Emergence,'
in which I discuss the significance of the contemporary practice of
reburial.

Through the documentation of writers like Christine Quintasket,
Verne Ray, William Elmendorf, Randy Bouchard, and Dorothy Kennedy,
we find that both aboriginal and ethnographic descriptions and historical
references of the Sinixt Interior Salish clearly exist. Yet for most people,
Sinixt Interior Salish people remain invisible. The Canadian Department
of Indian Affairs, for example, has a long history of mistaking the Sinixt
for other peoples in the region. In a 1903 report, the DIA (in Turnbull
1977: 116) reveals both its ignorance of the Sinixt and its confusion
between aboriginal groups that it does recognize. It says that the Sinixt
'are Shuswaps or Kootenays ... [who] speak the Shuswap language.' A
more recent letter from the Department of Citizenship and Immigration,
Indian Affairs Branch, to a late Member of Parliament, Herbert W. Herridge, shows no less ignorance of the Sinixt. The acting director states
therein that the 'Indians of the Arrow Lake Band were said to be
Shuswaps who married into a Kootenay family that lived and hunted for
years along the Columbia River' (Gordon 1963).

It is possible that Canadian ethnographers may have been influenced
by this governmental miscategorization of Sinixt people. James Teit
(1909b: 450), for example, asserts in an early publication that the Lakes
people are a political extension of the Shuswap. In fact, he published this
commentary on the Sinixt without ever having visited their territory. Teit
did have access to governmental records, but his initial information was
obtained at least in part from Shuswap sources. A few years later Teit did
fieldwork in the Arrow Lakes area. As indicated in his fieldnotes as well as
letters to anthropologist Franz Boas and various Indian agencies, he
changed his position on Sinixt ethnicity and territoriality (Teit 1909a;
1910–13; 1912). In an unpublished notebook, Teit writes:

In my paper on the Shuswap [1909a] ... I allowed the Shuswap the territory
along Arrow Lakes almost down to Robson. I had not then been in that district, and was misled by some statements of the Shuswaps of Shuswap Lake
region, which appeared to be corroborated by white testimony, to the effect
that the Arrow Lake country was former Shuswap territory, partly occupied
in recent years by Colville Indians chiefly for hunting and trapping purposes.
This is not correct. The Lake tribe occupied from very early times all the
country in British Columbia as outlined in the accompanying map [showing

the Columbia River valley north from about Kettle Falls and the general West Kootenay area], and I have been unable so far to collect any evidence that any part of the territory was ever occupied by other tribes. Further inquiry among the Shuswap confirms this. (Teit 1910–13)

Unfortunately, in his influential 'Salishan Tribes of the Western Plateau,' Teit (1930) does not offer this concise and clear retraction of his earlier published mistakes. Instead, new information on the Lakes is entrenched in a larger body of work on the Okanagan. While some good ethnographic information on the Sinixt does exist in this work, Teit nevertheless adds to the confusion by lumping them into the greater category of 'Okanagon' without sufficiently delineating their political and cultural life. In effect, he relieves them of one mistaken identity, that of the Shuswap, to bestow them with another. Verne Ray (1936b: 109) also criticizes James Teit for this brief treatment and overgeneralization of not only the Lakes, but of many northern Interior Salish peoples.[23] The damage Teit's vagueness does is considerable because, being ignorant of his omissions, later writers such as Graham (1945; 1963; 1971) and Lakin (1976) have taken his work as authoritative.

Despite the existence of Sinixt ethnography as witnessed in the work of James Teit and others, the record evidently lacks clarity and cohesiveness. As a result, some ambiguity about the Sinixt Interior Salish persists in the minds of anthropologists, bureaucrats, and the general population. Yet even with so flawed a literature, we have found that Sinixt ethnography points to this people's differences from their Plateau neighbours. However, as important as this ethnographic particularity is, we must remember the wisdom of Frederick Barth (1969): these quantifiable differences, these lists of ethnographic details do not themselves create the core of distinctiveness. Rather, ethnicity and identity emerge from how a people understands itself, how a people feels in juxtaposition to others.

Of People and Place

While the ethnographic oversights and contradictions of anthropologists are significant, another factor further contributes to the Sinixt's obscurity, especially in Canada. This factor is the people's changing pattern of winter residence. For reasons to be discussed in the next chapter, the Sinixt began a trend of decreasing utilization of their northern territories in the nineteenth century. For some generations now, Lakes people have not lived in permanent villages in the Canadian portion of their territory, a situation which has created a kind of vacuum of knowledge about local indigenous history and identity among both the Canadian bureaucracy and the settler communities of the West Kootenays.

Adding to the perplexity, various other First Nations in Canada now publicly claim what the Sinixt consider to be their own traditional territory. For example, Sophie Pierre, chief of the St Mary's Band (Ktunaxa Nation [Kutenai]), has been interviewed in local newspapers, the *Castlegar Sun* (Imhoff 1993a) and the *Trail Times* (Imhoff 1993b). Therein she claims that her traditional homeland 'spans the entire East and West Kootenays as well as the upper part of Washington State and Idaho,' from an area 'north of the Upper Arrow Lakes to the eastern slopes of the Rocky Mountains.' Articles in the *Castlegar Sun* (Morran 1997b; Norman 1995a; 1995b; 1995c) state that besides the Ktunaxa/Kinbasket Tribal Council (representing seven Shuswap and Kutenai bands, including St Mary's), the Westbank Band of the Okanagan has also applied for a treaty claiming a portion of the West Kootenays.

Such political wranglings over territory undoubtedly confound public and bureaucratic imaginations in regards to the history of the Arrow Lakes region. Likely some frustrated souls wish for clear and quantifiable aboriginal territories better suited to the needs of our present-day political dilemmas. 'Is it too much to expect simple reality?' they might ask. Of course, many of us forget that territory is a temporal entity, that a people's place changes over time. A territory and its borders may be either relatively new, as in the case of modern nation-states, or considerably older. Yet no matter what the depth of antiquity, drawing concrete boundaries is an acquiescence to a false idea of stasis; it is like stopping time at one point in a people's history. I need not emphasize that this is true for all peoples, not only for aboriginal peoples of North America. For example, neither the Soviet Union nor Yugoslavia exists now as it did in recent years. Closer to home, the boundaries of Canada have changed considerably both before and since Confederation in 1867, and in the current political climate those boundaries could quite radically change again if Quebec chooses to secede.

Anthropologist A.L. Kroeber (1963 [1939]: 5) agrees that drawing boundaries between cultural-political groups is the 'weakest feature of any mapping.' Unfortunately most methods of depicting time, space, and culture all together provide a most inadequate representation of the actual complexity on the ground. Gupta and Ferguson (1992: 6) find that today cultures continue to be envisioned as closed entities bound to closed territories. They say, 'Representations of space in the social sci-

ences are remarkably dependent on images of break, rupture, and dis-
junction. The distinctiveness of societies, nations, and cultures is based
upon a seemingly unproblematic division of space, on the fact that they
occupy "naturally" discontinuous spaces.' Evidently even in this decade,
the static, fragmented view of cultural groups continues to plague the
social sciences. Kroeber (1963 [1939]: 6) feels it is the reader's responsibility 'to translate what his eye sees into the dynamic aspects that are
intended. This difficulty inheres in all attempts to express in static two-
dimensional space terms, phenomena that have a sequential as well as a
spatial aspect; a flow as well as a distribution.'

Following Kroeber's (1963 [1939]: 6) lead, I have chosen to render
'cultural maps without boundary lines' (see Map 2). He and others working on the Plateau have found predicament in the definitive mapping of
cultures. For example, an anthropologist who studied with the Kutenai,
Turney-High (1941: 22–5) notes that his own field data on territorial
boundaries are inconsistent with those of earlier anthropologists who
worked in the region. He confesses, 'I myself feel serious doubt about the
claims of so much territory to the southwest, but since informants were
insistent, the map was drawn according to their directions.' Showing
rather little foresight for the land claims disputes to come, Turney-High
adds, 'In any event it is an unsettled point, and perhaps one of no great
importance.' Unsettled, indeed! But certainly more important than he
anticipated.

Historic evidence does show some of the give and take of boundaries
between the Sinixt and their neighbours. For example, in a conversation
with a 'Sinatcheggs' chief, fur trader Alexander Ross (1855: 171; cf. O.
Johnson 1969: 53; Bouchard and Kennedy 1985: 24) learned in 1825 that
the Kutenai had been pushed westward into the Sinixt region not long
before, 'in consequence of wars with the Blackfeet [sic], who often visited
[their] lands.' This anecdote carries some weight because the chief had a
Kutenai father, although he himself was Sinixt, presumably by way of his
mother's matrilineage. His political bias would likely have been relatively
neutral because he was descended from both cultural groups. According
to him, the Kutenai 'emigrated to this country about thirty years ago,'
around 1795. This sort of movement was not unique to the Kutenai, however. During the fur trade era, the Shuswap Kinbasket Band similarly took
up residence in new territory at Lake Windermere in the East Kootenays
(Graham 1963: 156). So too, the Sinixt made some changes to their residency pattern, gathering more often in the southerly reaches of their
territory by the late nineteenth century.

Changes in boundaries surely occur, but such territorial transitions are not easy, frequent, or even permanent. Conflict has definitely taken place in the Plateau as a result of incidents of intrusion. Recorded by James Teit (1930: 258) and corroborated by archaeological evidence (Smith 1930 in Bouchard and Kennedy 1985: 59), a battle between the Lower Kutenai and the Sinixt occurred in about 1800 over the Bonnington Falls salmon fishery on the Kootenay River near the mouth of the Slocan. Oral histories say that the Lakes eventually managed to drive off the Kutenai after sending war parties east to the south end of Kootenay Lake, near the place now called Creston. Especially since the Sinixt have been noted for an ethic of pacifism, this conflict may point to unusual resource pressure, perhaps a consequence of the Kutenai's endeavours to migrate westward as described by the 'Sinatcheggs' chief in 1825.

Such incidents suggest a hardness of territorial lines at the location of certain important economic resources, like fisheries. Other portions of a territory, such as in the more transient hunting areas, may have been less prone to similar regulation. Ray (1936b: 117–20) discusses the greater licence given in Salish hunting territory, for example, saying that 'the hunting territory of one group might be quite open to use by another even though the bounds be highly specific.' Further, he observes that

> Boundaries between groups of the Columbia Basin varied in exactitude ... Almost all villages were located on waterways, resulting in boundaries being most definite at points where streams or rivers were crossed. The greater the distance from population centers, the more vague the lines of demarcation grew. Thus, far back in hunting territory or far out in desert root digging grounds, boundaries sometimes completely faded out. (Ray 1936b: 117)

All of this commentary on change and ambiguity deflects from territorial longevity. My intention here is not to draw a line in the sand, as it were, but to examine some of the documentation on Sinixt territory. Past and present politics aside, the historical record does show that at the time of first contact with European fur traders, Sinixt peoples resided along the Columbia River valley, the Arrow Lakes, the Slocan Valley, Trout Lake, and to varying degrees, the Kootenay Lake area. Early Hudson's Bay Company maps show the Sinixt in this region. London cartographer John Arrowsmith (1859) compiled the original documents of fur traders and explorers to create his 1859 map, showing the 'Sin Natch Eggs Indians' in the area stretching from the Arrow Lakes to 'McGillivray or Flat Bow' (now Kootenay) Lake (see Map 1). He built upon the earlier work of Aaron

Arrowsmith (1814). Jesuit Pierre-Jean De Smet (c. 1842–8) includes this people on his 'Map of Northern Rocky Mountains and Plateau,' placing them on the Arrow Lakes as the 'Gens des Lacs de la Colombie.'

Various ethnographic scholars have similarly attempted to map the boundaries of Sinixt territory, including George Dawson in 1884 and 1892, James Teit in 1909, Franz Boas in 1928, and Verne Ray in 1936 (Bouchard and Kennedy 1985). Teit (1930), Ray (1936b), Elmendorf (1935–6), and Bouchard and Kennedy (1984; 1985; 1997) each document locations and names of Sinixt winter village and resource sites in the West Kootenays and Washington State.[24] In her autobiography, Christine Quintasket adds an indigenous view from the early twentieth century. She states that the 'Lakes were on Arrow Lakes primarily, but their villages and camps could also be found on Kootenay and Slocan lakes in British Columbia and in northern Stevens County in Washington' (Mourning Dove 1990: 146).

As Turney-High found with the Kutenai, inconsistencies between documents make a definitive Sinixt boundary impossible to consider. Of course, the differences are a reflection of multiple factors, including changing settlement patterns in recent times and scholars' inadequate access to the appropriate data. Ray (1936b: 117), for example, admits that 'in a few instances lack of definiteness [of map boundaries] is the result of insufficient data.' The presence of some ambiguity is usual and does not inhibit the recognition of a considerable time-depth of residence. Corroborating historic documents, archaeological evidence, and oral history allows for a fair picture of a core cultural territory at a given time.

Bouchard and Kennedy's (1985) unpublished 'Lakes Indian Ethnography and History' presents a thorough review comparing and contrasting about one hundred and fifty years of historical and ethnographic evidence which helps to define Sinixt territory. Here I briefly summarize Bouchard and Kennedy's conclusions, which are conservatively drawn from both published and archival data (see Map 3). These ethnographers place the northern limit of Sinixt territory at least sixty-four kilometres north of Revelstoke at the Dalles des Morts on the Columbia River, and the southern limit at least as far downstream as Northport or the Little Dalles (about forty kilometres upstream from Kettle Falls, Washington). Important to our contextualization of local fur trade and missionary history, it is worth noting that Verne Ray (1975: 127, 129a) considers Marcus and the upper rapids of Kettle Falls to have come under Sinixt jurisdiction. Bouchard and Kennedy also include this portion of the Columbia River between Northport and Kettle Falls since at least 1880, as well as

Christina Lake and the Kelly Hill region. Furthermore, they draw the western boundary along the height of the Monashee mountain range on the west side of the Columbia River, while the eastern boundary incorporates Trout Lake, the Selkirk Mountains west of Kootenay Lake, and the Kootenay River from just below the West Arm of Kootenay Lake, where the city of Nelson now rests.

It is significant that the Slocan Valley, in which lies the Vallican village and burial site, is well within the boundaries as drawn by Bouchard and Kennedy (1985: 25). They say that 'Lakes utilization of Slocan Lake, Slocan River, and the area where the Slocan meets the Kootenay River has been well documented' from 1826. Overall, Bouchard and Kennedy depict the Sinixt's boundaries aware of contention over areas which may have been shared by several groups, hence their conclusions are drawn with caution, dependent on historical data which they feel depict a core territory of the Sinixt people. References which point to a larger territory, such as the information provided by Ray (1936b: 110, 114), have been tempered by their renderings.

Identity, like territory, is temporal. It moves and flows, never static, growing out of the thoughts and practices and interactions of individuals in community. Ethnographers have captured moments in the history of Sinixt culture. They have shown us how this people shares some cultural characteristics with others on the Columbia Plateau, especially an ethic of pacifism and an observance of guardian spirits and shamanism, while also describing their own particular variations. Sinixt political leadership, for example, is uniquely centralized. But depictions of such distinctiveness come through an ethnographic haze. The categories by which Sinixt have been labelled – by name and language and culture group – have revealed almost as much about who the Sinixt *are not* as who they are. These errors, the incohesiveness and inaccessibility of written works, and the simple lack of attention to this people have caused confusion for scholars, governments, and non-Sinixt communities in Canada. In the final analysis, while imparting a foundation of knowledge about the Sinixt Interior Salish, many Columbia Plateau ethnographers have made a greater contribution to their obscurity.

chapter three

The Latent Land:
Towards a Lakes Diaspora

This was a Paradise. We had no hell, just a happy hunting ground. They made it hell for us ... When they landed here, they landed in heaven, and look what they did to it.

Robert Watt, Sinixt

It hurts too much to live here anymore! My heart aches! I feel bad! I miss my people! I wish I could have died with them!

Marilyn James, Sinixt[1]

Ethnographic categories (well defined or not) depict people in stasis rather than in flux, the movement by which all peoples perpetually live. Remember Kroeber's guidance: the historical method is crucial to understanding the complexity of cultures as they live, breathe, and wind together the current and the past through the perceptions of each new individual. How individuals perceive is always new. They take the available information from every part of their world and combine it with their own innovations and interpretations to create and re-create their culture. Yet the new comes in part from ideas and events of the past. Thus to understand something about the Sinixt today, about why they have chosen to come north to protect and rebury ancestral remains at Vallican, we must learn their history. In particular, we must learn what caused them to move out of the Arrow Lakes area in the first place. The history of this 'Lakes diaspora,' the nineteenth-century dispersal which created a kind of latent presence in their northern territory, gives us some insight into the lives of those people who are their descendants.[2]

Starting in the nineteenth century, the Sinixt began a trend of residing outside of their northern territory, a situation which has undoubtedly contributed to their obscurity in Canada in the twentieth century. Many although not all Lakes people now live in Washington State, a fact which has prompted the Canadian government to negate their legal status in their territory north of the 49° parallel. In fact, in Canada the Sinixt are officially 'extinct.' Yet, while this people has thus been forgotten by the dominant society, many of them are very much aware of their connection to the land in the north. Despite their comparative absence from their old villages in the West Kootenays, some Sinixt people have continued to cross the international boundary to fish, hunt, berry-pick, dig for roots, and visit important historical places. Their long residency in the territory thus became for some Lakes people an intermittent usage of various resources and cultural sites. In effect, their presence in the homeland was changed to a potential presence, to a kind of latency.

Today, the Sinixt have no legal or aboriginal rights in Canada according to the judgment in the deportation case of Robert Watt, the appointed guardian of the Vallican village and burial grounds. Referring to the Canadian Indian Act, Section 35 of the Constitution Act, 1982, and the Immigration Act in her 'Reasons for Order,' Madame Justice Reed (1994: 1, 3) of the Canadian Federal Court finds in Robert Watt's case that an 'aboriginal person who is an American citizen and is neither a Canadian citizen nor a status Indian under the *Indian Act* does not have a right to come into or remain in Canada,' even if that aboriginal person's traditional territory has been bisected by the international boundary. As with Robert Watt, this finding applies to most members of the Sinixt Nation.[3]

Sinixt people's efforts to obtain exhumed ancestral remains from Canadian institutions and to protect their burial sites have been frustrated by their lack of legal status in Canada, as illustrated in Robert Watt's deportation case. The international boundary between Canada and the United States separates those aboriginal territories which predate it, and the legal, political, economic, and cultural repercussions from this recent political obstruction have been harsh. In effect, through their late historical concentration of communities in the southern extreme of their territory, the Sinixt have been cut off from the northern 80 per cent of their historical territory, along with that land's significant cultural and economic benefits.

Why did the Sinixt choose to centralize in the southern-most portion of their territory? The reasons are complex. Many historical factors, including the kind of relationships the Sinixt have had with American and Canadian governments, have influenced a southerly focus, but it is possible that this trend may have been initiated as early as the eighteenth century. For millennia, the Columbia River valley has been a crucial transportation and trade route, allowing many different aboriginal ethnic groups to move back and forth by canoe from the interior of the continent to the Pacific. Sinixt territory was particularly strategic because it incorporated three major watersheds, the Pend Oreille, the Kootenay, and the Columbia, along which many peoples hold territory. It was a significant crossroads (Teit 1930: 250–3).

The advent of horse domestication on the Plateau in about 1700 and the relative ease of travel it heralded probably caused the trade routes to shift to land more amenable to overland travel (C. Miller 1985: 26). Teit (1930: 214) notes that such movement occurred among the Okanagan people, causing those who resided in the northerly reaches, where their territory is more heavily treed, to migrate southward. The rugged terrain of the Arrow Lakes and vicinity, while perfect for canoe travel, is far less suitable for horses than even the most forested of Okanagan territory. Hence it is likely that at this time traffic decreased on the Sinixt's mountainous portion of the Columbia and that main trade routes sprang up in formerly peripheral areas, in the open arid country which skirts the Sinixt homeland.

Meanwhile, the canoe continued by necessity to be the dominant method of transportation in the Arrow Lakes. James Teit explains:

Following the introduction of the horse, trade conditions changed rather suddenly, and the old trade routes became of minor importance. Trade now passed across country with the greatest ease ... The old Lake route to the north, being impossible for horses, was practically neglected. [Teit 1930: 252]

By contrast, Teit calls the trading centre which grew up among the Skoyelpi as a result of the new horse routes, 'the great trade emporium of the interior Salishan tribes.' The 'emporium' of which he speaks is presumably Kettle Falls, located a short distance downriver from the southerly terminus of Sinixt territory.[4] Once residing in a centre of economic activity, the Sinixt may have begun to spend more time seeking out their trade partners after the horse became the main method of travel. As a result, they may have begun to linger during the segment of their seasonal rounds which brought them south to the multiethnic Kettle Falls fishery, where the land begins to open up, making it more accessible to horses. The concentration of various Plateau peoples at this salmon fishery appears to have increased with the new method of travel.

The Northern Territory: A Refuge in Hard Times

While it is possible that the adoption of horse travel may have brought much trading activity to the south, the Sinixt nevertheless kept their semi-permanent villages and spent the majority of their seasonal rounds in the northern region. The upper Columbia fur trade began even before the establishment in 1811 of the general area's first fort, Fort Okanogan (A. Ross 1855; 1966 [1849]), and according to David Thompson (1971 [1811]: 313), the people of the Arrow Lakes had already participated in the changing economy by then.

Despite the Lakes' nominal participation, Hudson's Bay Company employees were vexed at the little success they had in initially encouraging the Sinixt to make more regular journeys south to Kettle Falls to trade furs at the new Fort Colvile, established in 1825. At first, the Lakes and other indigenous peoples in that region had little interest in trapping extra animals or disturbing their seasonal rounds in order to trade for European goods, many of which were at first of limited use to them (Chance 1973: 81–2). Indeed, Reichwein (1990: 268) says that as late as 1844, 'Columbia Plateau Native American populations in the Colville region near the Hudson's Bay Company's major northern supply post, Fort Colville, rarely visited the post.' Most Sinixt at this time continued to spend the majority of their year in the north.

The events that followed the advent of fur trading with Europeans may have actually strengthened the Sinixt's choice to reside in the northern portion of their territory. True, population loss from epidemics and the weakening of ecosystems due to fur trade overkill may have increased some logistical dependence on immigrant traders and later on missionaries, both of whom were mostly located in the south. Yet the north provided something else: refuge. Called 'population avoidance' elsewhere, this tendency to steer clear of newcomers was common among Plateau peoples (Reichwein 1990: 268). But the Sinixt's situation of isolation was uniquely advantageous. The West Kootenays' difficult terrain made this region one of the last to be populated by non-natives. On the area's perimeter, however, miners and pioneers began to move in starting as early as the 1840s. Land pressures and civil strife in eastern North America brought floods of immigrants of European descent, and the building of railroads introduced an influx of Chinese labourers. This inflow was prefaced by considerable violence, particularly that instigated by the United States Army during the Plateau Indian Wars, making life more than a little difficult for aboriginal peoples in the region.

Besides its segment of the important Columbia River route from the Rockies to the Pacific, the rugged West Kootenays drew little attention from non-natives. This region, especially the isolated Slocan Valley, therefore provided a potential retreat from the negative impact of immigration into the Plateau. Even the tireless explorer David Thompson did not venture into the lower Kootenay River loop between Kootenay Lake and the Columbia River, into which the Slocan River flows (Graham 1945: 30; Thompson 1994 [c. 1810]). The first reference to the mouth of the Slocan River appears to have been made in 1826 by a Hudson's Bay Company employee, William Kittson (Bouchard and Kennedy 1985: 103), but it is not until the Palliser Expedition of 1859 that any record of a European North American ascent of the 'Shlocan' Valley appears (Graham 1945: 116). As noted in the previous chapter, cartographers were ignorant of the Slocan, so it did not appear on maps until late. Even in 1872, a year after the colony joined the Dominion of Canada, British Columbia's (1872) Department of Indian Affairs published a map showing no sign of the large lake valley.

The Sinixt may have taken advantage of this sort of ignorance on the part of newcomers. Indeed, the remoteness of the Slocan and the rest of Sinixt territory may have offered a place of withdrawal from the fray. To be sure, the Slocan Valley protected a number of Sinixt villages within its precipitous walls. Both Teit (1930: 210) and Ray (1936b: 114, 125, 127–8) name six villages in the Slocan (see Appendix 2). These villages offered the Sinixt refuge, but also a choice – the choice to reach out and participate with fur traders, missionaries, miners, and settlers when it was advantageous to them, rather than having no option but to live in a continual relationship, enforced by the close proximity of immigrant communities. Not until 1882, when a large silver-lead ore seam on Kootenay Lake was claimed by Americans, did non-natives begin swarming the West Kootenays, arriving in large numbers to remain permanently, and thus encroaching upon and disrupting the Sinixt's northern communities.

This story of new immigration and the Lakes' subsequent southerly movement begins with epidemics. The first of these epidemics came like a premonition of the difficult years to come, affecting groups around the Kettle Falls area before the arrival of non-natives. Two smallpox epidemics accompanied aboriginal trade partners from east of the Rockies in about 1770 and 1780. Following these came many waves of measles, chicken pox, influenza, tuberculosis, and yellow fever. While the 1836 smallpox epidemic caused the deaths of over half the aboriginal people in the Colvile vicinity (Reichwein 1990: 258–9), the measles epidemic of 1847–50 was even more brutal (Boyd 1994; Galois 1996). David Chance (1973: 120) describes the latter epidemic, saying that it 'reached Fort Colvile ... with great force,' killing 123 in the winter of 1847–8, most of whom were children. The number of casualties from the next assault, the 1850–1 influenza outbreak, have gone unrecorded. Another smallpox epidemic arrived in 1853, and unknown diseases had their effect in 1857 and 1862. While one must remember that 'only the most massive epidemics have been recorded and ... we shall never know the full impact of European disease upon the Indians in the last century,' Scott (1928: 144) estimates that approximately 80 per cent of Columbia Plateau populations were decimated by the end of the nineteenth century.[5]

We must not underestimate the ravages of this relentless, rapid population decline. Many groups became less able to maintain the rigours of subsistence life as a result of survivors' physical frailty and smaller numbers – not to mention the intense fear and mourning that must have accompanied so much death. Hudson's Bay officials noted the desperation resulting from disease, manifesting itself in high rates of suicide and low fertility. Even so, 'the Lakes showed a surprising increase in population' in the latter part of the fur trade era (Chance 1973: 121–2). Of course, their population before the impact of disease cannot be stated definitively, but calculations range from five hundred (Mooney 1928: 15) to more than two thousand (Teit 1930: 211). Hudson's Bay Company records estimated the decreased Lakes population to be 138 in 1830. This rose to 229 in 1870 (Chance 1973: 124). According to census-takers, 325 Lakes people lived on the Colville Reservation in Washington State in 1882, while 25 'Colvilles' (that is, Lakes) maintained residence in British Columbia in 1881 (Bouchard and Kennedy 1985: 72).

Of course, we cannot be sure of how many Lakes people were overlooked by government census officials. However, it is clear that a number of Lakes people lived outside their territory during this time. Although Elmendorf (1935–6) claims that the Sinixt primarily married internally, exogamous marriage existed to some extent before the arrival of European disease (Ray 1939: 10). This lesser tendency to marry out increased in the nineteenth century so that the Lakes and other groups could augment their numbers and thereby help counter severe losses. Members of various groups joined the Lakes, such as the Kutenai, Shuswap, and Skoyelpi (A. Ross 1855; Teit 1909a; 1910–13). The Lakes themselves left the group to combine their forces most frequently with the Skoyelpi (Chance 1973: 121); however, Sinixt people also dispersed among the Kutenai, Shuswap, Okanagan, Spokane, and possibly other Plateau groups as well (Elmendorf 1935–6).

While this practice of exogamy may explain in part the modest recovery of the Lakes population, it may also have been the catalyst which set off the Lakes' eventual diaspora from their own territory. Further, this movement between groups reveals a heightened interdependence of aboriginal peoples that began as a result of the epidemics, and which played an important role in the later settlement period, especially during the Plateau Indian Wars which began in the 1850s.

Despite minor population recovery and intertribal support, the Sinixt and others became increasingly dependent on the Hudson's Bay outposts as the result of disease. While aboriginal peoples in the area seemed relatively indifferent to the presence of immigrant trade partners in the early nineteenth century, the trend slowly shifted starting by about the 1830s. Various entries in Hudson's Bay journals remark upon the devastation and resulting famine which caused people to gather at the forts to request food and sometimes medical assistance (Chance 1973: 104, 119–20).

John Work of Fort Colvile noted that for the first time the Sinixt, most of whom normally wintered to the north, remained at Kettle Falls among the Skoyelpi in 1830–1. Instead of dispersing to the hunting grounds as the fur traders wished, the Lakes had purposely remained until December to participate in Winter Dance ceremonies. The Columbia River unexpectedly froze, thus preventing them from travelling by canoe to their own winter villages in the Arrow Lakes region, where they had cached food stores. The unplanned stay and forced immobility resulted in considerable hunger and the first real instance of dependence upon Fort Colvile for provisions (Bouchard and Kennedy 1984: 64, 105).

While the relationship between the Hudson's Bay Company and the Sinixt became increasingly entwined, the draw southward during winter nevertheless was a sporadic rather than a permanent feature of the yearly economy. In fact, the fur traders encouraged the Lakes to stay in the north, but to hunt for pelts in the mountains rather than to winter as usual in their villages. In 1831, Fort Colvile Chief Factor Francis Heron (quoted in Chance 1973: 81) considered it to the fur traders' 'material advantage to get them off ... early to their hunting grounds where they will always do more than they can do if loitering away their time' in the winter villages or at Kettle Falls. The Hudson's Bay Company's attempts at 'encouraging ... industry' among the Lakes (that is, transforming their usual economic cycle to become advantageous to the European economy) degenerated into bribes of 'ammunition and traps as extra inducements' (Chance 1973: 81–2).

Regardless of the fur traders' efforts, many Lakes did remain in their habitual winter villages, and some did move southward. James Teit (1910–13) comments that over 100 Lakes people continued to reside in the northern Arrow Lakes area in the 1880s, over half a century after Francis Heron tried to implement economic change to his company's advantage. West Kootenay pioneer Edward Picard (quoted in Affleck 1976c: 107) gives us another example of nineteenth-century residence patterns: Picard's 'old friend,' Sinixt 'Chief Melture[6] and many of his tribe put in the ... winter [of 1886] across the river from Revelstoke' on the Columbia north of the Arrow Lakes, likely at the village Verne Ray (1936: 124, 126) has documented as skəx̣i'kəntən. The next year, that same group stayed across from Marcus, Washington, in the far south of their territory, probably at the major Lakes village, átstləktst'ctn. As well, a village of sixty or seventy Lakes people wintered at the southeast end of Slocan Lake well into the tumultuous mining era. They continued to occupy this old winter village site near Springer Creek, probably ka·ntca·'k (Ray 1936: 127), until 1896 when they moved to avoid the boomtown chaos of Slocan City and other nearby mining communities (Bouchard and Kennedy 1985: 99).[7]

Although some northern villages weathered the events of the nineteenth century, the Sinixt's extensive disease-induced population decline certainly caused difficulty in pursuing their usual livelihood. The sheer lack of numbers put stress on their labour-intensive seasonal round economy, obliging each individual to increase her work load in order to meet the requirements of subsistence. As populations became smaller and smaller, fur trade items became proportionately more important to aboriginal economies. Such items helped to reduce the work load and, contrary to the goals of the Hudson's Bay Company, may have actually aided the continued existence of normal winter village/seasonal round life. For instance, iron pots virtually eradicated the need to heat stones for boiling and baking, thereby eliminating some of the laborious steps in food preparation. As well, guns, steel knives, and iron arrowheads increased the efficiency of hunting and the processing of skins and meat, and decreased the need to manufacture stone tools. The time saved by using such implements freed individuals to complete other tasks which, before the epidemics, would have been shared by a greater population.

There was a catch however. Obtaining these helpful items required people to participate in the fur trade economy. Bouchard and Kennedy (1984: 104) note that 'by 1833 guns and ammunition were the most desired trade goods at Fort Colvile ... and gifts of the latter were regularly given to induce the Indians to return to their hunting grounds.' There may have been some tension between their own livelihood and the inclusion of hunting for the forts, yet initially the fur trade did not demand a radical change in the aboriginal economy.[8] Instead, it required an increased concentration on trapping during their seasonal rounds, particularly in the winter months. As early as 1811, David Thompson observed the changing winter routine. He writes that while he and his crew struggled to pull their canoes through ice on the Arrow Lakes,

> an Indian and his family came to us; he had been working beaver, when the snow became too deep; we enquired, if the snow was more than usual. He said he did not know, as he had never left the village at this season, but now many of them would leave it to hunt furs, to trade with us. (Thompson 1971 [1811]: 313)

With David Thompson's realization in 1811 that the Columbia River was the only navigable route from the Rockies to the Pacific (Belyea 1994: xi), Sinixt territory became a thoroughfare for fur traders. *Coureurs du bois* soon travelled regularly along the river. Even so, except for carrying out minor trade missions, none stayed to actually settle that rough portion of the Columbia. Fort Colvile, however, was established just south of their territory in 1825. Being the most productive of the fur trade outposts west of the Rockies, this fort precipitated a considerable amount of activity between aboriginal peoples and newcomers (J. Galbraith 1957). Significantly, the Lakes were the most prolific of the aboriginal peoples who trapped furs for that fort, providing up to two-thirds of all the beaver pelts received at Fort Colvile (Bouchard and Kennedy 1984: 105). This points to the possibility that the Lakes had been particularly hard hit by epidemics and had subsequently become more dependent upon fur trading for their livelihood.

During the course of the fur trade period in this region, three minor outposts were built right in Lakes territory. All north of what became the international boundary, they were Fort of the Lakes (or McKay House) at the north end of Upper Arrow Lake (Catholic Church Records 1972: 13–15; Québec Mission 1955: 7), Fort Fosthall midway up the same lake (K. Johnson 1951: 81, 94), and Fort Shepherd (Hudson's Bay Company

Archives 1939) on the Columbia across from the mouth of the Pend Oreille River.[9] Though none of them enjoyed a lengthy existence, the establishment of these smaller outposts in their territory suggests both a reluctance among the Sinixt to make regular journeys to Fort Colvile at Kettle Falls and a dependence of the Hudson's Bay Company upon the Sinixt for their fur hunting abilities.

Those same epidemics which aided the fur traders in their economic endeavours may have also facilitated the objectives of another kind of newcomer, the missionary. The first Catholic missionaries to Oregon Territory arrived by way of the Columbia River passage in October 1838.[10] Part of the Québec Mission (1955: 7–9), Jesuits Blanchet and Demers stopped en route at '*maison des lacs*' (that is, Fort of the Lakes) and there baptized thirteen Lakes children, among the earliest Christian rituals performed with aboriginal peoples in the Plateau region. Two years later at Fort Colvile, they also baptized Chief Kessouilih, who was then about forty years old (Catholic Church Records 1972: 13–14, 61). Thence recorded by his newly acquired Christian name, Grégoire, this long-serving, influential Sinixt chief later encouraged other Sinixt to follow suit. The 'greater part' of his people received baptism during the 1845 salmon season at Kettle Falls, where St Paul's mission had been established to serve the Skoyelpi and other groups who frequented the fishery (De Smet 1905: 482, 548).[11]

The Sinixt whom the missionaries encountered would have experienced much personal and communal loss as a result of disease. While they undoubtedly hoped to help the people, the Jesuits also knowingly took advantage of the ideological persuasiveness of vaccinations and other medical assistance. Father Ravalli, who was 'gifted in the medical arts,' served among the Lakes (De Smet 1905: 476, 483). Moreover, Fathers Joset and Vercruysee of St Paul's mission had inoculated the 'converted' against smallpox by 1853, and probably earlier (Chance 1973: 123). Joset (quoted in J. Ross 1968: 50) considered their efforts an effective method to 'garner a great harvest' of souls. Pierre-Jean De Smet, the Jesuits' superior and general overseer of their western missions, felt similarly:

> During the late prevalence of the smallpox, there were hardly any deaths from it among the neophytes, as most of them had been previously vaccinated by us, while the Spokans and other unconverted Indians, who said the 'medicine (vaccine) of the Fathers was a poison, used only to kill them,' were swept away by hundreds. This contrast, of course, had the effect of increas-

ing the influence of the missionaries. (De Smet 1905: 1235; cf. Bouchard and Kennedy 1984: 71)

Economy and place of residence are two areas over which De Smet and the other Jesuits hoped their medical powers would give them such influence. Employing a method of conversion specific to their order, the Jesuits attempted to dissuade Plateau peoples from following their usual nomadic economy of seasonal rounds. Writes historian Margaret Whitehead (1988: 15), 'Oregon's Jesuit missionaries used as a blueprint for their missionary developments the "réduction," or model self-supporting agricultural Christian mission village established by Spanish Jesuits in seventeenth-century Paraguay.' The function of reductions was primarily to provide controlled isolation as an aid to the alteration of behaviour and ideology. Further, the Jesuits believed that nomadism resulted in both moral ambiguity and poverty, two attributes they hoped to modify; they felt that 'stabilizing ... of the Indian society and economy was essential to further progress' in their 'civilization' and Christianization (Burns 1966: 51). Of course, this desire to settle the Indians into a sedentary agricultural lifestyle was at odds not only with the aboriginal economy, but also with fur traders' objectives.

The Jesuits attempted to impose 'a rigorous daily order from the very beginning,' combining religious instruction with training in agricultural practices and basic literacy (Burns 1966: 49). Yet in the Plateau, the reductions never really took root. Farming remained for decades only a minor component of the overall economy, hence the Jesuits were forced to adapt their approach. Unlike many of those around the world, the Jesuit missions among the Plateau peoples were

> seldom a true Reduction. Most of the tribes remained substantially nomadic from 1840 to 1880 ... [However,] there was usually a fair number forming a nucleus around [the mission], living permanently in cabins and tipis, and doing some farming. The rest of the families were scattered. They flocked to church on feast days, or managed to visit it for confession and advice, or stayed for a season now and again. The priest also made circuits through their camps and appeared at their gatherings ... Where an outlying situation seemed especially promising, a permanent station or sub-mission was erected. (Burns 1966: 52)

The Sinixt fit into this pattern, most being only occasional occupants of the Kettle Falls reduction. Some Sinixt evidently did take up residence at

St Paul's, and after 1869 also at the St Francis Regis reduction, not far away (Diomedi 1978: 38). But it is clear that many did not. While he notes that the 'Snaiclist' were 'principally attended from Colville Mission' (St Paul's), De Smet (1905: 548, 1302) also established for them an outlying mission called *La Station de Pierre Gens des Lacs de la Colombie*, or St Peter's Station for the Lakes People.[12]

This 'outstation' was built on the west side of Upper Arrow Lake as a place from which missionaries could instruct 'the duties and practices of religion' to those Sinixt unwilling to relocate permanently among the Skoyelpi. De Smet's (1905: 549) intention was to found a reduction alongside the mission, hoping to 'supply them with implements of husbandry and with various seeds and roots' as soon as the Jesuits had the means to do so. As well, he hoped to build a mission, church, and reduction at the mouth of the Kootenay River at the Lakes village kp'ítl'els, across the Columbia from what is now Castlegar. Neither endeavour transpired as far as we know, but the Jesuits' establishment of St Peter's Station, as well as their proposal for Lakes reductions, indicates that the Sinixt had not been entirely attracted to the Kettle Falls mission settlement of St Paul's as the Jesuits had hoped. A significant number must have continued to reside within their northern territories, forcing the missionaries to travel upriver in search of them.[13]

Missionaries and fur traders were a different species of newcomer to the settlers who followed in their trail. True enough, the Jesuits and Hudson's Bay Company personnel sought to change aboriginal peoples for their own theological or economic purposes. Yet these earliest immigrants did not endeavour to dispossess Plateau peoples of their land. In fact, the fur traders' own livelihood depended upon an only slightly modified version of the aboriginal economy, and missionaries, at least in their own minds, felt they had aboriginal peoples' best interests at heart.

By contrast, the second wave of immigrants came solely to improve their own lives. Says one Oregon Territory pioneer:

When we, the American emigrants, came into what the Indians claimed as their own country, we were considerable in numbers, and we came, not to establish trade with the Indians, but to take and settle the country exclusively for ourselves. Consequently, we went anywhere we pleased, settled down without any treaty or consultation with the Indians, and occupied our claims without their consent and without compensation ... Every succeeding fall they found the white population about doubled and our settlements continually extending, and rapidly encroaching more and more upon their pasture and camas [root-digging] grounds. (Burnett 1904: 97)

Similarly stated by John Ross (1968: 53), 'The threat posed by the early [fur traders and missionaries] was minimal by comparison to that posed by the miner and homesteader, with their military adjuncts. The success of their enterprise depended on removing the Indian from his aboriginal territory and placing him permanently on greatly reduced reservations.'

Movement came from what became the American side. With the signing of the 1846 Oregon Treaty which designated the 49th parallel as the boundary between the United States and British North America, the pioneers began to shift into Oregon Territory (Fisher 1977: 60). By 1854, about fifty thousand European Americans had arrived to the Plateau to stay, and clearing the way for them was the U.S. Army (Reichwein 1990: 275, 278). Indeed, violence between Plateau peoples and non-natives was quick to follow the instigation of the international line. By way of their trade routes, peoples of the Plateau had learned of the 'removals' of neighbouring groups onto reservations or to other parts of U.S. territory. They had an intense 'fear ... of losing their country and being forced onto reservations ... [They] knew about the [U.S.] government and settlers seizing Indian lands on the Plains. Now they feared their own turn had come' (Jesuit General 1858 quoted in Burns 1966: 169). Predictably, when the new U.S. Washington Territory[14] Governor Stevens proposed treaties, Plateau peoples were suspicious. And rightly so. Stevens intended to use the Walla Walla Council of 1855 as a vehicle to create a reservation in the southwest, far away from the peoples' own territories. This scheme was slated for the northern Plateau Indians as well, and those to be affected, such as the Sinixt and Skoyelpi, were greatly concerned for the safety of their territorial autonomy (Burns 1966: 78–9).

Colvile became a hot spot. After the infamous 1855 Walla Walla Council, Skoyelpi Chief Peter John 'closed his country to all Whites' (Burns 1966: 126). Wrote Angus MacDonald (quoted in Burns 1966: 138), manager of Fort Colvile in 1855, the peoples living in the vicinity of Kettle Falls 'were particularly determined that American troops never cross the Snake River,' which flows into the Columbia River in the southern Plateau. Following a trend which had intensified in response to disease-induced population decline, peoples of different ethnicities drew together as political allies.[15] They shared in common an 'extreme hostility' towards non-natives and a determination to join into the southern wars if the U.S. troops did not keep well away from their territories. Further, political convictions were supported by an intensifying religious observance, particularly among the followers of the 'Dreamer' or 'Prophet' religion which, in direct defiance of Catholic sentiments, denounced any association with non-natives.

During an 1855 council meeting at Fort Colvile, Governor Stevens (quoted in Burns 1966: 139) responded by reassuring the peoples of the northern Plateau: 'I have said to all the Indians, "it is for you to say whether you will sell your lands and what you will have for them," [and if you choose not to sell at all, that] is also good.' Only a few months later, in the spring of 1856, Stevens showed the little worth of his words by returning with a military escort to force a treaty-signing (Burns 1966: 148).

The Plateau peoples were well aware of the moral ambiguity of non-native negotiators. Writes Reichwein (1990: 294), 'One of several problems with the 1855 treaties ... was that many indigenous populations were neither present nor represented at the treaty meetings. Nonetheless, they were considered by Euro-American policy as though they had agreed to the United States government's terms.' Indeed, the signatures of absent chiefs were actually forged on some treaties (Peterson and Peers 1993: 138). Even the Catholics agreed that the U.S. government agents could not be trusted. In an 1857 letter to De Smet, Father Joseph Joset explains how the peoples around St Paul's Mission

> fear a treaty; in any event they protest they will yield only a part of their lands ... [The U.S. government agents] tell them one thing and have them sign something different ... For all the treaties concluded, though two years have passed, there is not an Indian who imagines that they have ceded the totality of their lands; they think that the government has acquired no title to their country. (Joset 1857 quoted in Burns 1966: 170)

The outcome of so much distrust and fear was violent resistance to U.S. encroachment. The 1848 Cayuse Indian War set the tone for the next three decades. After this came the 1855–6 Yakima War (the direct result of Governor Stevens's dubious attempts at treaty-making), the 1858–9 Coeur d'Alene-Spokane War, and the 1877 Nez Percé War. These 'Indian Wars' were largely fought in the southern Plateau area, the Coeur d'Alene-Spokane or 'Northern War' being nearest to Sinixt territory. Probably represented by a number of individuals rather than a larger contingent, Sinixt were certainly involved in the Northern War and likely the Yakima War and others (Burns 1966: 29, 147, 285–6; Reichwein 1990: 294).[16]

While no large battles ever occurred at Kettle Falls or further north, other disturbing incidents took place. These smaller conflicts had a terrible effect on Plateau–non-native relations:

> Skirmishes and incidents continued between the more noticeable outbreaks. Settlers, miners, soldiers, and travelers were involved in vicious little firefights, in murders, or in raids. Sparks of trouble frequently flared, to be swiftly extinguished by negotiators or friends of the tribe concerned. Where no trouble existed, the wind of rumor could agitate Indian and White, bringing them to the brink of fighting. (Burns 1966: 29)

Pioneers and especially miners did not wait meekly on the sidelines for the go-ahead from the U.S. Army. Non-native immigrants, some of whom were veterans of the Crimean and the American Civil Wars, fought their own way into Plateau country. Columbia Plateau peoples were thus forced to defend their territory on two fronts: the one military, the other civil (Burns 1966: 161, 277).

Gold was a major motivator for the immigrant push. The Colvile gold strike of 1855 brought hundreds, later thousands, and probably precipitated Governor Stevens's drive to obtain a treaty there at the close of that year. From then on, Colvile was dubbed the 'Eldorado of the North'; 'gangs of miners were feverishly at work on a Colville strike. Others were hopefully roaming the neighboring regions of the Interior, and more were on their way' (Burns 1966: 163).

Columbia River miners did not hesitate to reach their goal by way of violent methods, including lynching. One British colonial officer (quoted in Burns 1966: 163) called the miners '"Anglo-Saxon devils in human shape" whose crimes against Indians make one's blood boil.' Of course, the immigrants' behaviour towards aboriginal peoples would have varied greatly, but there was more than enough conflict for Plateau peoples to feel formidable threat.[17] Kettle Falls was soon roiling with tension. Adding to the strained relations, the newcomers had caused a significant disruption of fishing activity at Kettle Falls. By 1858, there were severe food shortages. The area became a powder keg, to the point that in 1859 the U.S. government established an army garrison there which kept up to two thousand troops in Washington Territory. General W.S. Harney (1859 quoted in Burns 1966: 352) chose this location because it was 'favorable to the restraint and control of our own Indians as well as those of British Columbia who cross over the border.' Yet despite these efforts at suppression, there was little ease in the hostilities for many years, even after the establishment of the Colville Reservation in 1872 (Affleck 1976b: 1; Burns 1966: 125, 260–1, 263, 352, 358).

Along with other aboriginal peoples in the region, the Sinixt evidently felt a considerable threat to their autonomy. As mentioned above, they did participate in wars in an effort to staunch the inflow of U.S. immigrants. To be sure, one U.S. Army lieutenant blamed aboriginal peoples from north of the boundary, presumably the Lakes, for the Colville troubles, 'many of whom came from British territory for the purposes of aggression and plunder.' The Sinixt's efforts to arrest the expansion of miners were not entirely successful, however, because miners forced their way north in 1856 when gold was found 'in paying quantities' at the mouth of the Pend Oreille River. That summer, one miner was killed in Sinixt territory. In 1861, another clash left three Euro-Americans and five aboriginal people dead. Through the 1860s and 1870s, other minor gold strikes in that watershed contributed to similar conflicts between the Sinixt and non-natives (Burns 1966: 357; Graham 1945: 102; 1963: 159; 1971: 81; Norris 1995: 18).

During these tense years, the northern territory was definitely used as a place of refuge by the Sinixt, and possibly by some of their allies as well. The Sinixt did spend considerable time in the south so they could participate in the politics of the Columbia Plateau and work their farms around Kettle Falls, but there is no doubt that many made good use of the territory north of the line to escape violence and political turmoil (Burns 1966: 277). Though largely unattended and unmarked until the early 1860s, the 1846 Oregon Treaty boundary had split Lakes territory in two, thereby providing sanctuary on the British side from U.S. troops.[18] The Sinixt did not consider the boundary to affect their own territorial integrity. In fact, they ignored British and American claims to jurisdiction and continued to live as though the boundary did not exist. Seeing the border only as 'a barrier against the approach of the Boston man [Americans],' the Lakes believed the boundary had been drawn specifically to prevent the northerly expansion of miners (Cox 1861 quoted in Bouchard and Kennedy 1985: 17).

The Sinixt and Skoyelpi Indians vigorously resisted the American influx, refusing to allow miners to travel upstream along the Columbia River and Arrow Lakes. Secretary of the North American Boundary Commission Charles Wilson (1970 [1861]: 111) noted the pride with which the Lakes chief recounted his people's successful repulsion of their American enemies. Probably Chief Grégoire, this 'most wonderful old man' continued to live with his people north towards the Arrow Lakes in

1861.[19] The Sinixt apparently still associated the 'King George men' with beneficial trade and respectful relations, no doubt partly because the British presence was minimal compared with that of the 'Bostons.' Indeed, the Sinixt actually provided protection for Hudson's Bay Company personnel in some hostile situations.

Gold finds in the West Kootenays during the 1850s, 1860s, and 1870s were insignificant in comparison to those in the East Kootenays, Similkameen, Okanagan, Washington Territory, or the most northerly reaches of the Columbia at the 'Big Bend.' The establishment of the army garrison near Kettle Falls had provided some stability, resulting in a quick expansion of immigrants south of the line. On the American side alone, Plateau gold mines yielded $140 million by 1867 (Burns 1966: 354). Boomtowns, railways, pack trains, and homesteads soon washed every side of Sinixt territory. Yet almost no non-native settlement took place in the West Kootenays at this time, although newcomers sometimes travelled through on their way to the uproar. In 1865, for example, a steamboat was launched on the Columbia River to ferry Big Bend gold-seekers from Marcus, Washington, to north of Upper Arrow Lake (Graham 1945: 106). Also in 1865, the Dewdney Trail construction crew came through to Fort Shepherd and continued eastward, leaving a considerable number of Chinese labourers who preferred to take their chances washing gold on the Columbia (Affleck 1976a: 34–5).

Despite these infringements, the activity within Sinixt territory remained marginal in contrast to surrounding regions, in part because of the Sinixt's own efforts. The relative quiet in Sinixt country allowed the territorial sanctuary from immigrant peoples to remain intact. According to the Jesuit General in 1878 (quoted in Burns 1966: 359), the people were still 'withdrawing into the mountain area and ... burying themselves in the vast solitudes' to escape the throng of newcomers. At this time more than any other, such refuge became an integral component of survival.

Before the 1880s, the Sinixt appear to have been in a unique position of territorial strength on the Plateau. Nevertheless, living off the land was not as viable as it had once been. Population numbers were still low and the fur trade was in decline. In fact, a half century of intense trapping had caused a crisis in the local ecosystem, and the Kettle Falls fishery was not as productive because of the political conflict in the area, making food increasingly hard to come by. It cannot have been easy to survive on disrupted and diminished seasonal round resources, even in the north country where there was little competition for land. Some aboriginal people took up gold panning themselves, and by the 1860s, agriculture was not so much optional as necessary (Bouchard and Kennedy 1984: 81–2; Chance 1973: 104–5; Reichwein 1990: 267).

Of course, most of the fertile, cleared land was in the Colville Valley on the American side. Consequently, the south continued to draw Sinixt settlement. Lieutenant Colonel J.S. Hawkins (1861 quoted in Bouchard and Kennedy 1985: 17) of the British Royal Engineers remarked in 1861 that 'the Lake Indians ... seem to live as much south as north of the 49th parallel,' but that their economic life was split between hunting in the north and farming around Kettle Falls and nearby Kelly Hill. Evidently, these people were still very much nomadic, frequently crossing back and forth over the boundary during their seasonal rounds.

Because the Sinixt often travelled between the Arrow Lakes area and Kettle Falls, Hawkins felt that they 'must be considered as much American as British subjects,' but the American and British governments seem to have disagreed. As early as 1850, government officials tried (with little consequence) to prevent aboriginal peoples from traversing the boundary, designating them wards of either American or British 'supervision' depending on where they wintered (Bouchard and Kennedy 1985: 17–18). In effect, this policy worked to formally divide the people as well as the land, but in practice it was not successful in isolating north- and south-wintering Sinixt from each other.

Notwithstanding the continual movement up and downriver, the pull southward may have been further encouraged by a certain U.S. governmental policy. The Americans hoped to facilitate agricultural development among Plateau peoples, including the Lakes, by giving 'gifts' of farming implements, supplies, and food (Burns 1966: 353). This effort did not appease hostile relations, but it may have contributed to an increasing divergence from the hunter-gatherer economy. To be sure, the U.S. government's intentions of fostering agriculture and a sedentary lifestyle were primarily to free up land for Euro-American immigrants. Ironically, when the Colville Reservation was finally set apart in 1872 – ostensibly to put aside farming land as a protective measure for aboriginal peoples – much of the fertile land therein was already in the control of non-natives (J. Ross 1968: 59, 61).

Fortunately, the first manifestation of the Colville Reservation incorporated the Lakes' southern territory, including many of the farms they had nurtured there. But other Plateau peoples were removed from their own country and squeezed onto that same land. 'Ethnic groups were thrown

together indiscriminately with no concern shown for their social or territorial integrity or traditional patterns of intergroup relations' (J. Ross
1968: 66). And the enforced close quarters did little to maintain any feelings of alliance that they might have fostered during the height of the war
years. In fact, the nationalism of separate ethnic groups and the resulting
unease strengthened in response to the crowding and decreased autonomy. In addition, the Lakes were a minority on the reservation. Thus,
when the U.S. government acted in 1891 to revoke the northern half of
the Colville Reservation (including the entire portion of Lakes territory),
the Sinixt were placed in the vulnerable position of being guests on their
own reserve (J. Ross 1968: 59, 63–4).[20]

The British Columbia government offered no alternative to the dicey
situation in Washington Territory, neither reserve nor economic aid to
help counter the devastating effects of immigration. Actually, unlike the
Americans, this government had a sparse presence in the region and did
not recognize the Sinixt's existence even though British surveyors of the
Palliser Expedition and the North American Boundary Commission
made note of their residence there.[21] The West Kootenays remained
open to the original occupants, but even with their northern territory relatively free of settlers and governmental encroachment, there must have
been a deep uneasiness among the Sinixt: sometimes wintering north,
sometimes wintering south, juggling too much governmental presence
south of the line and not enough north of it; all the time suspecting the
inevitability of immigrant seepage into the greater part of their territory.

The quality of seasonal rounds too would have changed considerably
by then, becoming undependable. The effects of epidemics, the loss of
land to settlers with the associated threat of violence, the tense relations
with coresidents of the Colville Reservation, the exhaustion of fur-bearing
animals, the new need for agriculture, and the general political uncer-
tainty each would have contributed to an economic and social life of significant hardship. True enough, wintering in the northern villages would
have provided some sanctuary. But it was hardly a sanctuary of serenity or
abundance.

The Trouble with Silver: Towards a Lakes Diaspora

Not every place of refuge has a silver lining. But the Lakes' certainly did,
and this silver has had definite consequences. Where for three-quarters of
a century the rugged inaccessibility of their northern territory had provided a safe haven from non-native immigration into the Plateau, by the

1880s its mineral wealth became a liability. Gold strikes had been modest there, but silver was something else. As early as 1844, the Hudson's Bay Company and the Jesuits had knowledge of the sizeable galena (silver-lead) ore shelf on Kootenay Lake, later known as 'Big Ledge,' but they made little of it (Affleck 1976a: 29–30). However, immigrant prospectors responded differently when they became aware of this and other galena deposits in the West Kootenays.

With the staking of claims on Big Ledge in 1882, the West Kootenay deluge began. By 1884, a small steamboat was already working on Kootenay Lake, bringing in the rush from the south, and the completion of the Canadian Pacific Railway through the British Columbia Rocky Mountains in 1885 made travel to Upper Arrow Lake easy to anyone from across Canada. The region soon teemed with prospectors, and finds were made all over the country. In 1887, claims were staked both on the West Arm's Toad Mountain, above what was to become Nelson, and on Red Mountain, the Sinixt's important berrying place down Fort Shepherd way, near what would become Rossland.[22] Numerous strikes were also made in the mountains east and west of the Arrow Lakes, in the Lardeau region around Trout Lake, and in the Beaver and Salmo Valleys between the Pend Oreille River and Kootenay Lake. The activity in the Slocan, initiated with Eli Carpenter and John Seaton's 'spectacular discovery' of enormous silver deposits at Payne Mountain in 1891, was perhaps the most intense of the whole West Kootenay mining era. By 1892, seven hundred and fifty claims were staked in the Slocan. Indeed, 'the country was seething with excitement' (Graham 1963: 81, 168, 180–1, 186, 191, 197, 215).

The non-native population exploded. Boomtowns mushroomed in the most precarious terrain. Previous to the silver finds, the community of Farwell (later renamed Revelstoke) had sprung up above Upper Arrow Lake during the construction of the Canadian Pacific Railway in the far north of Sinixt territory. Kate Johnson (1951: 62) describes the spot as lawless, full of drinkers, gamblers, dancing girls, and 'gunmen with sticky fingers.' The Chinese and young eastern Canadian rail workers who lived there were some of the first people to join the rush for silver in the West Kootenays. A more direct product of the rush, the town of Kaslo was established on the west shore of Kootenay Lake as the main point of entry into the Slocan: 'almost overnight, [it] became a surging, busy western camp. Each boat brought in hundreds of passengers and before many months the population had grown to more than 3000 people.' Within two years of Carpenter and Seaton's Slocan discovery, Kaslo had multiple hotels and saloons, a theatre, bank, government building, sawmill, and weekly newspaper (Graham 1963: 191–3).

Similar towns were wedged into every inhabitable corner (and some not so inhabitable ones) along waterways, in the crevasses between mountains, and up precipitous slopes. First established in 1892 as a tent city, Sandon grew up quickly as the epicentre of Slocan mining activity. Crammed under Payne Mountain in a remote, narrow, and heavily treed cleft in the Selkirk Range, it had its own water sewage system, hydroelectricity, dozens of stores and services, and a population of over two thousand by 1897 (Graham 1971: 12; 22–3). Another of many, Slocan City was a 'boisterous, flourishing town' during the 1890s, boasting a mining promotion office which pushed claims by the hundreds. It was also the point of departure for mining trails up nearby Springer and Lemon Creeks, and was likely a major contributor to the abandonment of the Sinixt winter village at Springer Creek after 1896.

The West Kootenay population during the height of the mining era exceeded its present-day level, and with that multitude of people came a rapid growth of industry and transportation. Canadian and American rail and steamboat companies competed fiercely for control of freight and passenger business. Linking this once-remote region to the main lines of the Canadian Pacific Railway and the Great Northern Railway in the United States, a spider's web of rail and steamboat shipping routes crisscrossed the area by the end of the 1890s.

Corporations were determined to surmount the roughness of topography to get that ore out; undaunted, they willingly built the eighty rail bridges required over the short distance between Robson and Nelson and etched rail lines into thousand-foot vertical rock cliffs which challenge engineers to this day. Besides taking out silver and bringing in a steady stream of settlers and miners, the new transportation routes also became an exotic attraction for tourists. More and more people arrived.

Besides transportation, other industries flourished in the wake of mining. Sawmills worked overtime in almost every town, bringing down the forests to keep newcomers supplied with construction materials. Forests were also denuded to fuel the smelters which processed ore at Nelson, Trail, and Kootenay Lake's Pilot Bay from the 1890s onward. The deforestation was profound, sometimes by design and sometimes by accidental forest fire; indeed, old photographs show boomtowns and mining sites surrounded in every direction by razed land. Further, in 1898 West Kootenay Power and Light built the first of many succeeding power facilities. An imposing dam was constructed that year at Lower Bonnington

Falls on the Kootenay River near important Sinixt fishery and village sites (Graham 1963; Smyth 1938).

In brief, within a few short years the West Kootenays went from quietude to ruckus. Many newcomers squatted rather than bought or pre-empted the land on which they lived (K. Johnson 1951: 50). However they obtained the acreage, immigrants certainly did not negotiate with native populations for the right to reside there. Even so, there were instances of community between settlers and the Sinixt. Stories recount how in 1902 the son of a Lakes man called 'Indian Joe' rescued a Euro-Canadian boy from drowning, and how pioneers were neighbourly with those Lakes people, asking them in for the occasional cup of tea when they came through during their seasonal rounds.

Yet the general trend of immigrant settlement in the West Kootenays, as in the American experience, depended on the removal of aboriginal people from the land of choice. The extended family group of Indian Joe came every year to Beaver Valley and East Trail to 'set up teepees on their ancestral camping ground very close to [historian Clara Graham's childhood] home and did some hunting.' But despite some friendliness between the groups and the mutual recognition of a long history of aboriginal residence, pioneers nevertheless felt adamant that the Lakes 'had no business to trespass' on land which settlers had taken for their own. Sometime after the turn of the century, the Indian Joe group settled at the Sinixt village across the Columbia River from Marcus, Washington (Graham quoted in Affleck 1976c: 29; Graham 1963: 243).

The dispossession of Sinixt land did not always come so innocuously. Following the pattern established since the time of the 1846 Oregon Treaty, many newcomers resorted to violence. The boomtowns were particularly volatile, unwelcoming places. Brooklyn, a short-lived CPR railway construction town, provides a good illustration: 'Before the town of Brooklyn came into being [in about 1890] there was a large tribe of Indians' that wintered in pithouses there, on the west side of Lower Arrow Lake (K. Johnson 1951: 128). However, those people were displaced by settlers, as many as five thousand of them by 1897. Like all the boomtowns, Brooklyn was rough and less than hospitable to the original aboriginal occupants. With a proliferation of red light districts, gambling halls, and other frontier services, Brooklyn proclaimed itself to be an 'all white town' (Graham 1971: 106). Such racial tension was hardly confined to the limits of Brooklyn. To be sure, the town of Salmo teetered on the brink of riot in 1905, spurred on by a sawmill's proposal to hire cheap Japanese labour (Affleck 1976c: 35). While this latter example of racial intolerance did not target the aboriginal community specifically, it does reveal a general atmosphere of contempt and hostility towards peoples of non-European descent.

Because of the scarcity of inhabitable land in the Columbia, Slocan, and Kootenay Lake valleys, land pressures worsened during the height of the boom. Certainly, Lakes people were adversely affected by this tension. One story recounted in 1994 at the Vallican burial site describes miners taking over valley bottoms, thereby pushing groups of Sinixt up into the steep mountain forest where it was difficult to survive; another story tells of miners setting fire to the woods where they knew Lakes people lived. Women were raped by miners and both women and men were murdered, according to oral histories passed down to a Sinixt man, Bob Campbell. Violence also occurred at the hand of pioneers who began clearing land for farming. Around 1890, for example, an altercation took place on Galena Bay at the northeast end of Upper Arrow Lake:

> Each year native Indians came [to Galena Bay] from remote areas ... They came with their families in several canoes arriving about the middle of August and stayed until about the middle of October. They caught Kokanee or red fish, also trout and larger fish, and did some hunting. They smoked the fish in cedar bark huts and carried them away to their winter quarters. They also picked and dried saskatoon berries taken from the shore areas.
>
> About 1890 they came as usual, but a settler named Sam Hill had built a shack on their camping ground. A party of them went over to the shack to order him off. The Chief, Cultus Jim, claimed that he had a prior right to ownership; Sam Hill claimed that he had the white man's privilege of squatter's right. The angry chief made a gesture with his rifle which he probably carried to scare Mr. Hill. However, Hill was an experienced hunter and quick on the draw; his rifle was up in a flash and he shot the chief through the heart. The rest of the Indians ran for their canoes and sailed south never to return. (K. Johnson 1951: 97–8; cf. Bouchard and Kennedy 1985: 86)

Well illustrated in this account, immigrant violence appears to have played a significant role in the Sinixt's reluctance to reside in their northern territory. Such clashes between the Lakes and non-natives, as well as the destruction of habitat caused by a rapid population growth and unrestrained industrial endeavours, transformed a former sanctuary into a place of danger. Even when they did reprimand miners for interfering with native people, government officials were far from the institutions which empowered them; their threats did not have much practical authority in the chaos of frontier life. Hence, with little or no assistance from the British Columbia government, the Sinixt were on their own to find a defence against the sudden changes brought by the manic rush for silver in their northern territories.

With the increasing settlement in the West Kootenays through the 1880s and 1890s, Sinixt people had two options: to leave the area and join a growing diaspora on the Colville Reservation and among other First Nations in British Columbia and Washington State, or to weather the problems of settlement and stay in their northern territory. The first option offered some safety as, both in Washington State and among Shuswap, Okanagan, and Kutenai neighbours in British Columbia, there were reservations which at least ensured a place to live. Several individuals whom I met at the Vallican burial site informed me that they were descendants of Sinixt people who had chosen to relocate to Okanagan reservations rather than live in the precarious conditions of their own territory. Other Sinixt people chose to live among the Kutenai and the Shuswap for similar reasons. Especially large numbers of Lakes descendants now live at two Okanagan reservations, the Inkaneep Reserve near Oliver and the Penticton Reserve, and at the Shuswap reservation called Head of the Lakes near Vernon. In addition to these British Columbia reserves, the fieldnotes of William Elmendorf (1935–6) indicate that some Lakes people have lived on the Spokane Reservation in Washington State. These people self-identify as Sinixt, although the governments appear to have no knowledge of this.

While providing some security, the option to leave of course denied the Lakes direct or easy access to the economic and sacred sites within their traditional territory north of the boundary, or to actively live in their own homeland. Further, the other peoples with whom they were forced to reside were not necessarily close allies. As previously noted, tensions on the Colville Reservation had definitely risen between various groups which had not previously coexisted in such close quarters.

The second option, to remain in northern Lakes territory, was also difficult. The choice to stay sometimes meant they were pushed out of hunter-gatherer livelihoods and subjected to the violence that accompanied the arrival of miners and pioneers in the West Kootenays. No reservation was established as refuge in the northern territory until after the turn of the century, following a number of years of rapid industrial, agricultural, and municipal development. Clearly neither of the Lakes' options was ideal; neither allowed these people to remain within their northern territory with security from the harassment and displacement of immigrants or other aboriginal peoples.

Those few Sinixt who did attempt to live in the West Kootenays after the mining boom were ultimately forced to leave later on. Their story details the failure of reservations to provide a secure land base for the Sinixt community. Perhaps most relevant to the present day movement at the Vallican burial and village site, the story of a particular group from the mouth of Kootenay River reveals how deep the cultural ties can be to Sinixt land – ties to not only a homogenous cultural territory, but to particular sites of land which have specific meaning for individual people.

Despite the difficulty which they faced with the encroachment of settlers in the West Kootenays, a number of Sinixt people continued to live north of the boundary well into the twentieth century. Some stayed on permanently while others continued to move back and forth across the line, engaging in their usual seasonal rounds of various cultural and economic pursuits as best they could in the newly populous region. As well, they sometimes participated in the wage-labour economy of the mining era, working as deckhands on steamboats, clearing and tending land for farmers, selling handwork and wildberries, hiring out packhorses, and labouring in the mines. In the Canadian government's view, these aboriginal people were squatters who cultivated their own gardens and orchards (Affleck 1976b; R. Galbraith 1914; Gordon 1963).

In Canada, the government never understood the Lakes to be a distinct Interior Salish people whose ancestral territory spanned the international boundary. Instead, they were considered to be either Colville or a hodgepodge of Shuswaps and Kutenais. Rather than acknowledging them to possess legitimate territorial rights north of the boundary, the governments perceived these 'Colville' Lakes to be American opportunists who took economic advantage of British and (after 1871) Canadian soil by illegally crossing the line.

Such a view is well illustrated in a letter from Inspector of Indian Agencies A. Megraw to a Lakes man whom he challenged for his regular sojourns down the Columbia River to southern Sinixt villages. Megraw (1915a) flatly states to Alexander Christie that 'British Columbia Indians should not be living in Washington State' and that if he were to receive any recognition from the Canadian Department of Indian Affairs, he must remain always in the north. In another letter, Megraw (1915b) claims that these people are 'Nomads and distinctively American in their affiliations.' Evidently, even though they had experience with similar problems among other cross-border First Nations such as the Mohawks, the government either did not understand or did not accept the predicament of this people divided by the late introduction of a political boundary between two colonial nation-states.

Anthropologist James Teit refutes the Canadian government's position on the 'foreign' citizenry of this people. Describing a particular incident in his unpublished fieldnotes, he writes:

> About twenty years ago, some slight troubles occurred between Lakes and Shuswap at Revelstoke over hunting rights, and the B.C. government officials took the position that the Shuswaps alone had rights in that district, the Lakes being American Indians from the Colville Reservation, and interlopers in B.C. This was entirely wrong, there being no more reason to deny the rights of [Lakes] people in B.C., than Okanogan and Kootenay which ... also inhabit both sides of the line. (Teit 1910–13)

The government's poor understanding of Sinixt identity and territory had resulted in no official recognition when the reserve commissions came through in the 1880s. The Department of Indian Affairs did count Salish people at the mouth of the Kootenay River during its 1881 census, but they considered them former residents of Colville Reservation. For unknown reasons, census-takers noted these 'Colvilles' under the Kutenai category rather than naming them separately (Bouchard and Kennedy 1985: 134). While British Columbia's historical ambivalence towards aboriginal peoples is well documented,[23] the Sinixt's particular situation appears to be unique. Like the majority of aboriginal peoples in British Columbia, they did not have an opportunity to negotiate a treaty, but the Sinixt's difficulty went further because the little recognition they did eventually obtain was thoroughly confused. As in Teit's (1910–13) example above, this confusion is further demonstrated in Indian Agent Galbraith's testimony to the 1914 Royal Commission on Indian Affairs:

> None of my predecessors or even the higher officials, knew when the reserves were allotted [in the 1880s], that there were any Indians in that locality [the Arrow Lakes region] with claims for land. In the early days, many of the Colville Indians had been in the habit of ascending the Columbia River to hunt and fish. In 1871 I found a small band of Indians under Gregory, a Chief, in this section. I ... found afterwards that they had drifted south of the line, and I heard no more of them. (R. Galbraith 1914)

Galbraith's statement reveals the government's blindspot in regards to the Lakes people. The officials of the Department of Indian Affairs, as witnessed in Galbraith's report, do not appear to know that 'Gregory' had been documented as the central Sinixt political figure from at least 1840 when he received baptism from the Jesuits (Catholic Church Records 1972: 61). Neither do they seem to understand that many of the so-called Colville Indians on the Arrow Lakes were actually Sinixt whose territory had been bisected by the international boundary. There is no mention of the effect of seasonal rounds in causing periodic, transitory use of territories rather than year-round use of sites, and they do not consider the impact of mining in causing them to 'drift ... south of the line,' away from the northern portion of their traditional territory.

This governmental befuddlement seems always to have existed. During conflicts with miners in 1861, Lakes and Kutenai peoples gathered at the confluence of the Columbia and Kootenay Rivers, working together to prevent non-natives entering the area. When gold commissioner and customs officer W.G. Cox arrived to mediate the tensions, the Kutenai took the opportunity to request a reservation at that spot, called kp'ítl'els by the Sinixt (Bouchard and Kennedy 1985: 112), and later Brilliant by Doukhobor settlers. This site had been noted as an important Lakes village, to the extent that in about 1845 De Smet (1905: 549) proposed to build a mission there.

Like De Smet before him, Cox knew that the Interior Salish Lakes headed by Chief Grégoire lived along the Columbia River, the entire length of the Arrow Lakes, and further north. He was also aware that the Kutenai's usual place of residence was further to the east, towards the southern part of Kootenay Lake. Cox nevertheless agreed to secure a reservation for the Kutenai at kp'ítl'els. Bouchard and Kennedy (1985: 114) deduce that 'the Kutenai ... wanted to take advantage of this site's strategic location.'

To be sure, being located at the crossroads of two large watersheds, kp'ítl'els was undoubtedly a major trade centre and important economic site. In any case, Cox's proposal for the reserve seems to have been overlooked because the Kutenai reservation at kp'ítl'els was never established. In fact, Dewdney registered that land as a townsite in 1865, just four years later, apparently without knowledge of Cox's previous agreement. The area was then opened for pre-emption by settlers. For whatever reason, the original application was never discussed in attempts to create a reserve at kp'ítl'els for Lakes people half a century after Cox's 1861 visit (Bouchard and Kennedy 1985: 115, 134–5).

Not until some forty years later, in 1902, was a reservation established about 115 kilometres north of the kp'ítl'els site, across the lake from the then recently founded town of Burton. However, this Arrow Lakes Indian Reserve, later commonly known as Oatscott Reserve, was never well settled by its would-be inhabitants.[24] Apparently, the people there did plant gardens and orchards, but much time was spent in Burton where some of them had lived before the reserve was allocated and where schooling and wage labour were available (R. Galbraith 1914). The particular location of Oatscott was not chosen because of cultural or economic significance, but rather because it was one of the only places the Department of Indian Affairs could find that was available for purchase in the Arrow Lakes valley newly crowded with miners and settlers. As stated by Indian Agent Galbraith (1914), the land 'was of very indifferent quality.' Important village sites exist to the north and south of this locale, but these areas, bearing mineral deposits and being good open places for settlement, had become bustling boom towns before the government had managed to allocate a reserve.[25] By 1916, people lived only intermittently at the Arrow Lakes Indian Reserve (Bouchard and Kennedy 1985: 155).

Although the Oatscott Reserve was designated for use by the 'Arrow Lakes Indians,' as previously noted the Canadian government did not understand the ethnic identity of those people to whom they referred. 'The Indians of the Arrow Lake Band were said to be Shuswaps who married into a Kootenay family,' according to the Indian Affairs Branch (Gordon 1963). Apparently, one Shuswap man did live on the reserve, but Bouchard and Kennedy (1985: 136) have confirmed that the remainder of the residents were Sinixt. James Teit (1910–13) discusses the confusion of identity at the Oatscott Reserve, saying that the Sinixt's 'rights have been ... partly recognized by setting aside a small reservation for them near Burton, but the Canadian Indian Department classes them as Shuswap which is quite misleading.'

Oatscott was a considerable distance from the group of Sinixt, principally the extended Christie family, who continued to live by hunting, fishing, trapping, berry-picking, and guiding in various spots downstream: at Champion Lakes in the mountains near Salmo, at the mouth of the Kootenay River, across from this site at Castlegar, and at several locations along the Columbia River down to Trail (Webber 1975: 86–93). They showed no interest in permanently relocating to the reservation so far to the north. Alexander Christie[26] (1915), a Sinixt man who lived at kp'ítl'els, told Inspector Megraw, 'the reason I did not live on the land ... [at the Oatscott Reserve] is it was not my home.' Megraw (1915b) counter-claimed that the Christie group would not take up residence at

Oatscott 'because of jealousy with the other Indians' and that kp'ítl'els should be of no special significance to them because 'They looked upon the entire length of the Arrow Lakes and the Kootenay River between Kootenay Lake and the Columbia River as hunting and fishing ground.' Christie nevertheless lobbied the government for years in an effort to make his home at the confluence of the Kootenay and Columbia Rivers an officially recognized reserve. In a statement to the 1914 Royal Commission on Indian Affairs, Christie says:

> I am one of the few survivors of the band of the Lake (or S-nai-tcekstet) tribe living at the mouth of Kootenay river. The lower Kootenay River has been occupied by my people from time immemorial. I have heard that our Indian Agent Mr. Galbraith has said that I have not always been at the mouth of Kootenay River, and that I have come there lately from parts unknown. I wish to state that I was born there and have made that place my head quarters during my entire life. Also my ancestors have belonged to there as far back as I can trace. Both of my parents were born there and three of my grandparents ... I want to stay in the home where I have always been and want that I have a piece of land made secure for me there. (Alexander Christie 1914)

Indian Agent Galbraith (1914) explains to the same Royal Commission how he became aware of the kp'ítl'els band and discusses the problems he experienced in attempting to gain a reserve for them:

> I spoke to Mr. Phillips, who was then Agent, but he knew nothing about [the Indians], and the fact of their being on the Columbia River did not crop up until Mr. Bullock-Webster, of the Provincial Police, notified me, as Agent, of the finding of the body of an old Indian on the railway track near Castlegar; and, upon making investigation, I found a small band of Indians camped on the Kootenay River near West Robson [kp'ítl'els]. There were in this band the families of Baptiste Christian, Alex Christie and one other ... I took up the question of the three or four families who had squatted at the mouth of the Kootenay River, and found that over thirty-five years ago, Mr. Haynes at Osoyoos had taken up that land ... I tried to get from the Haynes estate ten acres for them, as it was a favourite fishing ground of theirs and they had their graveyard there ... (R. Galbraith 1914)

As both Christie and Galbraith suggest, the site at kp'ítl'els is significant to the Lakes people. It had been the location of fishing and root-digging camps, winter villages, and burial grounds for many generations. Contrary to Galbraith's opinion that they were relatively new to the area, Superintendent General of Indian Affairs John McDougall (1910) notes that the group had 'occupied this part from time immemorial, the graves of their ancestors as also of their own families are here, and, while this is not a reserve yet these people have long established rights on this ground.' Indeed, the entire area of broad river benches on the Columbia River around the mouth of the Kootenay, at Castlegar, Brilliant, and adjoining areas were particularly heavily occupied. Land use and settlements in this vicinity have been recorded by non-natives since at least 1825, and archaeological evidence dates settlement to at least 4500 years ago (Bouchard and Kennedy 1985: 112, 113, 117).

Regardless of its importance to Sinixt people, that land had been preempted by J.C. Haynes. Initially this did not seem to inhibit aboriginal occupation (Alexander Christie 1914). However, in 1908 Doukhobor immigrants from Russia had purchased large tracts of land in the West Kootenays, including some sites of old Sinixt villages and burial grounds along the Columbia River (Bouchard and Kennedy 1985: 144, 149–50). After Haynes's death, the land at kp'ítl'els was sold in 1912 to the Doukhobors before the government was able to intercede and secure a reserve. The Doukhobors soon began working to put in orchards and communal buildings on that land, which they named Brilliant after the shining waters of the two rivers that met there. It was then that the kp'ítl'els group realized that the establishment of a reserve was crucial if they hoped to remain at their home village.

Galbraith was unsuccessful in his attempts to obtain any significant amount of land for a reserve at kp'ítl'els.[27] We have little information on the Doukhobors' position, but we do know that in response to the Indian Agent's requests, J.W. Sherbinin (1912) of the Doukhobor Society writes, 'Mr. [Peter] Verigin and Society ... do not wish to sell 5 or 10 acres to the Government for Indians. But they willing so as Indians can stay on the same spot, where they been staing for years, we would not mind if they will have garden two or three acres, as they wish, longer as they will be have him self, and from our side we will be good neighbours [sic].'

Galbraith later explains the circumstances to the Royal Commission on Indian Affairs, stating that he had arranged to buy part of the land after Haynes had died:

> but before I knew anything about it, it passed into the hands of the Doukhobors. I went to see the Doukhobors ... I asked them if they would sell ten or

fifteen acres of this piece which they had recently purchased ... Some time afterwards I received a letter from the Doukhobors in which they said they would not sell any of the land, but that the Indians might remain where they were. The Doukhobors have now fenced in the land, leaving the Indians with just about two acres ... they are so closely fenced in that they cannot do anything; in fact the Doukhobors have ploughed the land right up to the Indians' fence. (R. Galbraith 1914)

It is worth remembering that Indian Agent Galbraith's own negligence had led to the lack of a land base for the kp'ítl'els group and that it was in his own interest to present a picture to the Royal Commission that pinned the responsibility on a third party, namely the Doukhobors, who had legally purchased the land. In any case, the two acres on which the Christies remained were classified as a 'Temporary' reserve (Bergeron 1915), but the area was too small to support their livelihood. Antoine Christie[28] (1912) talks about 'crying everyday' after the Doukhobors took up residence at kp'ítl'els because the land on which she had planted gardens and fruit trees was no longer hers to cultivate. Alexander Christie states this problem to the 1914 Royal Commission thus:

When I returned [from a hunting trip,] half of my cleared land had been plowed up by the Doukhobours including all my young fruit trees. This spring they plowed the balance excepting a very little patch in which I put a few potatoes and oats. I protested and stopped them from plowing this little patch, but in walking around they trampled the oats and spoiled most of them. The fence I had around my cleared land the Doukhobours broke down, and only part of it is now left standing. I had five horses last fall and depended on wintering three of them on the grass land of my place, but the Doukhobours plowed this up before winter and thus I had no means of keeping my horses. I turned them in the woods, and two of them died. (Alexander Christie 1914)

Of particular interest here is the Sinixt's concern for the security of their gravesites. While Justice of the Peace Abraham Hirst (1914) writes that 'the Doukhobours are and have desecrated the Indian graves by tearing up the crosses and ploughing up the land over the graves,' Inspector Megraw (1915b) dismisses this allegation. Having gone to investigate the conflict, Megraw says that 'after a careful examination of the holding claimed by the Indians ... I saw no evidence of desecration of graves by the Doukhobors ... It is true these people have cultivated the ground up to the palings surrounding the graves, but there is no evidence of desecration or disrespect, unless it be that carefully tilled land is less respectful surroundings than if allowed to become overgrown with weeds.'

Alexander Christie expresses a rather different view of the situation:

> I know of four graveyards close to our houses, and there are other older burials I cannot point out. I know that Indians burying their dead there often came on the bones of other dead they had not known. The graveyards I know had sticks and crosses erected at the graves and rings of stone around the outside. In one of these cemeteries are buried my two children, my brother, my sister Mary[29] and my first Cousin. This graveyard has not been plowed up yet. In another graveyard are buried Frank's wife and some old men and women. The Doukhobours have plowed this graveyard ... These and other graves are now plowed over and no trace of the sticks and stones remain ... (Alexander Christie 1914)

Whatever actually happened to the burial grounds may never be known, but Alexander Christie was definitely not happy about the situation, saying 'There is a law against the despoiling of Indian graves – the Doukhobours ought to be prosecuted.'

Most of the Christie group were disheartened by their displacement from kp'ítl'els and soon relocated south of the boundary. Galbraith noted the Lakes' feeling of futility, saying

> there was no escape for the Indians or opportunity for them to do anything. Baptiste, the head of the Band, realized the situation and, his wife being a Colville Indian,[30] had gone to Marcus, just south of the Line, where he had been given 160 acres of land, horses, agricultural implements, &c. He had never, however, been taken off the rolls of the Agency and himself claimed that he held his American property for his wife as a Colville Indian, while he himself was still a King George man. (R. Galbraith 1914)

It is unclear how many Lakes people stayed on after the failure to establish a proper reserve at kp'ítl'els or how many continued to make sojourns into their northern territory from the areas to which they were exiled. For certain, Alexander Christie remained living around the mouth of the Kootenay River at least into the 1920s (Bouchard and Kennedy 1985: 155). With the help of anthropologist James Teit and Justice of the Peace Abraham Hirst, Christie continued to appeal for a proper reserve for a while, but their efforts had no positive results.[31]

James Teit observes the kp'ítl'els Sinixt's dilemma in his 'Salishan Tribes of the Western Plateaus,' writing:

> Since [the time of my visit in 1909] I hear that some of them have died, and others, owing to nonrecognition of their rights by the Canadian Government and to recent pressure of white settlement at this point, have followed the example of other members of their band (previous to 1908), and have gone to the United States, where they have been granted land on the Colville Reservation. (Teit 1930: 212)

Clearly, the late establishment of the Oatscott Reserve and the bungling of the proposed reserve at Brilliant resulted in little refuge for the Sinixt during the tumultuous pioneer era in the West Kootenays. As we have seen, some Lakes people remained in the north into the twentieth century, living through the peak years of West Kootenay mining. Yet most of the Sinixt had had little option but to join the diaspora and settle either to the south on the Colville Reservation, where they were recognized by the American government, or among neighbouring First Nations in Canada. The Brilliant Reserve was never brought to fruition and ultimately few people lived on the Oatscott Reserve. By 1937 only one person, Annie Joseph, resided on the Arrow Lakes Indian Reserve and she eventually moved to the Okanagan Reserve in Vernon. In 1956, after Mrs Joseph's death in 1953, the Oatscott Reserve lands were transferred to the control of the province and the Department of Indian Affairs pronounced the Arrow Lakes Band officially extinct (Gordon 1963; Weir 1973; cf. Bouchard and Kennedy 1985: 156–8).[32] Bouchard and Kennedy (1985: 158) note the irony of their new 'extinct' status, given that in 1959 the United States Bureau of Indian Affairs counted 257 Lakes Indians on the Colville Reservation alone.

The story of the people at the mouth of the Kootenay River, the Arrow Lakes Indian Reserve, and the 'Temporary' Brilliant Reserve does not offer specific information about the Vallican burial and village site. But the failure of reserves in the West Kootenays shows us something else: that specific locations hold great cultural and historical importance for Sinixt people. Although it is clearly within their territory, the Oatscott Reserve may have failed in part because that particular location seems not to have been an historic site as intensively used as others nearby. On the other hand, the Christie family's tenacious desire to live at kp'ítl'els, to stay where they were born and where their ancestors lived and were buried, reveals that certain areas hold a greater density of meaning. Territoriality for the Sinixt seems then not to be a blanket of homogenous importance. Rather, cultural importance intensifies with the historical understanding – the social memory – of certain areas. While the territory in its entirety is undoubtedly significant, particular places are home.

Despite having been designated 'extinct' by the Canadian government, the Sinixt community continues to thrive. Today the Lakes tell stories of how, even before the concern for the Vallican burial grounds, some of their people had continued to visit the northern territory from time to time, to pick berries, trade fish, and visit sacred sites. They have been present quietly and intermittently, although their presence has been nothing like it was before the arrival of Europeans or even at the end of the nineteenth century. While hostilities with the United States Army during the Plateau Indian Wars may have encouraged Lakes people to stay north, epidemics, fur trading, mining, the arrival of settlers, and the adoption of agriculture all chipped away at the feasibility of a Sinixt livelihood on Arrow, Slocan, and Kootenay Lakes. A late and ineffective Canadian governmental policy on the allotment of reservations in the West Kootenays seems also to have been a factor in the Sinixt's dispersal. Yet, the historic record shows that some Sinixt remained in the region into the twentieth century. The dominant society's belief that these people died off, that they vanished or perhaps never existed, contradicts this record. Not only this, it very much conflicts with the Sinixt's own vision of being an autonomous people deeply connected with their historical homeland which lies inside what is now Canada.

chapter four

Competing Prophecies:
The Case of the Vanishing Indian v. the
Resurrection of the Ancestors

*We have no record of these people. The band itself has been extinct for a long time.
We have never heard of the band ... We have absolutely no records on that band or
that area at all.*

Deborah Wilson, Department of Indian Affairs, Vancouver[1]

*We are still invisible, still extinct to them. Well, now we're back, looking for a place
to come and die.*

Bob Campbell, Sinixt[2]

Non-Sinixt in Canada seem to have mistaken latency of a territory for
the disappearance of a people. Such a perspective on the history of the
Arrow Lakes people fits very much into a nineteenth-century paradigm
with which our society, both academic and popular, continues to struggle.
Arising from Social Darwinist unilineal evolutionism, the Vanishing
Indian motif portrays aboriginal peoples as archaic, as misplaced relics
rather than peoples with a continuous and continuing historical consciousness and cultural identity. For years now, many European North
Americans have been anticipating the tragic demise of native peoples.
Yet, to the dominant society's confusion, these peoples have not disap-
peared. Rather, they have become increasingly vocal, asserting their cultural distinctiveness as well as their right to exist as viable socioeconomic
and political entities.

During my fieldwork among the Sinixt at Vallican, I found a world view
quite different from the nineteenth-century European evolutionary theories which encapsulate non-western peoples within static, unchanging cat-

egories. Discussions at Vallican incorporate ideas of prophecy, a coming apocalypse, and the resurrection of a healthy, working society. They assert the concept of world renewal. Such ideas may have their ideological basis in what anthropologists have called the Prophet Dance,[3] a movement which was prevalent in the Columbia Plateau in the nineteenth century. In conjunction with other cultural elements, memory of the Lakes' involvement in this movement is a key motivator of activity at the Vallican burial site.

Evidently, we have a conflict in the cosmologies of people like the Sinixt and the European North American society, and this conflict creates divergent expectations about the present and the future. Theoretically, paradigms of social evolution and world renewal clash over their perceptions of time, over continuity and change and how social change affects cultural identity. The one does not allow cultures, particularly non-western ones, to change without somehow dissolving. From this perspective, an Indian riding in a truck rather than on a horse is not really an Indian. The other view sees no conflict between continuity and social change. Rather, it proclaims cultural identity based on a connectedness with the past in an ever-changing world.

In effect, at Vallican, we witness a competition of prophecies: the European North American one which considers aboriginal peoples to be a Vanishing Race, a transitory phase in the Great March of Time, and that of aboriginal peoples which envisions their continued ancient existence – indeed, their resurrection into increasing cultural, spiritual, economic, and political vitality.

The Dance of Prophecy

With no little exasperation, Raymond Fogelson (1985: 81) writes, 'The Ghost Dance Religion ... has been studied and re-studied for so long that I will consider myself blessed if I never have to read another student paper on the subject.' Fogelson and others may be inundated with information on the subject, but I must admit that going into the field I had only vague recollections of nineteenth-century aboriginal prophecy movements from a second-year undergraduate anthropology class, and these I had not considered for a good long time. I certainly had no knowledge of the vast body of literature and the fiery debates over the Prophet Dance in the Plateau region in which I work. My naiveté was perhaps an asset, however, as I did not approach the Sinixt expecting to find particular views of death and resurrection or political prophecies. Actually, my

initial intention had been to study the effect of the international boundary on ethnic identity and cultural sense of place rather than ideas
around the reburials in particular. But the stories I heard at the Vallican
encampment had little specifically to do with my intended research; in
the end, the people there wanted to talk about little other than reburial.
Even when they were just sitting around drinking coffee among themselves, the conversation inevitably turned to the dead: the site of the latest
reburial, the graveyard on such-and-such a point of land, how many bodies there were in the fetal position, how many were lying in the extended
position, indicative of postmissionary burial, the need for a boat to access
the more remote sites, and so on.

When I returned from the West Kootenays to Toronto after my first
stint of fieldwork in the autumn of 1994, I was confused (as, perhaps, is
usual for anthropologists coming from the field). I wasn't sure what to
make of my time in Vallican, but couldn't help coming to the conclusion
that after listening to so much discussion on reburial, perhaps my focus
should turn to (what else?) reburial. Having made this decision, I nevertheless continued to fret over meanings until some months later when I
finally opened my fieldnotes again to discover that along with the Sinixt's
emphasis on reburial there had been much discussion on the impending
destruction of the world as we know it and the desire to create a healthy
and autonomous Lakes community. The academic trail eventually led me
to see some correlation between these ideas and those discussed in the
theoretical literature of the Plateau Prophet Dance.

The Prophet Dance has been a subject of intrigue for scholars, inspir-
ing decades of debate in the anthropological community. The literature
begins with James Mooney's (1896) late-nineteenth-century account of
the Ghost Dance, which focuses on the Northern Paiute prophet Wovoka,
a.k.a. Jack Wilson. Academics, government and military officials, and the
general public had a keen interest in the movement, especially after the
massacre of Sioux dancers at Wounded Knee in 1890. A long list of ethnographic and theoretical publications on this and other such 'revitalization
movements' ensued (e.g., Parker 1913; Linton 1943; Wallace 1956).

Details vary from example to example and theory to theory, but the
main characteristics of such movements are that an aboriginal person
returns from the land of the dead to foretell the coming destruction of
the present order, the resurrection of the dead, and the subsequent
establishment of a harmonious life of plenty. With the apocalypse and
world renewal, some prophets included an annihilation of European
North Americans. Whether or not this particular aspect of violence was

incorporated, many prophets nevertheless advocated an abstinence from European goods and ideas (Kehoe 1989).

In Mooney's opinion, these movements were a new response to the intense and often brutal changes which accompanied colonization by Europeans. As is true for the Lakes, drastic decreases in populations due to epidemics, the disappearance of game animals, and the encroachment of settlers and miners are among many factors which created severe crises in aboriginal communities. Mooney feels that they turned to supernatural means of escape from contemporary horrors, as have European societies in times of stress. Christianization, he contends, had proliferated a belief that hope arrives in the form of a messiah, and during this time, native peoples took on this foreign ideology to help express and cope with their intense situation. The result: aboriginal prophets rose up in every corner of North America.

Leslie Spier entirely disagrees with Mooney's interpretation. In *The Prophet Dance of the Northwest and Its Derivatives*, Spier (1935) attempts to show through the historical record that the Plateau was actually the cultural seed-bed for the prophet movements which swept the continent in the nineteenth century. His chief evidence is first or early non-native contact accounts of Plateau religious doctrines, strict moral codes, and a cultural preoccupation with the dead. For example, Spier quotes a Hudson's Bay Company employee, Alexander Ross, who was one of the first Europeans to travel up the Columbia River in 1811. Of the Okanagan, Ross (quoted in Spier 1935: 9) writes: 'They believe that this world will have an end, as it had a beginning; and their reason is this, that the rivers and lakes must eventually undermine the earth, and set the land afloat again, like the island of their forefathers, and then all must perish.' From similar historical evidence, as well as ethnography which describes the shamanic practice of travelling to the land of the dead, Spier claims that the Prophet Dance complex occurred in 'all the tribes of the northwestern interior, without exception' and arose from the Plateau peoples'

old belief in the impending destruction and renewal of the world, when the dead would return, in conjunction with which there was a dance based on supposed imitation of the dances of the dead, and a conviction that intense preoccupation with the dance would hasten the happy day. From time to time men 'died' and returned to life with renewed assurances of the truth of the doctrine; at intervals cataclysms of nature occurred which were taken as portents of the end. (Spier 1935: 5)

Spier's conclusions are corroborated by the ethnographic evidence of several noteworthy anthropologists such as Dubois (1938), Herskovits (1938), and Suttles (1957) as well as the excavation and analysis of pre-contact 'death cult' paraphernalia in the Columbia Basin by one archae-ologist, Strong (1945). Nevertheless, initiated by David Aberle's (1959) article 'The Prophet Dance and Reactions to White Contact,' a later school of thought espoused a new and improved materialist 'deprivation theory' not unlike Mooney's original thesis. Scholars such as Deward Walker (1969), David Chance (1973), and Christopher Miller (1985) began to criticize Spier for not recognizing the impact of devastating epi-demics and the possible transference of Christian concepts via trade routes into areas where no Europeans had yet arrived. Moreover, Spier's theories focus almost exclusively on the antiquity of cultural world view, and do not consider the many other possible facets of the Prophet Dance, including its political and economic dimensions.

Several ethnographers further criticize Spier (and those who sup-ported him afterward) for entering the field with Prophet Dance-coloured glasses and for subsequently pushing the data into a ready-made framework. David Chance (1973: 71–2), for example, notes how Spier wrongly interprets the dances with which Kettle Falls people greeted explorer David Thompson for the first time. Chance believes that Spier could have avoided such mistakes if he had done more careful archival research. De Aguayo (1987) outlines a similar problem in the early Prophet Dance literature, demonstrating how Spier and others have ignored the long-established indigenous political and economic hierar-chy which motivated the prophet movement among the Wet'suwet'en.[4]

True enough, Spier seems to defend the purely spiritual nature of the Prophet Dance, shifting any political message about the eradication of whites to postcontact 'derivatives.' Spier (1935: 40, 48) actually draws close connections between these so-called offshoot movements (like that led by the prophet Smohalla) and the 'Indian Wars' in the Northwest, while still claiming that the Prophet Dance proper had no such political impulse. Spier (1935: 46) asserts that such action never reached the 'cen-tre' of Plateau among the Sanpoil and Sinkaietk (and presumably the Skoyelpi and Sinixt). Rather, despite the influences of missionaries, these peoples 'still clung to the old shamanic religion and the Prophet cult.' Yet, Spier does offer discussion on the Christianized version of the Prophet Dance (a 'second wave'), in which he focuses on such innocuous European additions as bells and flags and the incorporation of the idea of Sabbath. He insists that no real conceptual transformation occurred

(Spier 1935: 37), even though later anthropologists, like Jay Miller (1989: 163), note that aboriginal peoples in the area of the Colville Reservation (including the Sinixt) 'professed both native and Catholic religions, a spiritual dualism tolerated by the Jesuits.'

In Spier's view, this kind of adaptation is not properly aboriginal. Indeed, Spier seems more defensive about his assertion of an unchanged conceptual motivation than is perhaps appropriate. It is as though Spier felt that if he admitted to any adaptation of non-native theology, to political or economic content (even that which may have existed prior to contact), or to any hostility towards European immigrants in the Prophet Dance, it would undermine his argument of the movement's cultural antiquity. By contrast, Spier (1935: 41) has no qualms in agreeing with Mooney that the political affectations of the Ghost Dance and Smohalla cult 'derivatives' are 'wholly intelligible as the result of the drastic interference with native life during the decades following 1850.' It is odd that Spier, educated as he was in the Boasian historical school of anthropology, could not allow for native peoples' changing worlds and ideologies within the context of their continuous relationship with ancient beliefs and practices.

Undoubtedly, Spier's theory falls short both in isolating mythological frameworks from political and economic systems and in understating the probable intensification of the movement during difficult times. Certainly, Spier is unrealistic if he expects to show definitively that all messianic movements in North America diffused from the Plateau and that such movements were of an entirely aboriginal ideological source. Yet, despite some obvious problems with his arguments and evidence, despite his unwarranted defensiveness to others' criticism of his thesis,[5] Spier's basic idea has merit.

As Spier asserts, it is unlikely that even extreme social and material upheaval would actually replace millennia of home-grown cosmology with an essentially new set of ideas. Instead, long-held cultural views probably coloured the response to new situations. Spier (1935: 16) does not view aboriginal peoples as entirely static. Indeed, he concedes that a conceptual field of ancient shamanic ideas and the Plateau peoples' 'constant concern with the dead' were probably the two ancient cultural principles which laid the 'groundwork from which the Prophet Dance complex could arise' in more recent times.

It is noteworthy that David Aberle (1959; 1966), unlike some of Spier's other critics, does not disregard the importance of pre-existing cultural beliefs in his 'deprivation theory.' Aberle, although rather single-minded in his materialist perspective, also offers a complex depiction of the tensions between continuity, change, and the negotiation of difficult circumstances. To be sure, as Aberle (1959) says in his argument for a deprivation theory, there is no reason why both cosmological continuity *and* distressing new circumstances could not have been motivators in the nineteenth-century Prophet Dance.

Some later theorists have been less flexible than David Aberle in their views of continuity and social change. Confronting Spier and his resistance in accommodating the changing perspectives of aboriginal peoples, Deward Walker (1969) and Christopher Miller (1985) seem to have taken the other extreme. These authors appear unreasonable in their claims that foreign goods and diseases, the horse, and rumours of Christianity (all of which arrived before the actual European immigrants) caused a *radical* dissociation from indigenous thought-ways. One exemplary quotation illustrates their belief of aboriginal peoples' severance from the past during times of change:

> Epidemic disease was merely the last of the many destructive waves that swept across the land in the eighteenth century, but it was the most devastating of the lot. The conjunction of sickness with the coming of horses, guns, climatic deterioration, and near constant war put an unbearable strain on the Plateau world. In response, the Plateau people abandoned many of their most treasured ideals ... in exchange for a chance at survival. (C. Miller 1985: 35)

Such a claim suggests that indigenous North American cultures are fragile and, in times of trouble, must be radically transformed if the people are to continue to exist at all. As well, ideas like this imply that such cultures could not withstand the brute force of European technology and beliefs in particular, that they fall like flies before Christian ideology and cut themselves off from the past forever.

In effect, these scholars advocate a kind of world-systems theory in which the conceptual (as well as the economic) life of the aboriginal 'periphery' has fallen to the mercy of a European colonial 'centre.' Two macroeconomists in the field of political sociology, Frank and Gills (1993), have written extensively on how capitalistic colonial 'centres' have subjugated and made dependent their so-called peripheries. While it is useful in understanding the power relations between disparate peoples with unequal access to economic resources, such a theoretical perspective seriously neglects the agency and resistance of those in the

'hinterland.' Moreover, it disregards the endurance of ideological continuity and the historical consciousness of peoples who have lived through
difficult times, like those of the North American Plateau.

As we have seen, some theorists appear to make excessive claims in
regards to radical discontinuity as a result of colonialism. However, it is
also untenable to assert that aboriginal peoples remained essentially
unchanged by the unprecedented circumstances in which they found
themselves by the nineteenth century. But the historical trends of the pre-
and early European contact eras may not necessarily have caused a turn
from local to more Europeanized thought ways, as Walker and Miller
suggest. Rather than an *abandonment* of ancient beliefs and practices in
peoples' desperate measures to defend themselves against social and
environmental chaos, it is conceivable that drastic change might have
promoted an actual *deepening* of already existing cultural perspectives (cf.
Basso 1984: 45). Others have noted such an intensification in economic
relations, despite the often severe alteration in a people's cultural and
material production. Sahlins (1993: 17), for instance, asserts that in a
colonial situation the first 'impulse of the people is not to become just
like us but more like themselves. They turn foreign goods to the service
of domestic ideas, to the objectification of their own relations and
notions of the good life.'

Fogelson, who has worked with the Sinixt's Shuswap neighbours, supports a similar theoretical framework of continuity in changing circumstances in his view of the Prophet Dance. Citing the prevalence of
'Orpheus-type tales' in which people travel to the land of the dead in
order to bring relatives back to the living, Fogelson (1985: 79–82) agrees
that prophecy movements were probably 'less keyed to the adoption of
Christian ideas of millenarian resurrection and more to indigenous conceptions that consider death to be a potentially reversible process.' Yet,
while recognizing a strong continuity, this anthropologist does not deny
the incredible symbolic impact of epidemics.[6] In fact, he has postulated
that the high numbers of casualties over a short period of time may have
caused a conceptual crisis because the living may not have had the means
or strength to perform proper mortuary rituals.

Fogelson (1989: 144–5) further contends that among many North
American peoples, death is seen as an ongoing process, as another social
role which mortuary rituals mark and facilitate. Hence, if proper ritual
action were not taken, the dead may not have been able to make the
social transition to their new role. In fact, 'given the premises of native
metaphysics and the paralyzing horror of the situation, it is perhaps con-

ceivable that for many Indians the victims did not really or fully die.' In the minds of the living, the dead may have been left in a kind of limbo, inhabiting a liminal field which allowed them to travel back and forth between their roles of life and death; perhaps, without the proper rite of passage, they were unable to initiate their journey into death.

Fogelson's idea can only be tested at the local level, by inquiring about concepts of death and the impact of epidemics. Among the Sinixt Interior Salish at Vallican, this idea of a disruption in the dead's normal social role certainly appears to have merit in situations where ancestral remains have been exhumed, as we shall see in the following chapter, 'Emergence.' If Fogelson's basic premise is correct among some people, as it seems to be among the Sinixt, it shows how indigenous cosmology responded to the pressures of unusual circumstances. It does not show a 'breach' of continuity.

Change as Continuity

Theoretical arguments about continuity and change like those of Fogelson, Walker, Mills, Aberle, and Spier have been an issue of debate for years in the anthropological community. At the forefront of such deliberations, though not uncontroversial, Marshall Sahlins has attempted to demonstrate how people employ their local world views to interpret unprecedented occurrences.

Asking 'whether the continuity of any system ever occurs without its alteration, or alteration without continuity,' Sahlins (1981: 67) presents a more balanced perspective on the tension between cultural variation and structure during colonial times. In a recent essay, Sahlins (1993: 4–5) vigorously opposes the 'post-modern' idea of 'invented traditions' which assumes that colonized peoples' 'ideas of ancient custom are developed out of the colonial experience' and that they therefore 'have nothing to do but recreate themselves in the image others have made of them.' He believes such analyses suggest that

> the main historical activity remaining to the underlying people is to misconstrue the effects of such imperialism as their own cultural traditions. Worse yet, their cultural false consciousness is normalizing. In the name of ancestral practice, the people construct an essentialized culture: a supposedly unchanging inheritance, sheltered from the contestations of a true social existence. (Sahlins 1993: 6)

Sahlins's chief criticism here is that many analyses of colonial power relations, with their 'sentimental pessimism,' deny peoples' agency as well as their historical consciousness and cultural identity. People do not forget who they are so easily, and who they choose to be is not entirely constructed in reaction to colonialism. Rather, it is we anthropologists who forget that, colonized or uncolonized, 'local people integrate the world system in something even more inclusive: their own system of the world.' Indeed, we neglect the fact that people of *all* cultures 'must construct their own existence in relation to external conditions, natural and social, which they did not create or control, yet cannot avoid.' In other words, all of us think, feel, respond, and create in an environment which shapes us and which we, in turn, shape. Hence, even in oppressive circumstances, interaction with a foreign system is not capitulation, but a part of peoples' continued cultural, economic, and political negotiation with a complex, ever-changing environment. Cultural continuity does not mean stasis or blind repetition of ancient custom; rather, variation is an inseparable part of structure in human societies (Sahlins 1993: 7, 11, 13, 16).

With Sahlins's theoretical position in mind, the terminology of 'change' and 'continuity' becomes problematic. Of course, we have for years used 'change' to connote a breakage in the link with the past while 'continuity' evokes images of the seamless, wavy flow of an unhindered time-stream. Neither image is correct. There is no direct line to the past and there is no absolute rupture. As Sahlins suggests, change *is* continuity, and vice versa. Every individual newly experiences and creates her culture. Every individual responds to the multiple forces and influences in her life, including ideas which have in some form endured for generations. Those ideas are obviously not the very same ideas thought by great grandparents, grandparents, or parents. What child thinks exactly the way her mother or father does? Surely, ideas are imagined in a living person's own way, with her own cognitive innovations, her own interpretations, and her own applications to her own current context.

As we know, ideas are not objects. They cannot be handed on like an antique set of china, as palpable forms which persons from another era possessed. Rather, ideas are new every time someone thinks them. They change over the course of individuals' lives as well as through generations. Thus, living persons' perceptions of how other generations behaved and thought are perceptions which help to make sense of the lives they live now. Ideas are our own, yet we do inherit something; there is some 'social memory,' as Fentress and Wickham (1992) call it.

Perhaps we inherit memory of ideas more like weather than fine bone china. There are kinds of memories like there are kinds of weather; there is rain, but no rain is alike. Intangible and fleeting, memory, like weather, constantly moves and changes, returns in sometimes similar but always unreplicable forms, takes on our moods, surprises us, frightens us, helps us, and destroys us. Different kinds of weather are storied by culture too: think of monsoons and twisters, mist and ice fog. Communities lay great value and meaning upon them; they are metaphors by which we live. And, of course, there are individual preferences for weather. Familiar forms – and some not so familiar – are experienced by each of us anew. How we conceive of and respond to memories, as to weather, depends on cultural and individual influences.

Though never the same, there is no doubt that in some way ideas come down through generations by way of individuals. Indeed:

> Individual memory is not simply personal: the memories which constitute our identity and provide the context for every thought and action are not only our own, but are learned, borrowed, and inherited – in part, and part of, a common stock, constructed, sustained, and transmitted by the families, communities, and cultures to which we belong. No human group is constituted, no code of conduct promulgated, no thought given form, no action committed, no knowledge communicated, without its intervention; history itself is both a product and a source of social memory. (Moore 1992: viii)

Fentress and Wickham (1992: 7) believe this social memory 'is structured by language, by teaching and observing, by collectively held ideas, and by experiences shared with others.' Primarily transmitted through oral accounts, social memory is 'an expression of collective experience ... [which] identifies a group, giving it a sense of its past and defining its aspirations for the future.' More than this, 'Social memory is a source of knowledge. This means that it does more than provide a set of categories through which, in an unselfconscious way, a group experiences its surroundings; it also provides the groups with material for conscious reflection' (Fentress and Wickham 1992: x, 25–6).

Authors like Fentress and Wickham have written a considerable amount on the mechanics of social memory – the actual methods by which individuals transmit and obtain aspects of certain persistent cultural ideas. However, this aspect of inquiry is of lesser focus in my work among the Lakes people at Vallican than is their current application of social memory. Nevertheless, it is worth noting one aspect of transmission: it is *historical consciousness* that makes us 'experience the present as connected to the past. Our experience of the present is thus embedded in past experience. Memory represents the past and present as connected to each other, and consistent with each other' (Fentress and Wickham 1992: 24). However, such conscious memory of history has its limitations: no individual is entirely aware of the genesis of her ideas or the multiple current and historical factors which motivate her. In addition, cultures encourage critical thought among individuals in different ways, and certainly, individual awareness varies from person to person.

Perhaps obvious but still important to emphasize, just because someone has historical consciousness of one's cultural identity and cultural world view does not mean that she understands how historical figures actually thought. In other words, such consciousness does not necessarily provide accurate ideas of an 'objective history.' We are conscious of what we *believe* to have been the past. But neither does this mean that there is no continuum of ideas in what we believe. As Fentress and Wickham (1992: xi) say, 'Social memory is, in fact, often selective, distorted, and inaccurate. None the less, it is important to recognize that it is not necessarily any of these; it can be extremely exact, when people have found it socially relevant from that day to this to remember and recount an event in the way it was originally experienced.'

True enough, social memory is a participatory activity, not a static thing. We engage it as necessary. Nevertheless, we must not overly accentuate the agency involved in remembering and constructing thought. Neither historical exactitude nor selectivity of memory arises only through our *consciousness*. Humans are hardly so omniscient. The way we think comes too from any number of changing and continuous individual and cultural influences of which we are quite *un*aware.

Clearly, the oppositional terms 'change' and 'continuity' do not encompass the integrated concepts found in a theory of social memory. My colleague Gastón Gordillo (personal communication 1997) suggests other words like cultural 'resignification' and 'reformulation' in an effort to properly combine the two concepts as a dialectic. However, in my view, these words underemphasize the potential staying-power of ideas. In fact, they emphasize change. Fentress and Wickham (1992: 201) similarly accent change, stating that ideas about the past are really only products of a current context, that is, recent 'inventions.' They say, 'For many groups, [having social memory] means putting the puzzle back together: inventing the past to fit the present or, equally, the present to fit the past. We preserve the past at the cost of decontextualizing it, and partially blotting it out.'

It is true that every cultural creation and interaction is new and current, always at work to make sense of the present in light of the past. Yet, not necessarily in a transparent or direct way, these creations are also always influenced to varying degrees by the *actuality* of cultural history – what people actually thought and did in historical times. Here, I am more closely identified with Marshall Sahlins in his feeling that academics have gone too far in reversing social science's old view of an undisturbed, direct connection between peoples and their pasts. As we shall see among the Sinixt at Vallican in the next chapter, it is possible to have reformulated ideas about the past while also possessing strong elements of historically cultural ideas. Therefore, we should not talk about change *and* continuity – that is, in opposition – but rather change *as* continuity – as dialectic. In drawing maps, Alfred Kroeber resigned himself to the necessary evil of using boundaries as an heuristic device symbolic of a more dynamic actuality. Like him, I resign myself to the overused terms change and continuity, dependent upon the reader's ability to imbue them with the subtleties of cultural history.

Let's be clear: on the ground, ideas about change and continuity are political. To be sure, the concept of change has actually been used as a political tool against aboriginal peoples. For instance, in the British Columbia Supreme Court *Delgamuukw* case,[7] Chief Justice Allan McEachern (1991) declared the plaintiffs' aboriginal rights extinguished in part because the Gitksan and Wet'suwet'en of today are so different from those Gitksan and Wet'suwet'en who had first contact with new European immigrants generations ago. Even though the Supreme Court of Canada (1997) has found McEachern to be in error and has ordered a retrial, in certain legal circles aboriginality evidently means stasis. While we may acknowledge that every culture is always changing, change is thus used as a political weapon to delegitimize the identity and privileges of aboriginal peoples.

The relationship between colonizer and colonized is not an easy one. Some manner of self-defence is often critical for those living with change instigated in part by colonial or imperialist regimes, but negotiation with the dominant society is an inevitable part of colonized peoples' continued cultural existence. As Sahlins (1993: 19) says, aboriginal peoples have often been 'prepared to make compromises with the dominant culture, even to deploy its techniques and ideals – in the course of distinguishing their own.'

But a conflict arises in the dominant society's view of such adaptation strategies. The problem comes in part from the colonizers' tendency to imagine non-western worlds as frozen in time, having no real historical depth and thus being unable to change without losing their identities. They perceive peoples, particularly those from oral societies, as of the past – archaic, obsolete, even invisible. From this perspective, one which has its roots in old social theories of unilineal evolutionism, if Indians act like anything other than their ancestors at the time of contact with Europeans, they are not really Indians. In other words, they cannot be both 'modern' *and* 'indigenous.'

Yet for aboriginal peoples living all over North America today, historical consciousness and a sense of cultural identity continue to hold strong, even through centuries of colonization and attempted acculturation. These people easily conceive of themselves as both modern and indigenous. Despite others' incredulity, they are quite aware of their own continued existence as cultural entities.

The position of apparent extinction in which the Sinixt find themselves today is a graphic example of this conflict of cultural views and of the political quagmire which can result from it. Yet there is a glimmer of poetry, a poignant irony in the invisibility of the Sinixt. Not only anthropologists but European North American society as a whole have expected and thus facilitated – even concocted – their disappearance. For how long now have Euros been wringing their hands over (or delighting in) the Vanishing Race? How many decades have passed in watching the stoic backs and swishing horse tails move graciously off into Edward Curtis's last sunset? Anthropologists and archaeologists have been chasing after salvage operations for generations, scurrying to write up passing worlds before the prophesied clap of doom, the end of an age, the seal of the tomb behind them. And how many missionaries have dragged children through European concepts of the evolutionary stages of agriculture, industry, and Victorian orderliness – away from the past and into a bright, shiny future? How many nomads have been forcibly settled, how many hunters and fishers made farmers, transformed from autonomous political groups to uniform band council bureaucracies directed at every turn by federal agencies? How sad, we seem to have said, but how necessary and inevitable: the future is before us; we can't live in the past.

Yet there they are, and aren't we surprised. Aren't we incredulous. To think that all this time the Sinixt ('the *who?*') have known themselves without our expertise. We non-natives in Canada, on the other hand, have known them only through their ancestral remains – the only kind of documentation we thought available. We have made them real for ourselves by beholding them, their tangible skeletons, a whisper from the past. Like wizards, we conjure them into existence through formulations and analyses, through our anthropological gaze. Obedient familiars, they take shape and voice only through our power, lie still in crates when our interest wanes.

Indeed, we have relegated the Sinixt to the past, to extinction, only to be startled when they rise from the dead to reclaim their own. Ironic, yes, that the living only appear so that they can take from us the bones of their ancestors, all that have been previously visible to us. The invisible arise, materialize, to set the world in order: to conceal from us their dead, to make invisible our material proofs of their former existence, and to be themselves named living again. An exchange of death for life, so to speak. A resurrection. As though, to our astonishment, the prophecies of the nineteenth-century aboriginal visionaries are coming to fruition at last, the Earth Woman has turned round on herself and offered up her dead.

But the point is, they were never dead in the first place, not as a people. They were just somewhere else. Then, is it *our* vision which enlivens them, our fieldnotes, maps, photos, computer printouts, and publications – our power/knowledge, to use Foucault's term – which wash away the vanishing cream? Or is it *their* desire, their choice to be known at a time when anonymity among others has felt dangerous?

At issue here is the tension between written and oral, or material and temporal, expressions of history. For certain, material documents (archaeological artefacts included) take precedence in North America. This is especially true in 'official' arenas like the court system and governmental bureaucracies, causing a terrible imbalance in the legal and political credibility between oral and literate versions of history. Even though the recent Supreme Court of Canada (1997) decision on *Delgamuukw* has given weight to oral history as evidence, we have yet to see how much substantial difference a single legal decision will have on centuries of bias in favour of documentary evidence.

Regardless of *Delgamuukw*, time has shown that those who hold and create documents have become the owners and caretakers of history (Fogelson 1989: 142).[8] As we have seen in the case of the Lakes, having incohesive documentary evidence is as good as not existing in the dominant society's view. Yet the source of conflict between ideas of the disappearance and the resurrection of aboriginal peoples goes deeper than the mere material objectification of histories. It is rooted in our ideas of time – or more precisely, oversimplified depictions of our ideas of time.

Nineteenth-century unilineal evolutionary schemata are largely responsible for placing different cultural, political, and economic lifeways into hierarchized time sequences. Herbert Spencer and other European Social Darwinists who advocated such paradigms felt that looking upon non-western peoples was like looking back in time to their own societies' formative stages of development. R.H. Pearce sums up how evolutionary views of progress have impacted on North American aboriginal peoples:

> Westward American progress would, in fact, be understood to be reproducing this historical progression [of unilineal evolutionism]; the savage would be understood as one who had not and somehow could not progress into the civilized, who would inevitably be destroyed by the civilized ... For the Indian was the remnant of a savage past away from which civilized men had struggled to grow. To study him was to study the past. To civilize him was to triumph over the past. To kill him was to kill the past. History would thus be the key to the moral worth of cultures; the history of [North] American civilization would thus be conceived as three-dimensional, progressing from past to present, from east to west, from lower to higher. (Pearce 1953: 49, quoted in Lake 1991: 127)

Initiated with Franz Boas's historical methods, anthropology has soundly trounced ideas like these, that various peoples around the world are stuck on their alloted rungs ascending an evolutionary ladder. Unfortunately, much of our society still adheres to unilineal evolutionary views to a great extent, but at least we scholars have come to terms with the idea that all living peoples are current. Or have we?

In my search for sources on time perspectives of Plateau peoples, I discovered that theories of timelessness continue to proliferate in the Native Studies literature. True enough, the current antihistoricism is hidden, usually in simplistic dichotomies of cyclic and linear time. Mircea Eliade (1954), for example, has been a proponent of this idea, seducing many with romantic talk of archetypes, regeneration of the world, and myths of the eternal return in his theoretical drafts of non-western peoples. Using the Ghost Dance as an exemplary model, he has attempted to show how 'archaic man acknowledges no act which has not been previously posited and lived by someone else ... His life is a ceaseless repetition of gestures initiated by others ... [which] acquire meaning, reality, solely to the extent to which they repeat a primordial act' (Eliade 1954: 5). In other words, the 'archaic ontology' places them in a kind of time-eddy – sloshing round and round in their mythical origins unable to escape to the newness of it all.

Now, you might wonder why I would resort to an old chestnut like Eliade to state my case. Believe it or not, he continues to have followers, and Calvin Martin, an historian from Rutgers University, is perhaps one of his keenest disciples. Under the rubric of cultural relativity, Martin believes that

the Indian is usually shoehorned into the dominant culture's paradigm of reason and logic, its calculus of viewing the world and manipulating its parts. The traditional historian colonizes the Indian's mind, like a virus commandeering the cell's genetic machinery. The typical procedure is to make Amerindians into what might be termed a 'people of history,' such as we have become in our civilization. Let it be said bluntly and forcefully that Native Americans traditionally subscribed to a philosophy of history, and of time, profoundly different from ours and that of our forbears. (Martin 1987: 6)

What is that 'philosophy of history, and of time' to which aboriginal peoples adhere? Quoting from Lévi-Strauss's *The Savage Mind*, Martin (1987: 15; 27) proclaims that the 'characteristic feature of the savage mind is its timelessness.' He calls Indians a 'people of myth' and Europeans a 'people of history,' believing that we can 'refer to and discuss an overarching cosmology, or world view, seemingly distinctive to Native American societies – all of them – just as one may describe Western thinking in similarly gross terms.' In this, he follows Eliade's opinion that there are '"two distinct orientations" in human society, "the one traditional ... that of cyclical time, periodically regenerating itself *ad infinitum*; the other modern, that of finite time."' The world, then, according to Martin (1987: 194–5), is split into temporal orders which divide along aboriginal/western lines: 'The one is eternal, cyclical, endlessly repetitive, powered by Nature, and cosmogenic. The other, a linear segment, remorselessly historical, profane, and anthropological [anthropocentric].'

There is no little irony in Martin's (1987: 24) scolding of our tendency 'to invent Indians for all seasons.' Indeed, why he cannot see his own theoretical formulations as inventive is difficult to imagine. While attempting to show how historians have colonized the so-called Indian mind, forming it in their own image, Martin has perpetuated the 'gross' (his word) and unsophisticated stereotype of a homogenized and reified 'Indian,' a stereotype which is truly a product of colonization. Surely, 'great divide' theories like Martin's which isolate European and aboriginal North

American cosmologies into bounded, disparate, and internally congruous units are probably one of the greatest sources of historical and contemporary misunderstandings of North American indigenous peoples.

As Comanche writer Paul Chaat Smith (1994: 38) puts it, more than anything else, 'What has made us one people is the common legacy of colonialism and diaspora.' Beyond this shared history, North American societies grew up as a 'riot of vastly different cultures.' Yet this 'amazing variety of human civilization that existed five hundred years ago has been replaced in the popular imagination by one image ... The true story is simply too messy and complicated. And too threatening. The myth of the noble savages, completely unable to cope with modern times goes down much easier.'

Extreme as his theories of homogeneity are, Calvin Martin isn't alone. Other scholars, from a wide variety of disciplines and ethnic backgrounds (including aboriginal North American), draw similar conclusions of homogeneity. Two examples are N. Scott Momaday (1976), who believes in a mythic 'racial memory' common to all North American peoples, and Jamake Highwater (1981), who studies their 'primal mind.' The latter has carefully avoided the word 'primitive' because of negative connotations, but his renovation of the term cannot hide its theoretical basis in nineteenth-century unilineal evolutionism – it still derives from the idea of a *primary* stage of evolution.[9]

While this stereotype is profoundly influential, it is more than the homogenization of North American peoples which denies the complexity of the current and historical cultural worlds on this continent. It is also the utterly simplistic and monolithic views of time. The problem here is not that ideas about cyclical and linear time do not exist, but rather that there are not only *two* kinds of time, and that these are not split neatly between the constructed categories of 'western' and 'non-western' peoples.

Truly, the idea that western peoples think exclusively in a profane, linear time frame is as much a bastardization of cultural complexity as the idea of cyclic, mythic Indians. If we shun received knowledge on the matter and question linear time's label of 'profanity,' we may find that the ideal of linear progress is as mythical and archetypal – indeed, as *cyclical* – as any seemingly exotic rituals and exotic hunting lives of exotic tribes. One possible interpretation for the idea of progress is that it originates in a desire to return to Paradise, to be flawless and perfect, as in the origin stories of Genesis. From this perspective, the goals of the Enlightenment are actually rooted in a desire for world renewal, akin to seeking Christ's resurrection, a recurrent, cyclical drive to return to our place of grace at the right-hand side of God. Adherence to linear time and the quest for progress shows that we are forever in the mythic struggle of getting back to the perfect state in which we dwelled at the original moment of our Creation.

Let's take a recent popular media event as an example. In the company of friends a few summers ago, I rolled my eyes in disdain when the conversation turned to the O.J. Simpson trial.[10] ('What could be more profane?' thought I.) One in the gathering, a lawyer, reprimanded me for being so closed-minded and shallow. After all, wasn't the public appeal of the trial based entirely in the archetype of the Fallen Hero? Wasn't it Lucifer? Wasn't it Greek tragedy and hubris and Oedipus all over again, an enactment of the most central mythic themes in western culture? I had to concur that his was a credible interpretation. If we follow this logic, in the apparently charmed life and subsequent infamy of O.J. Simpson we see archetypal motivations in everyday life: reliving Eden, re-experiencing the disaster of Original Sin. Surely, we could thus view even the most material, nonspiritual pursuits – like the Marxists' Great March to Utopia – as mythic, sacred, cyclical ventures, if we so choose. But then, where are all the Mircea Eliades and Jamake Highwaters and Calvin Martins to proclaim the primitivism of 'western thought'? What specialist in mythology will acknowledge that the sacred and the profane cohabit the daily workings of the 'western mind'?

A considerable number of academics have been guilty of thus approaching aboriginal peoples with the lens of spirituality. We *make* Indians primitive and sacred and archetypal with our framework of interpretation and by our presuppositions of 'non-western' views of time. At the same time, we assume that, since the Enlightenment at least, Europeans have been secular and free of myth. I agree that important root myths inform and motivate culture, but not only outside the bounds of the 'west.' True, Indians have their mythic motivations, but so do peoples of European descent.

Commenting on the enforced spiritualism of aboriginal peoples, Paul Chaat Smith (1994: 34) says that the 'discourse on Indian art or politics or culture, even among people of good will, is continually frustrated by the distinctive, romanticized type of racism that confronts Indians today. This romanticism is a highly developed, deeply ideological system,' ever tenacious in academic and popular renderings alike. He adds:

Some will always find white inventions of Indians preferable to the real thing. There will always be a market for both nostalgia and fantasy. The cottage industry of Native Americana, formerly the province of hippies and enterprising opportunists, has become mainstream and professional. Today, in the average chain bookstore in the United States, most of the Indian titles are in the new-age section. Well-meaning feminists conduct Indian rituals and the men's movement appropriates Indian drumming for their get-togethers. The myth-making machinery that, in earlier days, made us out to be primitive and simple now says we are spiritually advanced and environmentally perfect. Anything, it seems, but fully human. Over time these cartoon images have never worked to our advantage and, even though much in the new version is flattering, I can't see that it will help us in the long run. (Smith 1994: 39)

A similar sentiment is expressed by Gerald Vizenor (1986: 328), a professor of Chippewa descent, in regards to the contemporary reburial movement among North American aboriginal peoples. He feels that purely spiritualist interpretations of the repatriation and reburial of indigenous ancestral remains amounts to 'primitivist simplification.'

It is worth noting here that aboriginal peoples of the West Kootenays have not avoided this kind of Noble Savage imagery. In his *Historic Nelson*, John Norris (1995: 20) uses the metaphor of 'primeval serenity' to an extreme, actually equating the peoples of Kootenay Lake with animals. He says that upon the first signs of spring, the Indians

like the animals, would respond to the ancient rhythms of rebirth by shaking off winter's lethargy and moving outward from confinement. Soon they would paddle northward onto the lake in their canoes, family by family, seeking out the hunting, fishing, and berry-picking locations allotted to each by tradition. Their activities, like those of the animals, would hardly ruffle the great flow of nature. (Norris 1995: 19)

For Norris, Indians are products of nature, not creators of culture. In fact, they are timeless, living only in response to the cycle of the land's seasons. On the other hand, the activities of Europeans (unlike the animals) are outside of nature, that is, cultural. Norris (1995: 20) says that with the late-nineteenth-century Silver Rush, 'Europeans ... [would] initiate in earnest the destruction of [the land's] primeval serenity.' Time apparently begins with the rupture of 'primeval' cycles, only possible at the hand of Europeans. Norris's words are proof that the romantic racism of one-dimensional nature/culture oppositions is hard to shake.

If we force our way past stereotypes like these, we find that *all* world views are motivated by myths to some extent, and as cultures have differ-ent stories, cosmological perspectives vary from people to people. But cosmology and temporal analysis do not start and end with myths and archetypes. To be sure, we live by multiple interconnected views of time which are motivated in a number of ways. One theory, offered by Ben-jamin Lee Whorf (1983 [1941]), proposes that grammatical structures influence views of time. With the incredible linguistic diversity in North America, one can only imagine the temporal possibilities.[11] Other schol-ars, like E.P. Thompson (1967), have demonstrated how views of time and history are altered by changes in economic practices. In addition, Maurice Bloch (n.d.) has been very critical of those who attempt to bestow a people with a single generalized temporal conception and has demonstrated, to the contrary, that cultural views of time are internally heterogeneous, fitting into categories such as those appropriate to either formal or informal social contexts. These may be used on different occa-sions for different social purposes, and the exclusive expression of one kind of time, Bloch stresses, does not preclude the simultaneous acknowl-edgment of any of the others. Similarly, Fogelson points out that in writ-ing history, we

> must take into account the complex interaction of several concurrent sys-tems of time. A non-exhaustive list could include: cosmological time, social structural time, seasonal time, life cyclical time, prophetic time, and experi-ential time that can often be classed as time-out-of-time. Most of these temporal orientations are oscillating and repetitive, and non-lineal, if not curvilinear. (Fogelson 1985: 84–5)

So too, long sweeps of time are dependent on a multiplicity of com-partmentalized times, all of which 'provide the interwoven threads that result in rich tapestries of human history' (Fogelson 1989: 137). Thomas Overholt (1974) reminds us that we are not passive victims to our tempo-ral conceptions; rather, we participate in and negotiate with our systems of time. Our understanding of temporality is both conscious and uncon-scious, both metaphoric and literal.

Land as Memory, Land as Identity

Scholars have noted that conceptions of time cannot be separated from space, and that space is in fact the anchor of time. Much has been made of the association of aboriginal North Americans and their connection to land, perhaps to a romantic extreme, as Paul Chaat Smith notes above. However, all people find cultural and historicized meaning in space. Exploring the cultural symbolism of the forestlands of Poland and Germany, for example, Simon Schama's *Landscape and Memory* (1995) offers an eloquent discussion of how western European history and historical consciousness are embedded in various places. In his study of the Inuit of Kangersuatsiaq, Northwest Greenland, Mark Nuttall (1992) also considers how people imbue land with time. Nuttall proposes a concept called 'memoryscape [which] is constructed with people's mental images of the environment, with particular emphasis on places as remembered places.' In Nuttall's view, humans perceive the physical world through their senses while simultaneously culturally modifying, ordering, and conceptualizing it through experience, thought, and language. Around Kangersuatsiaq, for example,

> the places a hunter frequents are stamped with the indelible marks of community. These marks are not visible, but are manifest in place names, memories of hunting and of past events. All give a sense of a bounded locality distinct from the memoryscape of neighbouring communities. To borrow the often used Lévi-Strauss phrase, places are 'good to think with' and nurture a feeling of belonging. (Nuttall 1992: 39–40)

In this example, hunting is not simply an economic act, but an interaction of the hunter with space and time during which geography takes on 'physical, mythical, factual, and historical meaning' (Nuttall 1992: 51). The author claims, 'Events, whether contemporary, historical or mythical, that happen at certain points in the local area tend to become integral elements of those places. They are thought about and remembered with reference to specific events and experiences ... Memories take the form of stories about real and remembered things. They cannot be separated from the land ...' (Nuttall 1992: 54).

While Nuttall's notion of memoryscape captures elements of peoples' relationships to land, it is limited to established communities which currently live in the landscape they culturalize. Noncommunity land is land *without* memory or a 'memory-desert where "each little place with its name and legend produced a vivid pause in the imagination"' (N. Gunn 1969: 34). An area, while familiar to those who hunt and live there, none the less becomes unknown territory to those who have no knowledge or memory of it' (Nuttall 1992: 57). Thus, through a kind of geographic archives, memoryscape defines a community's living boundaries.

Not many of the people at Vallican had personal living memories of the landscape of the Sinixt's northern territory before 1989. How then does memoryscape apply to displaced peoples' ideas of land in which their ancestors lived? What of people outside the homeland? Gupta and Ferguson (1992: 10) believe that the 'natural' geographic boundaries on which anthropology has depended so heavily to define culture groups are dubious. With so much movement around the globe, all cultures – even those which remain in homelands of antiquity – are in a sense displaced. In other words, we can no longer pretend that culture groups are discrete, easily definable spots on the map.

Gupta and Ferguson (1992: 10) say that 'even people remaining in familiar and ancestral places find the nature of their relation to place ineluctably changed, and the illusion of a natural and essential connection between the place and the culture broken.' Of course, this does not preclude peoples' living and working memory of place; rather, it is *anthropologists'* illusion of a simple connection between land and culture that is broken, our presumption that people could ever be divided into uniform, bounded geographic units.

Memory is constantly changing, perhaps even more rapidly for those who do not live daily in remembered places. Hence, for many such people, identity becomes threatened and geographic repositories of social memory become safeguards of that identity. 'Remembered places have often served as symbolic anchors of community for dispersed people,' write Gupta and Ferguson (1992: 11). That is, remembered places become imbued with cultural power that might not be so potent if the integrity of those places were unthreatened. Around the world, '"Homeland" ... remains one of the most powerful unifying symbols for mobile and displaced peoples, though the relation to homeland may be very differently constructed in different settings.' The irony of the current era is that 'as actual places and localities become ever more blurred and indeterminate, *ideas* of culturally and ethnically distinct places become perhaps even more salient.' Indeed, 'displaced peoples cluster around remembered or imagined homelands, places, or communities in a world that seems increasingly to deny such firm territorialized anchors in their actuality.'[12]

Points of land, from this theoretical perspective, become iconic, emblematic for a culture and its identity. More than having an extensive, detailed, and unified conceptualization of every corner of the land, as expressed in Nuttall's memoryscape, peoples jarred from a place of antiquity are more likely to distinguish specific geographic markers which embody cultural identity. Perhaps more sensitive to this pinpointed relationship of people with their historicized sites, early-twentieth-century literary critic Mikhail Bakhtin's (1981) concept of the 'chronotope' shows how time can be geographically concentrated. By way of Basso (1984), Nuttall actually formulates his concept of memoryscape partially from the more elaborate work of Bakhtin.

In his literary theory of novels, Bakhtin uses the term chronotope for the fusion of time and space. A chronotope is time which

> takes on flesh and becomes visible for human contemplation; likewise, space becomes charged and responsive to the movements of time and history and the enduring character of a people ... Chronotopes thus stand as monuments to the community itself, as symbols of it, as forces operating to shape its members' images of themselves. (Bakhtin 1981: 7)

Bakhtin took this concept of the chronotope (literally, 'time space') from physics and applied it to the study of time and space in literature. Writes Bakhtin (1981: 84), scientists' use of the chronotope 'is not important for our purposes; we are borrowing it for literary criticism almost as a metaphor ... What counts for us is the fact that it expresses the inseparability of space and time (time as the fourth dimension of space).' So too, anthropologists like Basso (1984) have appropriated the term for their own uses. For the anthropologist, a chronotope is taken out of the literary context and placed in the social one. What counts in our case is not the fusion of time and space in the novel, but instead in the community.

Basso applies Bakhtin's concept generally, but perception of time and space is never uniform. Bakhtin uses the concept of chronotope to uncover the *specifics* of time in space. He discusses how in ancient literary forms time-space becomes a concrete metaphor like a building or public square. For example, often represented by the chronotope of the 'road' ('spatial and temporal paths'), adventure-time or the 'epic past' is the dominant form of time in the genre of the Greek Romance novel; it works to push characters relentlessly through space by way of escape, persecution, and quests. Though the characters are perpetually on the move in their own personal time-space, there is never any reference to other times in this literary form – no past, no future. 'Walled off from all subsequent times, the epic past is absolute and complete. It is as closed as a circle; inside it everything is finished, already over.' Thus, the epic past is inaccessible to the reader or listener; it is a distant and closed time-space embodied in the road on which the characters travel (Bakhtin 1981: 87, 105, 243; Morris 1994: 182).

As in Bakhtin's exploration of literary chronotopes like the road in Greek Romance novels, anthropologists must similarly seek out the specifics of how people variously experience time-space. Chronotopes as applied by the social sciences are specific places with historical weight. They are sites of cultural identification, places like the English cathedral altar where the Archbishop of Canterbury was murdered, or the Hebrew mountain-top fortress of Masada, or the Blackfoot's etched walls at Writing-on-Stone near the Sweet Grass Hills – places to which people can point in demonstration of their history and identity.

But chronotopes need not be so famous as these. Indeed, places all around us are fraught with cultural memory and social meanings – sacred, economic, political, ethnic – although some hold more power than others. To participate with such a place, to acknowledge one's historical connection to a chronotope, is in fact a form of synchrony, the merging of oneself with all the significant historical events and all the people who ever passed that place. Most often specific to a particular culture, they are portals to both past and future, places of communication and identification with those who came before and those who will come after. But it is important to emphasize that to solidify time in this way is not to homogenize the memories of individual people. A chronotope may be like the set of bone china dishes one inherits, but the *ideas* about those dishes are still weather-like. The chronotope is merely a concrete symbol onto which are projected the more elusive and ever-changing concepts of cultural identity and history.

We will see in the next chapter how the chronotope applies specifically to the Vallican village and burial site, how it functions 'as the primary means for materializing time in space, emerges as a center for concretizing representation' for a displaced people (Bakhtin 1981: 250). For now, however, as described by Alexander Christie in the previous chapter, the kp'ítl'els burial ground at the confluence of the Kootenay and Columbia Rivers will suffice as an example of a chronotope in the anthropological context:

> I know of four graveyards close to our houses, and there are other older burials I cannot point out. I know that Indians burying their dead there often came on the bones of other dead they had not known. The graveyards I know had sticks and crosses erected at the graves and rings of stone around the outside. In one of these cemeteries are buried my two children, my brother, my sister Mary and my first Cousin ... In another graveyard are buried Frank's wife and some old men and women. (Alexander Christie 1914)

Through the kp'ítl'els graves, Alexander Christie distinguishes between the recent past and the distant past. Though all exist in the same place, the graves have different connections to Alexander Christie depending upon time-distance and personal relationships with or knowledge of the person interred. For Alexander Christie, kp'ítl'els holds a *personalized* time-space as well as a more distant and generalized *cultural* time-space.

To be explored in the next chapter, this kind of multilayered chronotope similarly exists at Vallican. A distant or epic past occurs in conjunction with communal and personal pasts, the former time concept surfacing through localized myth and undisturbed ancestral graves, the latter ones by way of family stories and individuals' remembrances of the Slocan. But there is also another kind of time layer at Vallican. Unknown ancestors are personalized through the exhumation and subsequent reburial of the bodily remains of individuals who lived in the distant past. That is, reburial brings living people into direct, tangible contact with ancient ancestral remains, thus drawing together the distant past and the present. At Vallican, exhumation and reburial have caused distant time to break out of its epic capsule and, metaphorically, enter into current time.

All humans are not conceptually the same in regards to time and place. True, everyone lives in a variety of temporal spaces, but these vary from society to society and person to person, thus reinforcing cultural and individual identity and historical consciousness. The differences between groups come from the cultural specifics, however, not from a great divide between stereotyped and essentialized western and non-western peoples. The detail and complexity of our cultures shape us – our history, land, language, mythology – not vast racial categories.

It is a shame that some see themselves only as 'linear' thinkers when a multitude of conceptual riches is everywhere around them. So too, the bestowal of aboriginal peoples with a label of cyclic mysticism is criminally simplistic, condemning them to the anachronistic, untimely role of the Noble Savage, doomed to vanish at any moment. To be sure, such one-dimensional views rub off on our theoretical formulations of cultural movements such as the nineteenth-century Prophet Dance and the contemporary efforts of aboriginal peoples to repatriate and rebury the exhumed remains of their ancestors. But this oversimplification is not merely a poor representation of cultural complexity. It is also political. Surely, to consider a people 'extinct' is a political matter, and Indians can only really vanish – that is, become extinct – if we believe in the prophecies of an exclusively linear, evolutionary time.

For those of us who have taken the prophetic voice of doom to heart, indigenous peoples have surprised us. Many have had their own prophecies which allow for their continued existence in spite of so much social change. The historical consciousness of people like the Sinixt at Vallican binds their present lives with their ethnic past. But the result of our incredulity at their resurrection is not merely an interesting conflict in metaphysics; it has caused them economic and political and, yes, spiritual hardship. Even so, they continue to defy European prophecies and emerge from the chaos as a people tied together in place and time through the strength of cultural identity.

chapter five

Emergence:
Distress, Memory, and the Re-creation of
Morality among an Invisible People

*It's going to be hope or death. We can't live the way we are now. My people will be
living zombies in another twenty years.*

Jim Stelkia, Sinixt[1]

*It's really comforting and peaceful here. You go into the mountains and you can get
completely away from the modern world. You can bend down and pick a berry and
know that your ancestors were here picking the same berry, and you feel at home.*

Bob Campbell, Sinixt[2]

Now this place is a kind of Mecca.

Vanessa Holloman, Sinixt

Degrees of historical consciousness and cultural identity vary from group
to group, just as they do from individual to individual within groups.
Every person juggles her ideas of the past with her concept of identity in
the present, even though there are undoubtedly some people who have a
mere thread connecting them with their past. Yet, many North American
aboriginal peoples do have a strong sense of identification with their
ethnic past, a past in which their ancestors often lived quite differently
than they do today.

Among the Sinixt Interior Salish, history also means different things to
different people. Individuals apply their ideas of the past and identity to
themselves and their situations differently. Of course, there is no single
Sinixt way of thinking or acting, just as there is no single idea of what it
means to be Canadian or French or Bengali. But this does not mean

there are no larger cultural ideas which inform groups of people. It does not mean there are not certain aspects which bind a group by identity.

Identity is the basic capsule of unification, even though people do not necessarily agree what it *means* to have that identity. Both diverse and unified, this kind of historical consciousness has encouraged an emergence of Lakes people into their formerly latent northern territories, eclipsing the larger Canadian society's idea that they had vanished. Although not in exact replication, certain aspects of Sinixt culture endure among the people at Vallican, especially social memory of the Slocan Valley and of ideas similar to those found in the nineteenth-century Plateau Prophet Dance movement. Cultural sense of place and certain ideas, including references to prophecy, destruction, and resurrection, motivate the Lakes people's desire to come to the north in order to rebury their ancestors in the Vallican graves from which they had been exhumed by archaeologists.

As strong as these world views are, other factors influence the Sinixt's activity at the Vallican village and burial site as well. Indeed, their ideas are continually enriched by change, but change has its difficulties too. As we have learned from the Prophet Dance literature, both cultural continuity and social upheaval have been influential in the lives of aboriginal peoples since the arrival of Europeans. Similarly, the Sinixt's desire to protect gravesites appears to come in part from deprivation – a disruptive history as well as current challenges to their political, economic, and spiritual well-being.

From this people's perspective, the world has become chaotic, has gone past the boundaries of decent and moral living, and the disruption of graves is symbolic for the larger devastation which occurs everywhere around them. The Sinixt's response is to plan their own cultural community which will act as a refuge from the destruction they anticipate will result from the immoral actions of others, a community based on their moral ethics of reciprocity, egalitarianism, and peace. The reburials at Vallican are very much connected to this endeavour to build a working Sinixt society, to resolve the distressing circumstances of the present day. The commemorative act of reburial, of returning ancestral remains to their proper place, seems to be symbolic for setting the world in order. It is an act which resurrects a life lived well, which asserts the proper moral relationships between land, people, and ancestors, as well as ethnic and socioeconomic vitality.

As of November 1998, the Sinixt have repatriated and reburied fifty-five ancestral remains. All but four of these were reburied at the Vallican grave site, even though many of these had originally been interred in other parts of their territory (Sinixt/Arrow Lakes Band 1996b). Vallican has become the major location of reburial largely because most other Lakes burial sites have been inundated by West Kootenay Power's hydro-electric projects. Slower and shallower than others, the Slocan is the only major river in Sinixt territory which has not been dammed.

The Vallican site is located about forty kilometres northwest of Nelson in one of the very few leisurely, winding river valleys in the West Kootenays (see Map 3). Though tightly bound by the eastern and western ranges of the Selkirk Mountains, the comparatively slow-moving Slocan River has carved a narrow, flat streambed – a protected spot just right for winter villages. People definitely took advantage of the conditions of that valley: alluvial terraces along the Slocan River host the highest known densities of archaeological village sites within Lakes territory. Vallican itself has 61 housepits while upstream Lemon Creek has 84 housepits and downstream South Slocan has 63. In addition to those in the Slocan, two other major housepit clusters exist at Deer Park (58 housepits) on Lower Arrow Lake and at Kettle Falls (33 housepits). Six minor clusters of between 10 and 17 housepits are located on the lengthy stretch between Kettle Falls and Edgewood on Lower Arrow Lake (Mohs 1982b: 6, 44). In addition, historical Lakes winter village sites were documented by Teit (1930), Ray (1936), and Elmendorf (1935–6) as far north as the Revelstoke area.[3]

It is important to remember that many sites were destroyed for archaeological survey when the Arrow Lakes were flooded after the Hugh Keenleyside Dam was built in 1968 on the Columbia River above Castlegar. Similarly, the Kootenay, Lardeau, and Pend Oreille Rivers have been extensively dammed. As a result, the extent of village densities in the affected areas will never be fully understood. For this reason alone – for their rarity – Slocan River village sites are significant. The Vallican site is particularly important to archaeologists because of its large size and its unusually wide variety of representative Plateau cultural features at a single location. Dates of occupancy at Vallican are estimated to be from about 2200 BP to possibly as recent as 110 BP (AD 1840) (Eldridge 1984: 39, 47). Over six hectares in area, the village at Vallican consists of a burial ground, shell middens, five hillside residential and food preparation terraces, and seventy cultural depressions which are all that remain of semisubterranean houses (pithouses), mat lodges, storage pits, earth ovens, and underground tunnels or trenches (Mohs 1983: 1).[4]

Morley Eldridge, an archaeologist who has worked at the Vallican site, has made some astute observations regarding the significance of this village for Lakes people. He writes:

> Most of the known features and deposits at the Vallican site ... are probably associated with the Lakes Indians in whose territory the site is located. The people speaking this language are believed by many Canadian specialists to be extinct. This is emphatically not the case. According to Bloodworth (1959: 56–7), there were 257 members of the Colville Confederated Tribes who were identified as Lakes in 1959. Although their precise numbers are not known today, the Lakes still maintain a strong ethnic identity and are very much aware of their original homeland in British Columbia ... Because most of the Lakes Indians' former winter village sites have been destroyed by hydroelectric developments (both in British Columbia and Washington State), the Vallican site may hold special significance for the remaining members of this ethnic group. The site is one of the last heritage resources which can resolve inconsistencies and gaps in the ethnographic record of these people. (Eldridge 1984: 50)

As Eldridge anticipated, now Vallican does indeed hold special significance for Lakes people.

The Politics of Reburial

As mentioned, Sinixt people have reburied most of the repatriated remains at Vallican even though many were not originally disinterred there. The Sinixt located and obtained these bodies from a variety of institutions. The Royal British Columbia Museum, Simon Fraser University, the University of British Columbia, the Nelson Museum, the Boundary Museum in Grand Forks, and the Arrow Lakes Historical Society in Nakusp each gave remains to the Lakes people based at Vallican. Five other bodies came from private individuals in the West Kootenays (Sinixt/Arrow Lakes Band 1996b). At present, the Sinixt are seeking other remains which may have been exhumed from gravesites in their territory, inquiring in particular at the Royal Ontario Museum, the Smithsonian Institution in Washington, DC, and several European museums.

While some institutions and private citizens have now begun to voluntarily return remains, the Sinixt had a long battle in their initial repatriation from the Royal British Columbia Museum. Six remains had been given over to the provincial museum from the British Columbia Heritage Trust, the institution which conducted archaeological surveys beginning in 1981 in preparation for road construction near the site. To recount the story briefly, when archaeologist Gordon Mohs discovered the large extent of the Vallican village and burial site, he suggested that the Heritage Trust notify the Lakes people on the Colville Reservation in Washington State. However, according to Mohs (1988), 'this was over-ruled because the Branch did not want to become involved in international jurisdictional matters. Consequently, they were never contacted. The Kutenai Indians from Creston and St Mary's were contacted when the dig was in progress to show that the human remains were being treated with respect.'

About 1987, when the Sinixt finally heard of the archaeological dig and the plans to build a road, they attempted to stop the construction through the courts (Sinixt/Arrow Lakes Band 1989b). The British Columbia Heritage Trust was convinced that the site was far enough from the proposed road and that it would not be disturbed. By this time, the Trust had purchased the Vallican site and intended to build an interpretive centre there (Hewitt 1989). The Sinixt disagreed with the Trust's approach, and when their legal challenge failed, they set up a blockade. Nevertheless, the road went through in March 1989, and part of the site, a terrace of pithouses, was damaged in the process (C. Gunn 1989).

Meanwhile, the Sinixt had been attempting since 1988 to repatriate the remains which had been taken from Vallican (Gunn and Morgan 1989). However, the Royal British Columbia Museum was reluctant. Museum personnel felt jurisdiction over the remains was unclear, partly because they believed the Slocan Valley may have been a transitional territory in times past and partly because the Lakes are not officially recognized in Canada (Barkley 1990). They could not make a legal transaction with a nonlegal entity like the Arrow Lakes Band, so any legal correspondence had to go through the Colville Confederated Tribes rather than to the individual band directly.

Furthermore, the Sinixt were required to show evidence of support from First Nations in Canada, so that they might receive the remains through a legal Canadian entity (Colville Confederated Tribes 1990). First Nations in Canada were hesitant to support the Sinixt's claim to the burials as this might compromise their own land claims efforts. After many meetings, much correspondence, and the Sinixt's initiation of a 'protest caravan' which travelled to the Royal British Columbia Museum in Victoria, several bands agreed to support the Sinixt's efforts. Some gave their support only with legal disclaimers. One such group is the Kootenay Indian Area Council, which passed a resolution saying that they 'fully support the release of the remains to the Sixixt [*sic*] people for the

purpose of reburial, without prejudicing our Land Claims to the Arrow
Lakes area in B.C.' (Pierre 1990). In the end, the contract transferring
the title of the exhumed remains was made between the museum and
'the descendants of the Arrow Lakes people representing the Okanagan
Tribal council.' Francis Romero, grandson of Lakes Chief Aropaghan,
signed for the bodies on 25 September 1990 (Romero 1990; Royal British
Columbia Museum 1990).

Despite their difficulty in overcoming both native and non-native bureaucratic obstacles, the Sinixt have shown considerable perseverance in their
efforts to repatriate ancestral remains. Their communal resolve suggests
that having jurisdiction over one's dead is symbolic of self-determination
and cultural identity. The control of one's dead is in effect the control of
one's self, one's community. Obviously political, the right to determine
the state of the dead actually defines the current state of one's own autonomy. More than this, taking responsibility for the dead is also culturally
definitive.

How one defines death and ritualizes it, even in normal uneventful circumstances, is often an important marker of ethnic identity. In China, for
example, among the enormous cultural variation in a huge population,
death rites are the one social entity which distinguish the Chinese from
the non-Chinese. They are the common bond which unite the Chinese as
a people (Watson and Rawski 1988). Similarly, death rites are a source of
ethnic differentiation and identification among the Confederated Tribes
of the Colville Reservation in northeastern Washington State. Anthropologist Jay Miller (in Mourning Dove 1990: 210–12) describes burial
grounds there as an 'important link with a tribal past ... [where] people
are buried by family and tribe.' Peoples' sense of cultural place is marked
by the location of cemeteries, and although there is intermingling among
different peoples in many other aspects of reservation life, ethnic identity
is strongly segregated when it comes to mortuary rituals and sites.

Funerals on the Colville Reservation are occasions for people to
reunite from their disparate residences, to sit vigil through the night, and
to feast together afterward. They are a focal point of social cohesion, not
only between the individual who has passed on and those people of certain ethnicity whom she left behind, but also between that ethnic group
and the land in which they have deep history. Jay Miller (in Mourning
Dove 1990: 212) remarks that the peoples of the Colville Reservation 'are
justly proud of the care shown to their dead, their heightened sense of
community, and their strong ties with the land.'

This rite of connectedness between people, living and dead, and the land in which they dwell is not confined to the Colville Reservation, however. It also extends to ancestral lands from which they have been alienated. Jay Miller (in Mourning Dove 1990: 212) writes, 'In some cases, as with the cemetery at Manson on Lake Chelan, these links continue with ancestral land that is not part of the main reservation.' Bouchard and Kennedy describe a similar commitment among the Sinixt to a cemetery at Kelly Hill (Pia), Washington, part of the Lakes territory which was removed from the Colville Reservation in the nineteenth century. Even though some of the detailed knowledge about this historical territory seems to have diminished, this lack of clarity

has in no way detracted from their strong sense of identity as Lakes Indians. Today this identity is expressed by holding events such as the annual clean-up of the Kelly Hill cemetery, or celebrating root feasts there. Kelly Hill remains the focal area for the 'Lakes experience' today, even though only a handful of Lakes people still live in this vicinity. (Bouchard and Kennedy 1985: 5)

Like the cemetery at Kelly Hill, the Vallican burial site has taken on ethnic importance despite the fact that Lakes people had not resided in villages there for generations.

Given that Vallican is one of only a few village and burial sites which has not been destroyed by the inundation of hydroelectric damming projects and that it is a sizeable site with continuous occupation for over two thousand years, it is not entirely surprising that the Sinixt hold special reverence for it. Yet the site has been unattended for some time. Many have only recently become aware of it. How is it then that these graves, along with the associated village site, have suddenly become so important? Even if funerals and cemeteries are significant markers of identity for people on the Colville Reservation, as Jay Miller and Bouchard and Kennedy attest, most Lakes people had not visited the Vallican site before they knew about the exhumation of bodies. What motivates these people in their strong desire to repatriate and rebury ancestral remains in a place which many had never seen before the crisis erupted in 1989?

Jane Hubert, a British scholar who has written at length on reburial in various cultures, holds that strong sentiments about reburial come from

the *current* beliefs of the living populations. These beliefs may be rooted in ancient tradition, or be of comparatively recent origin. Similarly, cultural practices are continually changing and may develop with or without concomitant changes in beliefs, merely expressing old beliefs in new ways. Although it is not possible to totally disentangle them, there are two distinct bases for opposition to the disturbance of the dead. The first ... are the beliefs, attitudes and emotions of living descendants regarding their ancestors. The second are the wishes and intentions of the dead themselves. (Hubert 1989: 57)

It may be difficult to know precisely what the ancestors themselves wanted. Yet, if whole communities of people are buried in a particular manner at a particular site, one might logically deduce that this was considered the appropriate place for the dead. There is no reason to believe those people had a desire to later be exhumed. As for the living, encapsulated in their rituals of reburial there are not only current *ideas* about the past, but there are also current *motivations*, motivations which, among other things, often seek to reinforce strength of cultural identity through commemoration.

A rite of connectedness with people from the past, reburial is a truly commemorative act. According to Edward Casey (1987: 217–19), commemorative ceremonies are public rituals of 'intensified remembering.' As in the reburial of unknown ancestral remains, these ceremonies commonly make greater reference to group identity than to the actual individual or event that is commemorated. In fact, there is often a complete absence of such detail since commemorative ceremonies frequently recognize events which occurred earlier than current living memory. The emphasis is not historical *detail* but rather historical *connectedness*; that is, the longevity of the group, its existence through a considerable depth of time.

Using a United States Memorial Day service as his example, Casey discusses how commemoration takes the hazy details of historical persons and events and converts them into familiar, culturally unifying entities in the present:

The First World War, which occurred some seventy years ago in forlorn trenches in France ... was fought by soldiers whom I did not know, indeed could not have known, personally. Nevertheless, neither such distance in space and time nor such anonymity in identity detracts from the efficacy of commemoration as I and others now celebrate it on Memorial Day. The distance and anonymity do not matter ... [Commemorative rituals] make even the most alien presences available to me as a commemorator ... Through the appropriate commemorabilia, I overcame the effects of anonymity and spatio-temporal distance and pay homage to people and events I have never known and will never know face-to-face. The mystery of the matter – but also an insight into its inner working – resides in the way I remember the commemorated past through various commemoratively effective media in the present. It is as if this past were presenting itself to me translucently in such media – as if I were viewing the past in them, albeit darkly: as somehow set within their materiality. (Casey 1987: 218–19)

Through the ritual acts and the paraphernalia of commemoration, the distant past is thus perceived as directly identifiable with the present, directly tangible. Further, the cycle of repetition common to commemorative ceremonies regularly reinforces a current idea of that past, implying or explicitly claiming continuity between the commemorators and the history which is commemorated (Connerton 1989: 45).

To effect this kind of group identification with the past, commemorative rituals must have certain qualities. They must offer the commemorators adequate time to reflect on their connection with the historical events or persons which are commemorated, they must be collective, and they must embody certain belief systems through ritual action. Commemorative rituals are always solemn, taking the past seriously by re-enacting a former circumstance. This 'reactualization' brings something that is temporally removed into an active present.

Important to commemorative acts is their 'lastingness,' their ability to memorialize through time. We often find events and individuals commemorated in places of tribute like stone war memorials and graves of unknown soldiers, structures meant to endure the passage of time. However, longevity of memorialization is primarily dependent on the memory of living individuals. It is not dependent upon the 'living memory' of individuals, but rather on their *historical consciousness* of that which is commemorated. For this reason, commemorative ceremonies must be repeated regularly, continually fortifying the social memory of individuals without which the event or person commemorated has no value in unifying the group. The dominant time mode of commemorative rituals, 'lastingness' or 'perdurance' is 'a combination of sameness or permanence over time with a capacity to modify or evolve.' Affirming the connection of the past with the present and pointing forward to the a group's continued cohesion through future rituals, commemorative ceremonies are 'an especially efficacious remedy against time's dispersive power' (Casey 1987: 222–30). True, time may have 'dispersive power,' as Casey puts it, but time can also unify if living individuals perceive it as connecting them to temporally distant individuals who are identified as part of their culture.

Reburial, as a commemorative ritual, certainly provides a venue for living persons to reflect on their place in a time continuum with deceased ancestors. They are solemn, collective events which express deeply held communal beliefs about re-establishing and maintaining proper cultural order through the re-enactment of death rites which have previously been violated. The commemorative quality of reburial is intensified because usually the commemorating group had lost control over their dead when others exhumed them, an act which is an affront to their political and cultural autonomy. It does not matter that those dead may be anonymous and time-distant, as Casey points out. Historical detail is inconsequential. It matters only that living commemorators find historical connectedness.

Known or unknown, ancestral remains actually become charged tangible symbols, the commemorative paraphernalia of cultural and political continuity. Those who rebury them re-enact the original burial, thus symbolically embodying people from another era. The graves of newly reburied ancestors (and by extension, the land in which they lie) become lasting symbols of the community. Thus, the rite of reburial becomes a temporal enactment of continuity and cultural identification while also creating a physical monument for future generations to contemplate.

The act of reburial may only be repeated as many times as bodies have been exhumed, yet it points to other frequently repeated commemorative rituals, namely the act of burying the newly dead. The reburied and the buried become connected in time because their mortuary rituals are contemporaneous. Reburial enhances a feeling of cultural time-depth by placing everyday burial in direct temporal contact with the remains of the distant past.

Because reburial and ordinary burial both occur in the present, living people are prompted to reflect upon the relationship between anonymous, temporally distant ancestors and their own family members and friends who die. In this way, reburying disturbed ancestral remains makes the anonymous past not only communal, but also personal. As Casey (1987: 219) says, it is as if we 'were viewing the past' through the ancestors, 'albeit darkly: as somehow set within their materiality.' Whether or not there is living memory of those ancestors does not affect the outcome: an intensive identification between past and present.

This kind of connection is certainly true among the Sinixt, who often refer to ancestral remains in a personal and familiar way. Of a skull which was repatriated in 1998, one Sinixt member inquired over the telephone, 'So how's he doing?' While acknowledging the anonymity of such time-distant people, the Sinixt at Vallican nevertheless feel a deep relationship between the remains' quietude and their own well-being. Evidently, commemoration of ancient graves which have been alienated from living peoples, like those at Vallican, can have as much symbolic power as death rituals for personally known individuals in personally known land.

The meanings and motivations behind the *original* method of burial are harder to grasp than those behind reburials as enacted by living peoples. Indeed, they are impossible to understand in any definitive way. This is an important distinction. As I have said, people alive today cannot live the ideas, feelings, and beliefs of the individuals who came before. Nevertheless, the actuality of historical ideas and practices does have impact upon the ideas of living people. Living people interpret with contemporary cultural tools, including a pool of modified historical ideas which informs the individuals of a group to varying degrees. As always, continuity and change are at play to create meaning for people now: continuous yet perpetually negotiated and renegotiated by living people in the present.

Of course, specific culturally historic ideas never surface exactly as they existed among people from the past. They come in various shades of grey, get grainier or sharper depending on all the other knowledge and experience that a living person brings to her conceptual world. A person burying their dead in Vallican in 1800 didn't include telephone conversations or AIDS or a trip to the Ukraine in the range of possibilities. She didn't live on a reservation. She didn't teach at college or grapple with the ethics of cloning or shop at Safeway or give up her deceased loved ones to a funeral home. Certainly, there are pools of ideas originating in the past that inform those living in the present, but how those ideas are interpreted, either critically or implicitly, is always varied and complex.

In light of this complicated dance between the conceptual present and past, one must acknowledge that to a certain extent the Sinixt at Vallican *feel* they know what their ancestors wanted in their afterlife. Robert Watt (1993: 1), the Lakes' guardian of the Vallican site, explains that 'The burial sites which identify our territory are extremely unique and significant to my people. Our burial practices included the placement of the body in a sitting, semi-fetal position, most often facing west, covered with moss and then cedar bark and placed in a cedar basket.'

This distinctive premissionary burial posture is a mark of Sinixt ethnicity, according to spokesperson Marilyn James, and ideally the remains should be replaced, using archaeological notes, in the exact location where they were found. When that is impossible (when the grave site is flooded, for example) the Sinixt have reburied remains at Vallican (Hogan 1991). 'We have a cultural law,' says Marilyn James, 'From the earth we come, and we must go back. When the archaeologists dig us up, they are keeping us from going back and following a law' (Hamilton 1992). Yvonne Swan (1989), a Sinixt woman who was the organizer of the 1989 protest at Vallican, agrees that 'These sacred remains ... must be returned to us so that we can return them to Mother Earth, as is proper and respectful.' A document written by the band outlining the 'Sinixt Cultural Zones' formally states:

> It is a belief of the Sinixt that there is a cultural law that states that, when one dies, the physical form must return to the earth. When the physical form of a human is not allowed to return to the earth then the law is being broken and the person whom the remains represent must be vindicated. The only clear way that the living can rectify the mistake is to return the remains to the earth and let the law be followed. (Sinixt/Arrow Lakes Band n.d.)

Bob Campbell says that his mother, Eva Adolph Orr, a Sinixt elder born in about 1910 who has overseen the activity at the Vallican site, has requested that no priests or Christian ceremony be allowed at the rites of reburial because those ancestors were buried before any missionaries had arrived to encourage a European-style burial practice. Speaking on behalf of his mother, Bob Campbell says:

> Those people were Sinaistxt, they were Arrow Lakes Indians who prayed that one way. They didn't have anything to do with this new way that came in. They died before that. So in all, honoring them – I think we should just have the Elders who know how to speak the language, talk to the Spirits and tell them what we're doing. We'll do it closest as we can to the old way, because I'm sure they weren't Catholics, those people. (Sinixt/Arrow Lakes Band 1989a)

Evidently, even though they acknowledge that they can only 'do it closest as we can,' the Sinixt currently attempt to offer the mortuary rites that the ancestors would have wanted, rather than what might be considered appropriate today. Yet they honour their idea of the ancestors' desires not by attempting to replicate the rituals of long ago, but instead by leaving them untouched. In fact, they have chosen purposely to perform reburials in an utterly simple fashion so as not to take away from the power of the original ceremonies, modifying them only if the ancestors 'speak' to individuals, making certain requests. Eva Orr (quoted in Walter 1991) says, 'We can't do anything else for them but put them back.' Thus, the people at Vallican 'keep the Lakes' way' – in this case, keep the 'cultural law' – while simultaneously acknowledging the differences between current practices and those of ancestors from another time.

Since only contemporary people enact the rituals, it can only be contemporary beliefs and desires which motivate the reburial of disinterred ancestral remains. As noted above, Jane Hubert (1989: 57) writes that such current beliefs may be ancient *or* comparatively recent. She sets the two in opposition even though influences on current belief systems and practices are *both* historic and contemporary. Indeed, social memory incorporates both new and old, and social memory clearly influences the activities of reburial at Vallican. The evidence indicates that a continuity of beliefs around death and burial does influence the activity among the Sinixt at Vallican. However, such *contemporary* beliefs have both ancient and recent influences. The Sinixt have neither remained on a static rung of the evolutionary ladder nor completely severed their historical cultural knowledge and identity as a response to an ever-changing world. Among other recent factors, part of the Sinixt's involvement in the repatriation of ancestral remains has been motivated by the larger, highly politicized debate of reburial that goes on in North America today, but this does not preclude the influence of the social memory of their own ethnic mortuary practices and beliefs. Indeed, social memory contributes to the Lakes' practice of reburial as well as to their understanding of who they are today. At the Vallican reburial site, we find a place which has become a kind of repository of ethnic identity, both historical and current.

Versions of History, Versions of Place

At the Vallican site, both historical consciousness and historical ideas work to inform the present activity of Sinixt people. The social memory of the Slocan region itself and the influence of the ideas originating from what has been called the Prophet Dance have been perpetuated by oral histories. However, contrary to the doctrines of scholars like Calvin Martin, Lakes people do not rely only on oral accounts and archetypal myths to create a contemporary understanding of Vallican's history. They also use written documents, archaeological data, and other media to gain knowledge. Young adults at the Vallican encampment are well versed in literary traditions and linear history.

For one, Marilyn James is a counsellor at Caribou College in Kamloops, British Columbia. In her professional capacity there, she emphasizes the need to teach high academic standards while still upholding the central importance of oral history. She and the others who come and go to the Vallican site find no conflict in making reference to historical and archaeological documents and websites on the internet to confirm or augment their oral histories. In fact, they have filing cabinets full of archival documents, including copies of early maps of the area, fur trader diaries, legal transactions, newspaper articles, and various correspondence concerning the Lakes. Many also read theoretical and historical works, particularly on the global effects of colonization and the capitalist world economy.

At 88 years old in the spring of 1998, Eva Orr was reading a history of the Jews, comparing their diaspora to her own people's. In similar manner, other Sinixt regularly analyse and debate the relative credibility of various versions of history. True enough, much of their interest in these documents lies in the corroboration of Sinixt oral history. In their view, their oral history, and its manifestation in the physical landscape, takes precedence over written history.

Robert Watt makes a significant distinction between oral and literary histories. Unlike literary histories, according to him, oral histories are private. He says, 'Our stories, they're not for paper.' In part, it is stories of the Slocan that make the connection to Vallican itself so private and significant. Bouchard and Kennedy (1985: 5) say that their Lakes informants could independently identify only five specific place names north of the international border; instead, these researchers say, Lakes informants had more general impressions of that land. By contrast, I have found that both specific and more general stories of the northern Lakes territory exist.

Eva Orr (quoted in Walter 1991) has childhood memories of the areas around Nelson, Trail, and the Slocan Valley: 'I remember as a young girl, riding horses north into the woods, on trails that only our adults knew about. I remember we camped around here and picked huckleberries and they said this was where we came from.' In fact, Mrs Orr was born on one of these crossborder huckleberry-picking trips. She says the journey by horse from around Marcus, Washington, to the lower Slocan Valley took about three days. When she returned by car decades later, her son, Bob Campbell, asked if she recognized anything. Her response was 'Of course not! I came up here on a horse path, not any paved road!'

Marilyn James says that her mother, Alvina Lum,[5] continued to gather berries nearby at Salmo right through to the 1960s. In addition, Alvina Lum and Eva Orr both knew people who had lived in pithouses in the Slocan Valley and Arrow Lakes. To be sure, Bouchard and Kennedy (1985: 99) have noted that a Sinixt village existed in the Slocan as late as 1896, only fifteen years or so before Eva Orr was born. Perhaps it is the stories of that village's former residents that Mrs Orr and Mrs Lum had heard as children.

Besides the general area of the Slocan, Eva Orr is also aware of some of the area's historically important sacred places. For instance, Mrs Orr tells a creation story about an unusually shaped mountain close to the Vallican site – the same Frog Mountain which Robert Watt pointed out to me on the first day of our acquaintance. Even before Lakes people became aware of the existence of the Vallican burials, another sacred site had been the cause of Eva Orr's concern. In about 1987, she sent Bob Campbell and Manny MacDougall to check on a particular site on the Arrow Lakes near Edgewood which was apparently being used by other native peoples for ceremonial purposes. During this trip, Campbell first learned about the archaeological activity at Vallican. Sinixt people from all over soon heard of the disruption of the graves via 'the moccasin telegraph,' as Marilyn James calls it, and in time many began going to see the site for themselves. Annie Kruger (quoted in Hamilton 1992), a Sinixt elder living at Penticton, British Columbia, remarks that 'Vallican had everything ... We had our territories and our ancestors knew the boundaries. My mother's people were born and raised in the Slocan Valley. It's like going home.'

Some of the younger Lakes people have said that they came up to the protest camp unsure, even ambivalent about Vallican, but when they arrived they had profound experiences which connected them and their stories to the landscape. For example, Eva Orr's granddaughter, Vanessa Holloman, visited Vallican along with her husband and young children while I was there in the summer of 1994. She says that her grandmother encouraged her to come up to Vallican 'to see where we're from.' Before the trouble when the road went in, Vanessa feels:

People didn't really realize. People accepted where they were. Until you're made aware of it, it's really just another place. There are all these stories. It's just a story until your have something to connect you to it. The stories of this area were always around – just Grandpa's stories: so much air – but they solidify when you find the place. Now this place is a kind of Mecca.

Suddenly having a place to which she can connect the stories of her child-hood, Vanessa Holloman has taken much greater interest in Sinixt his-tory. For Vanessa, Vallican is the crystallization of history, the once merely plausible made real.

Marilyn James, also of the younger adult generation, offered me an anecdote to illustrate how she feels Sinixt oral history has been verified in the Vallican site. Paraphrased, she says: Somewhere in Egypt there was a legend of a woman, a priestess or noblewoman of some sort who was asso-ciated with a certain symbol. Her story was passed on orally for hundreds and hundreds of years. Recently discovered in an archaeological site were the remains of a woman who had that same symbol on her necklace. The woman must have been of high rank because she had had two servants executed and buried with her. She was the same woman from that legend. This archaeological discovery was like an anchor for the people to have faith in their own stories. It showed them that their own histories are not 'just stories' and that the knowledge they had passed down for many gen-erations was reliable. It gave them something to point to. The Vallican burial site is like this for the Lakes people. It makes our history real for us.

Through accounts like those of Vanessa Holloman and Marilyn James, we find that Vallican is a chronotope revived – space where time and people come together, a fusion of place, time, and community. This bench of land nestled among conifers at the edge of a clear rushing river, pitted as it is with ancient houses and graves, has become a physical manifestation of present-day ethnicity in which time 'thickens,' that is, 'takes on flesh and becomes visible for human contemplation' (Bakhtin 1981: 7, 84). Where Sinixt historical consciousness and identity had been strong, it has become stronger with their embrace of the living, breathing land which, because of colonial circumstances, had been confined for many Lakes people to the realm of oral history and imagination. This parcel of land, where their forebears dwelled and were buried and from which they had been alienated, strengthens the Sinixt's historical consciousness because it shows that their idea of themselves – their history, their sense of place, their identity – *really* exists, in *real* time and *real* space. As Marilyn James says, the people can have faith in their own histories; indeed, those oral histories for which the dominant society has so little regard become liter-ally true in their eyes.

Yet Vallican, despite its central importance, is not the only site which holds this kind of power for the Sinixt. There are other chronotopes in the Slocan and Arrow Lakes vicinity, including cemeteries, places of ritual, sacred mountains, hunting grounds, berrying spots, culturally modified trees, and pictograph sites. Many have been destroyed by deforestation, road-building, and hydroelectric inundation. Nevertheless, by following oral history accounts and written documents the Lakes are becoming reacquainted with some of the important places in their history – places which were not so much entirely forgotten, as have been left latent for some years.

Of all these places, Vallican is a chronotope of particular significance. It is a place charged with history. This intense feeling is revealed in the complex multiple time perspectives and associated cultural identity it holds for many Sinixt. To be sure, at Vallican there are four distinctive layers of chronotopic time. I define these as the distant epic past, the communal past, the personal past, and the resurrected past.

The first chronotopic layer at Vallican is akin to Bakhtin's epic time which he explored in ancient Greek novels: a closed time, already finished, distant, and inaccessible to living peoples. Epic or mythic time is manifested in the ancient undisturbed graves and houses of people from another time as well as in Frog Mountain, which overlooks Vallican and which embodies the oral history of how Frog saved the Sinixt during a time of famine in ancient days.

Sinixt elder Eva Orr is very much aware of the difference between the Sinixt now and the Sinixt then. She reveals her recognition of a distant epic past when she recounts the story of Frog Mountain as an ancient mythic event enacted by archetypal characters rather than by ordinary people. Eva Orr (quoted in Walter 1991) also showed distant time-reckoning just before reburying the remains that were repatriated from the University of British Columbia. She said at that time, 'Today, we're here to put these people back where they belong. We can't do anything else for them but put them back. We can't do anything from our day. They were a different people.'

At later reburial ceremonies, Eva Orr and several other Sinixt members have made similar comments to me about the time-distance of ancestors. They definitely segregate their own temporal reality from that of these ancestors; they acknowledge a lapse of time and all the changes that have occurred since these individuals' deaths. Not only this, some Sinixt at Vallican depict the time of those people as inaccessible to the people of the current era. The ancestors they rebury belong to a distant and unreachable time, another Vallican time-space which is closer to the mythic time of Frog Mountain than to the temporal realities of living Sinixt.

The second chronotopic layer at Vallican is the communal past. This is a relatively near past, the living memory which arises through personal remembrance and the oral and literary accounts of family and friends in the Slocan. Cindy Fry, for instance, knows through oral history and written documents (e.g., Graham 1971: 80–2) that, from the mid-nineteenth century until her death, her great grandmother, Justine Soqu-stike-en Fry, went on hunting excursions in the Slocan with her husband, Richard Fry. Annie Kruger (quoted in Hamilton 1992) remembers the area around Vallican as the home of her mother's family. Members of Mrs Kruger's family were 'born and raised in the Slocan Valley.' For both Cindy Fry and Annie Kruger, the Slocan is a personal family place which embodies personal family history. Eva Orr similarly finds familial memory in the Slocan: she recounts riding there by horseback as a child, remembering the trails that led to places 'around here.'

For Eva Orr, this too is an important place of communal, but also personal past, so much that she has encouraged her granddaughter, Vanessa Holloman, to visit Vallican to discover 'where we're from.' Thus, Eva Orr's personal memory of the area is not merely her own; the place is handed to a later generation almost as a gift. Because the personal and communal past is embodied in the Vallican area for Eva Orr, she can pass it down almost as an amulet of identity. She can pass the *place* down like family china, even though individuals' *meanings* behind that place are less easily transferred.

Vallican may be a place where history is made tangible, easily passed on like a concrete inheritance. However, as discussed in the previous chapter, ideas and meanings, the interpretations of a chronotope, are more like weather than fine bone china: highly variable, ever-changing, taking on familiar forms but never in exactly the same way. Ultimately, the way the individuals of a younger generation conceive of the Vallican chronotope is dependent upon multiple cultural influences and their own interpretations. Their way will, of course, differ from Eva Orr's way.

Yet think here of Vanessa Holloman's own account: 'The stories of this area were always around – just Grandpa's stories: so much air – but they solidify when you find the place.' Like her grandmother, Vanessa's grandfather also has memory of a communal past in the Slocan area which he has passed on to his granddaughter. Not only this, Vanessa herself sees the significant symbolism of this time-space. She sees how stories – that is, accounts of time – 'solidify.' She may not have the same memory or ideas or interpretations as her grandmother and grandfather, but she perceives a similar cultural importance of having family stories embodied in place. Although she does not use Bakhtin's terminology, her description is profoundly similar to Bakhtin's ideas: time taking on flesh through space. Vanessa Holloman's own theoretical conceptions of Vallican, employing the oral accounts of her grandparents, depict it as a chronotope revealing a time layer of a communal past.

The third time layer of the Vallican chronotope is the personal past. This is the recollection of individual, mostly recent contact with the site. Sinixt individuals have visited, worked in, lived at, and protected the Vallican site since the late 1980s. The personal past is a kind of working time, incorporating the complex current time-reckoning of people living in complex societies. Multiple times are thus associated with present day life at the site.

I have already mentioned the keen engagement of Lakes people in historical (linear, event-centred) debates, but there are many other times at work in Vallican. Some of these are the bureaucratic time of court proceedings and land claims efforts, the shift schedules of wage labour, the cycles of celebrations and rituals (the annual community Thanksgiving feast, the Winter Dance, and personal sweatlodge ceremonies, for example), the school year, and seasonal cycles, including hunting and gathering.

Those who make pilgrimages to Vallican rather than actually live there also take time out of their usual schedules. For these individuals (the majority of Sinixt who participate in life at Vallican), the site has its own distinctive daily time rhythms, different from those of their ordinary homelife in other communities.

The significance of the personal past time layer is that individuals build personal histories in the place beyond the collective histories of the communal past and epic past. True, there are a few, like Eva Orr, who have some personal time-depth in the Slocan, but most have only recently made personal contact with this land. For these Sinixt, recollections of the personal past help create their own connections with that spot in addition to those connections found through community history.

Finally, Vallican's fourth time layer, the resurrected past, arises from a breach in the contained or closed quality of the distant epic past. This rupture in the epic past has occurred as a result of the exhumation of ancestral remains and their subsequent reburial. Nameless, faceless culture from a generalized mythic Sinixt past has come into direct physical contact with living Sinixt when *individuals* from the past were dug up by archaeologists and road-builders. The repatriation of these remains and the ensuing commemorative rituals of interment make intimate what was once a closed, distant, and anonymous past; this newly resurrected past, as I call it, contributes to a personalized relationship between living Sinixt and people of ancient times.

As we learned earlier in this chapter, Edward Casey (1987) sees this collapse of time and anonymity as an integral part of commemorative ceremonies like reburial. Certainly, among the Sinixt this telescoping of temporal distance has occurred as a result of the commemorative re-enactment of burials performed long ago. Indeed, laying an individual to rest, even an unknown ancestor, wakes individuality of the distant past, and in its way, this act creates a time layer that is synchronous. As already mentioned, repatriated remains become contemporary individuals for whom the Sinixt have much concern; they ask about a skull, 'So how's he doing?' Note also Marilyn James's use of the present tense in her admonishment of the excavation of Sinixt grave sites. Archaeologists 'dig *us* up' – 'When the archaeologists dig us up,' she says, 'they are keeping us from going back and following a law' (James quoted in Hamilton 1992).

The archaeologists do not remove mere physical objects, bones from the earth; neither do they remove abstract 'culture.' Rather, they remove individuals. Yet these individuals who have thrown off the anonymity of the ancient past are also part of a collective. Thus, when they exhume the remains of people who lived long ago, archaeologists disinter that collective, or the Sinixt as a category, an ethnic group which exists now as then. Hence, to disinter these remains is to defile both living and dead, and metaphorically, the living and dead become a single temporal entity through a resurrected past.

For some Sinixt, resurrection is literal. Recall Fogelson's (1989: 144–5) comment that people may not have been seen to 'really or fully die' without proper mortuary rites. Similarly, when those rites are disturbed by exhumation, the dead again cross to the world of the living. For example, Eva Orr has dreamt that one of the ancestors visited her, displaying great displeasure at having been exhumed from his original grave and reburied elsewhere. The night before the reburial of some other remains in April 1998, Eva Orr heard the 'ancient Indians' singing from their graves at the Vallican camp. They sang the 'skeleton song' of the man to be reburied, the song associated with his guardian spirit. Mrs Orr then remembered that song from her childhood and offered it to him at the next day's ceremony. For Eva Orr and others, time has the capability of folding so that people from the past make direct contact with people living today.

Bob Campbell (quoted in Walter 1991) reveals a similar collapse of time when he refers to general life at Vallican camp: 'You go into the mountains and you can get completely away from the modern world. You can bend down and pick a berry and know that your ancestors were here picking the same berry, and you feel at home.' Robert Watt, too, shows a kind of synchrony when he emphatically states, 'I'm *from* here' even though he had never personally been to the Slocan before the discovery that burials had been disturbed. In Robert Watt's and Bob Campbell's words, we find that to occupy the same space and to act as those from a distant time is, in a sense, to occupy that time. It is to fuse past and present and embody, even become, those ancestors. It is to become rooted in an entanglement of land and history, to be entwined and grow within them. It is to learn the meaning of a deep cultural sense of place, to learn the meaning of 'home.' It is, in its way, to participate with a resurrected past as embodied in the chronotope of Vallican.

Seen in isolation from the other temporal layers at work at Vallican, a depiction of the Sinixt's 'resurrected past' time perspective might be mistaken for the romantic aboriginal stereotype of mono-temporalism as advocated by Mircea Eliade and Calvin Martin, among others. It seems that an idea of synchrony (cyclical or archetypal time, call it what you will) does exist, but as I have made clear in my discussion of the four temporal layers of the Vallican chronotope, this is far from the only kind of time operating among the Sinixt. As is true of all peoples, the Sinixt live with multiple times, times which work simultaneously, and these are taken both literally and metaphorically. But through the various temporal worlds – working shifts for the Parks Service, wrangling the snail pace of bureaucratic agencies, or engaging with individuals who lived long ago – a connection of space and time persists. Many Lakes people feel a distinct sense of cultural continuity, and for a considerable number this continuity rests very much in the relationship they have with their land, particularly at Vallican.

Reburial makes Vallican especially important, causing the distant past to come closer, creating a heightened relationship of Sinixt ancestors with their living descendants. Like the Lakes man, Alexander Christie, who lived at the confluence of the Kootenay and Columbia Rivers in the early twentieth century, living Sinixt find burials to be important cultural markers in the present, indicative of cultural time in space. A more personalized relationship with ancestors through their remains intensifies the connection of place and people of divergent times. As was true for Alexander Christie, it is *particular* places that hold special meaning – particular places are home. So too, Vallican became charged with meaning, with cultural and personal significance when *individual* ancestors were exhumed and subsequently reburied there. The distant past was breached to create a new, deepening level of meaning in the Vallican chronotope.

Prophecy of Chaos, Desire for Utopia, and the Moral Code

The effects of mythic, communal, and personal histories in the Slocan
have connected Lakes people to Vallican, as has the commemorative act
of reburial. Social and personal memory of cultural place have motivated
a desire to care for the dead of long ago. Similarly, the loss of control over
the dead has heightened a desire for cultural and political autonomy
among the Lakes. Less obvious than these factors is the effect of historical
ideas on reburial. Yet, whether living Sinixt are aware of it or not, the
actual history of ideas seems to play a part in the importance of the
graves. At Vallican, ideas proliferate which are similar to those associated
with shamanism and the Plateau Prophet Dance. A preoccupation with
the dead and ideas of prophecy, apocalypse, and renewal, as well as the
importance of moral living, are prominent at Vallican. These are ideas
basic to both shamanism and the Prophet Dance, a movement which was
prevalent in the Columbia Plateau in the nineteenth century, as we
learned in the preceding chapter. Aspects of Lakes' shamanism and their
involvement in the Prophet Dance I shall discuss below.

First, however, it is important to establish that the ideas in question also
arise through other cultural media, ones that have had immediate influence in the living memories of Lakes people. A great diversity of social
interaction exists at Vallican; visitors such as Quakers, Doukhobors,
Tibetan monks, and expatriot American draft dodgers all contribute to
an exchange of ideas at the site. To be sure, the presence of ideas about
prophecy, apocalypse, resurrection, and a moral code are not mere repli-
cations of nineteenth-century religious movements. Although the Sinixt's
historical involvement with the Prophet Dance surely makes its mark,
these ideas exist at Vallican as a result of multiple ideological influences
in the present, two of which are the environmental movement and the
Native American Church.

Many residents of the Slocan Valley have for years been involved in
environmental activism. The Valhalla Wilderness Society, for example,
fought at length to establish a park on the west side of Slocan Lake, protecting the watersheds and old growth forest of the Selkirk Mountains'
Valhalla Range from logging. Since then, they have won battles over
other parts of the valley, such as the White Grizzly (Pic-ha-kee-lowna) Wilderness Park in the Selkirks' Goat Range. Similar concerns continue to
involve many advocates of environmentally responsible forestry practices.

Soon after they came to Vallican in the late 1980s, the Sinixt worked
alongside the environmental groups in an effort to eradicate clearcutting

in the Slocan. Furthermore, they have participated in official government forums on the development of forestry planning and have submitted statements outlining their 'Sinixt Cultural Zones' in hopes of averting the destruction of what they consider culturally and environmentally sensitive areas within their territory (Sinixt/Arrow Lakes Band n.d.; Valhalla Wilderness Society and Slocan Valley Watershed Alliance 1996: 10–11).

In one exemplary publication, the environmental groups write articles which clearly reveal their ideas of utopia, apocalypse, and moral living. Indeed, they predict terrible destruction of the world as we know it, the world as they consider good and right:

> If parks continue to be used to justify [logging outside of their boundaries], the [Slocan] valley, the province and the world can expect an ecosystem collapse of disastrous proportions. This year, south of the border, massive flood damages resulting from clearcut logging forced 30,000 out of their homes. To avoid this kind of disaster, there have to be rules for ecosystem protection everywhere logging takes place. (Valhalla Wilderness Society and Slocan Valley Watershed Alliance 1996: 1)

Similar publications describe the unlogged land as containing 'the primeval values of nature.' Such land 'holds some of the last great, magnificently scenic wilderness pockets in the world ... Preservation of such areas ... must be demanded on behalf of present and future generations as well as for the animal and bird forest inhabitants that are being mercilessly driven into extinction by over-cutting.' The Valhalla Society (1993: 1, 7) further warns against the 'ruinous' and 'catastrophic' behaviour of 'an ever rapacious timber industry' which has been given *carte blanche* by unethical governments. Nevertheless, all may not be lost: the 'threat to the integrity of this area' can be halted; the 'treasured ... ancient forests' are 'there for us today, and hopefully, if we are wise, we will see it all preserved for future generations.' Indeed, the strength of the forests will rise again if we reverse our immoral behaviour.

Plainly, environmental groups working in the Slocan like the Valhalla Wilderness Society adhere to views of wilderness as utopia. Not only this, they actually prophesy 'collapse' and flooding of mythic proportions if our immoral economic behaviour is not altered. So too, if we transform ourselves through ethical practices, the strength of the wilderness will reassert itself. Here are clear ideas about prophecy, the destruction of utopia, and its possible resurrection through a moral code.

Because the Slocan's environmentalists have connections with Lakes people at Vallican, the beliefs of each group are readily exchanged with the other. In the publications of the Valhalla Wilderness Society and the Slocan Valley Watershed Alliance (1996: 10–11), the Sinixt express their own views on the importance of preserving their traditional land for current and future subsistence purposes. In turn, the Valhalla Wilderness Society and the Slocan Valley Watershed Alliance present the Sinixt as examples of upright environmental living, examples of thousands of years of responsible inhabitation of the land.

Both environmentalists and the Sinixt themselves consider the Sinixt people to be 'an intrinsic part of the environmental and cultural landscape of the largest and northernmost interior rainforest zone in North America.' As such, they are depicted as successful, moral residents who 'used the entire landscape within their traditional territory to sustain themselves for thousands of years.' Non-Sinixt, including multinational forestry companies, are expected to follow their example by implementing ecologically sustainable practices. The Valhalla Wilderness Society has been a political force in the West Kootenays for over twenty years, some time before the Sinixt made themselves heard to non-native residents of the area. While the Sinixt are more recent contributors to the environmentalists' views, each group evidently influences the ideas of the other. Each contributes to the other's ideas about an ideal world, its catastrophic destruction, and potential resurrection through righteous living.[6]

Besides the environmental movement in the Slocan Valley, another contemporary factor, the Native American Church, may influence the ideas of Lakes people in regards to the Vallican burial grounds. While I have been told that no Native American Church rituals have ever been performed at the Vallican camp itself, some Sinixt and other peoples on the Colville Reservation have been adherents. Bob Campbell was one of the people who brought the Native American Church to the Colville Reservation after having attended meetings with Navajo members in 1976. On 20 October 1977, Bob Campbell and others officially incorporated the first Washington State chapter, calling it the First Native American Church (Stewart 1987: 321–5). Bob Campbell subsequently became a Roadman, a ritual officiant who symbolically leads fellow worshippers along the Peyote Road, or the ethical way 'to the good life both in this world and the next' (Slotkin 1975: 71–3).

The ideas behind the Native American Church are difficult to describe definitively since each congregation takes on considerable individuality from the culture of local participants. Historically, the Native American Church arose largely from the merging of two earlier religious movements, Peyotism and the Ghost Dance. As mentioned in the previous chapter, the Ghost Dance that culminated in the massacre at Wounded Knee in 1890 is generally considered to have spread from the Plateau Prophet Dance (Kehoe 1989).[7] Wovoka, the prophet of the Ghost Dance, taught his followers that 'instructions were received from supernatural powers ... during trance or unconsciousness. Faithful dancing, clean living, peaceful adjustment with whites, hard work, and following God's chosen leaders would hasten the resurrection of dead relatives and the desired restoration of the "good old days" of Indian prosperity. During world renewal, whites would quietly be removed' (Stewart 1987: 66).

In the 1890s, there was much intertribal participation in the Ghost Dance, which helped to spread other ideas, including the Peyotism that was native to the American Southwest and Mexico. The Peyote religion contributed many ritual elements to the Native American Church. Remarkable among these is the partaking of peyote, which inspires the ritual trance and visions that allow participants to communicate with dead ancestors, heal the sick, and see into the future (Stewart 1987: 24–5, 31, 41).

The first legal incorporation of the combined religion, later called the Native American Church, occurred in 1909 as a defence against American antipeyote laws. Followers of the religion hoped that defining their ritual practices in an official capacity would make the use of peyote a legitimate religious freedom in the eyes of the American government (Slotkin 1975: 58). Nevertheless, the Native American Church has struggled with the legality of peyote and people on the Colville Reservation have not escaped such difficulty. In 1978, three men were arrested for the possession of peyote and jailed for thirteen days, but were later acquitted when their lawyers pointed out to the Ferry County judge that the ritual use of peyote was specifically exempted from the United States Drug Abuse Control Acts (Stewart 1987: 324–5).

Peyote continues to be an integral component to the ritual life of the Native American Church. It provides a method of seeking revelation and unification with the Great Spirit. Taking peyote is often described as an arduous endeavour, as choosing a difficult path. Yet the results are important: visions illuminate how one has strayed from the Peyote Road and cause healing as well as an ability to look into the future. Indeed, visions are said to be the instigators of both personal and cultural renewal (Slotkin 1975: 74–6).

In 1977, Leonard Crow Dog, a Brulé Teton Sioux from the Rosebud Reservation in South Dakota, performed the very first peyote ceremony for new followers of the First Native American Church on the Colville Reservation. Leonard Crow Dog reveals some of the ideas associated with the Native American Church in a 1986 interview conducted by Ruby and Brown (1989: 199–203). Involved in the 1973 Wounded Knee battle, this man actually uses the name 'Ghost Dance' for the religion he practices. Much of his discussion surrounds surviving the effects of European colonialism. 'We survive on this land to preserve our way of life and culture that will never change,' he says.

Survival comes largely from following an ethical life, and the rejuvenation among the righteous is now being seen: 'When I was a little boy in this valley [on the Rosebud Reservation] there was only one sweatlodge. Today we have twenty-six sweat lodges. Families have them. They have understanding [through spiritual visions] from their [dead] grandmothers and grandfathers.'

The use of peyote is among the practices which invoke 'dreams and visions.' Peyote offers prophetic messages and the basis of a moral code which will help aboriginal peoples to survive the chaos brought by the arrival of non-natives. Not unlike Marilyn James, Leonard Crow Dog says, 'We have laws' which are communicated to the living by way of dead ancestors. 'Our message today come when we speak with our ancestors, who bring messages from the Creator. I speak with my grandfather. I speak with my [dead] father in a ceremony. I relate to my people the message from the Great Spirit.'

Leonard Crow Dog shared these ideas with adherents of Colville's First Native American Church when he helped them to establish their new worship practices. The survival of which Leonard Crow Dog speaks is of the apocalypse that aboriginal peoples have already experienced through colonization. Through the mediation of dead ancestors, through their instructions on leading a moral life, adherents to the Native American Church are now experiencing the initial stages of renewal. This renewal is fragile, however, dependent upon the upright living of Native American Church followers.

Leonard Crow Dog's ideas – the prophetic role played by deceased ancestors, as well as concepts of destruction and resurrection – are very similar to those which accompany the reburial practice of Sinixt at Vallican, a few members of whom have participated in the First Native American Church. While there has been no Native American Church activity at Vallican, these cultural elements may have nevertheless taken a roundabout route from the Rosebud Reservation to Vallican through exposure to ideas on the Colville Reservation. If the nineteenth-century Plateau

Prophet Dance did influence the Plains Ghost Dance as scholars like Leslie Spier (1935) claim, then those ideas, transformed and adapted through the new Native American Church practices of living peoples, may have made a full circuit in their recent return to Plateau peoples. Indeed, the interest of some of the Lakes people at Vallican in the Native American Church, as well as in environmentalism, likely exists in part because of the prevalence and longevity of similar ideas indigenous to their own region, ideas which appear to have their foundation in Sinixt shamanism and the Columbia Plateau's historical Prophet Dance.[8]

Perhaps we should establish here whether the Prophet Dance movement and related shamanistic customs are actually a part of Sinixt cultural history. Leslie Spier, you will remember, argues that the Prophet Dance rose out of the ancient practice of shamanism. As discussed in the chapter reviewing Sinixt ethnography, Ray (1939: 94) confirms that shamanism is an important aspect of Sinixt culture, the skills of which are sought through vision quests and the subsequent attainment of certain powerful guardian spirits.

The autobiography of a Sinixt-Skoyelpi woman corroborates Ray's data. Christine Quintasket had two women guiding her in her spiritual training, her mother and a spiritual counsellor, who persistently encouraged their novice to go on vision quests throughout her puberty so that she might eventually become a powerful medicine woman.[9] She says that 'Indians had a staunch belief that God made the world according to a divine plan that gave power from the animal world to our ancestors and now to us'; one could only come to that power by obtaining a guardian spirit (Mourning Dove 1990: 128). Though not successful in her own pursuit for a spirit guide, she notes that 'Finding a spirit gave a child a future in medicine, with the ability to cure the sick or to foresee things that would happen to others' (Mourning Dove 1990: 37).

Further, Christine Quintasket remarks on the social importance of shamans, saying that her people's 'interaction with different tribes was generally through intermarriage among important families and through religious events held most often during the winter under the direction of shamans.' Indeed, shamans, 'with [their] knowledge of spirit guardians and animal guides, had greater influence among the natives than did the chief' (Mourning Dove 1990: 31).

She notes also that the arrival of non-native immigrants did not quell the people's faith in the shamans. Shamans continued to perform important mortuary rites, such as brushing the dead with rose branches so that they would not rise again to take away the living. (Evidently, the cultural view of death as described by Christine Quintasket included the possibility of resurrection.) In regards to their healing practices, Christine Quintasket says, 'People will try white doctors only when they cannot get native ones' (Mourning Dove 1990: 94, 128).

Elsewhere, Quintasket describes a religious gathering in Lakes territory near Northport, Washington. This 'seancing rite' was hosted by three Sinixt shamans, one of whom was Conequah, a man considered to be 'the greatest shaman of the Sinschirst' or Arrow Lakes people. During the ceremony, Conequah was bound hand and foot into a fetal position. He then went into a trance and was overtaken by an important spirit which offered the gathering several prophecies. After laying unconscious for some time, Conequah revived (Mourning Dove 1990: 132–4).

It appears that shamanism among the Lakes, as illustrated in these examples, incorporates the skill of prophecy as well as the concept of resurrection after death. The use of a ceremonial fetal position mimics the burial posture which the Sinixt formerly employed, thus symbolizing the shaman's movement into the world of the dead during the trance state. That fetal death posture itself suggests that the concept of resurrection is not confined to the specialized activities of shamans: the dead themselves are like the unborn, awaiting emergence from the earth-womb into new life. Christine Quintasket depicts these earlier methods of burial, writing:

> It was the ancient custom to bury the dead wrapped in tanned buckskins and fur robes. The body was placed, in compact form, in a grave lined with spread-out robes, lying on the back with the knees doubled back toward the chest, breaking the hip sockets, placing the arms between the shins and thighs, and doubling back the feet. The body was bound with thongs and sewn into the first robe. Other robes were added, depending on the wealth of the family. The bundle was placed on a high scaffold in the trees for ten days while the family watched and waited to make sure the person did not revive. When there were no certain signs of life, the body was taken to a sandy knoll and buried in a seated position. Some were buried in shale talus slopes under cliffs to prevent intrusion from enemies. (Mourning Dove 1990: 93)

Note the similarity between the binding of the dead during mortuary rituals and the binding of shamans into a fetal position during religious ceremonies. Both suggest an unborn state, with the obvious potential for and expectation of new life. Both shamans and the deceased experience a destruction of life, and both are eagerly watched for any sign of revival. Shamanistic ritual enacts death and the potential revival of the dead. Hence, just as shamans return from the world of the dead with prophetic offerings, so might the deceased provide shamanic prophecy upon their awakening.[10]

It is worth remarking that many of the people of whom Christine Quintasket writes did not see a conflict in following both the spiritual leadership of shamans and Catholics. Of course, there is no line in time where Sinixt ideas and practices ended and Christian ones began; rather, these ideologies were integrated to varying extents among different individuals. So too, some Sinixt may have feigned an adoption of Christianity so they could practice their indigenous beliefs in private without provocation from church officials.[11] For example, Chief Andrew Aropaghan (the grandfather of Francis Romero, who signed in 1990 for the legal transfer of ancestral remains from the Royal British Columbia Museum) tried to downplay indigenous practices to the Jesuit priests. The missionaries did not approve of shamanism, but Aropaghan told them, 'Let my children enjoy their Medicine Dancing as their ancestors did for so many years. It is not harmful. We all go to your church first and only dance later for our own amusement.' In his diplomatic way, Aropaghan appeased the priests while both asserting the possibility of being simultaneously Sinixt and Christian and protecting a crucial part of Sinixt cultural life (Mourning Dove 1990: 130–1).

In addition to shamanism, the Prophet Dance movement itself had influence on the concepts and practices of Lakes people. There is little historical citation of the Sinixt's own participation, but Robert Watt comments that his uncle told him that the Lakes had 'dreamers' who prophesied the coming of Europeans and all the destruction that would ensue. The Prophet Dance did exist everywhere on the Columbia Plateau, including within the Lakes' own territory. During the mid-nineteenth century, for example, the Jesuits at St Paul's Mission referred to the 'dreamers' of the 'prophet religion' who dwelled among peoples at Kettle Falls and to the movement's occasional threat or hindrance to Catholic gains.

Interestingly, the Jesuits were aware of how the Prophet Dance related to territoriality and thus fuelled the conflict between Plateau peoples and immigrant settlers; to be sure, they made note of the dreamers' participation in land talks, such as the 1877 Wheaton Council which took place at Spokane Falls between the United States government and upper Columbia Plateau peoples, including the Lakes. The Jesuits believed that the prophet movement 'taught a mystic identification of the Indian with his tribal land. Though borrowing elements from Catholics, Protestants and Mormons, it abhorred agriculture and White civilization as an offense to nature' (Burns 1966: 365, 377, 417).

Offering a more detailed example, ethnographer James Teit (1930: 292) documents a Thompson woman prophet who died about 1850. She journeyed among the Similkameen and the Okanagan which, by Teit's linguistic reckoning, likely include the Lakes. With the amount of trade and travel between peoples, the Sinixt would have at the very least heard her teachings second-hand and may have actually been adherents. According to Teit, this woman went about the country 'telling the people about the spirit land, and also relating how the coming of whites would result in the destruction of the Indians. She prophesied the stealing of the Indian's lands and the destruction of the game by the whites, and stated that they would destroy the Indian while pretending to benefit them.' He adds that this woman encouraged her followers to engage in a war to drive non-natives out because it would be better to die than to be 'reduced to the conditions they would have to endure, once the whites became dominant.'

Leslie Spier (1935: 55) specifically cites the Lakes' participation in the Prophet movement, although he does not offer many details. He may have come to his conclusion by associating the Sinixt with peoples to the west and south for whom there is considerable documentation of such practices. Verne Ray (1936a) gives a closer account, writing on a prophet named Kolaskin. While Ray places the late-nineteenth-century movement among the Sanpoil, Skoyelpi, Spokane, and Sinkaietk, Bouchard and Kennedy (1984: 16–17, 187–8) have noted that 'Joseph Skolaskin' is generally still very much remembered on the Colville Reservation. In fact, during their research on place names in Skoyelpi and Lakes territory which has been flooded by the Grand Coulee Dam, Cecelia Pichette showed them a pictograph which is said to be the hand of Kolaskin:

Slowly and deliberately Cecelia walked right up to the rock and put her own hand over the handprint of Skolaskin – this was something she had never been allowed to do as a child and as a young woman. But her action was more than just doing something that she had never been allowed to do. It was clear to us as we watched her that this was her symbolic way of putting herself in touch with the past generations of Sanpoil people. This united her with that time when her ancestors had special powers. (Bouchard and Kennedy 1984: 17)

Ray (1936a: 75) says that Kolaskin was undoubtedly 'the most powerful figure the Sanpoil had known for generations.' But his influence was not confined to the Sanpoil alone. Being active from about 1870 to the time of his death in 1920, Kolaskin certainly must have been in contact with, if not also had followers from, the rest of the multiethnic Colville Reservation to which he belonged, including the Sinixt. Besides Kolaskin and the Thompson woman, there were several other renowned prophets in the central Plateau region, such as Smohalla (Ruby and Brown 1989). Given that aboriginal peoples in the Columbia Basin were then being pushed ever closer together because of the encroachment of settlers and the creation of reservations, it is almost certain that the Lakes had knowledge of as well as direct connections with one or more of those spiritual leaders.

In an earlier discussion, I reviewed Leslie Spier's argument that the Prophet movement is an ancient, defining aspect of Plateau cultures. Certainly, proving the actual extent of the movement's antiquity is not really possible. Yet, if we take Ray's (1936a) portrayal of Kolaskin as an example, we find older traditions in a complex mix with newer ones. Kolaskin appears to combine shamanistic ideas of death, resurrection, and prophecy and winter ceremonial practices along with Christian rituals such as Sunday prayer meetings and an avoidance of work, dancing, or gambling during the Sabbath.

In his youth, Kolaskin suffered a painful and incapacitating illness for two years during which his legs became involuntarily flexed into a fetal position. Towards the end of his infirmity, he lost consciousness. Ray's informants say that the young man experienced 'death' and that his relatives and neighbours began preparations for burial:

> Kolaskin's best clothing was made ready and the morrow was set for the actual interment. However about nightfall he regained consciousness and all present began to rejoice because their friend had 'come to life' again. Kolaskin began to sing. The song he sang was a new one; no one had ever heard it before. He spoke to the assemblage, declaring that his pains were gone and that he was well once more. He told them that he had experienced a great revelation in a dream while he had been dead. (Ray 1936a: 68)

As would a shaman, Kolaksin had taken on the fetal burial posture, journeyed to the land of death by way of altered consciousness, and revived with messages for the living. He later became famous for prophesying (with some accuracy) cataclysmic events such as floods and earthquakes. Dictating the methods he had discovered about leading a righteous and exemplary moral life, he became a powerful leader. But Kolaskin turned tyrannical, exploiting his followers' labour and wealth and using force against them when they did not obey his directives.

Such behaviour is clearly not in keeping with the long-held cultural ethics of pacifism and egalitarianism in the Plateau, and hence some community members balked. After spending three years in a federal penitentiary for being implicated in a murder, Kolaskin reverted to a leadership role which adhered more closely to that of a 'traditional' shaman and chief. He preached wariness against non-natives, but unlike other prophets such as Smohalla, he nevertheless kept the ethic of pacifism when he discouraged his followers from joining the Northern Plateau Indian War of 1858–9. Instead of employing violence as a tactic, he travelled to Washington, DC, on two occasions and led the political battle in protecting his people's interests, rights, and land against American intrusion. Continuing to impress people 'by the miracle of his "return to life,"' as well as his prophetic statements and profound oratory skills, Kolaskin regained popularity as a leader (Ray 1936a: 70, 75; Burns 1966: 286).

Clearly, Kolaskin's success depended at least in part on his adherence to old cultural symbols, particularly prophecy of apocalyptic events, pacifism, and resurrection from death. However, he was also a dynamic character who brought together *all* the cultural resources available to him in an effort to achieve his goals. Truly, in this religious leader's life we find a *mélange* of ancient and recent ideas, of political, economic, and spiritual motivations, and of moral and immoral behaviour – a situation perhaps more elaborate than Leslie Spier allowed in his theoretical framework which depicts the Prophet Dance as an historical cultural form directly replicated by contemporary people.

Sure enough, there are some concepts that endure through history by way of historical consciousness and cultural practices, but these are not isolated from other newer ones. Rather, the behaviour and beliefs of Kolaskin reveal how a great multitude of influences inform our ideas of the world. As we have seen, any individual must continually negotiate recent cultural additions as well as ideas that have come through generations, interpreted and reinterpreted. Like everyone, Kolaskin and his people played with ideas deliberately, implicitly, and unconsciously, envisioning similar principles in different ways and drawing together all the tools at hand to find meaning in life. In other words, like everyone, Kolaskin and his people lived change and continuity simultaneously.

This is also true for Lakes people who now rebury their ancestors at Vallican. Their ideas and motivations come in part from the actual history of cultural phenomena like shamanism and the Prophet Dance, but they also likely come from newer influences such as environmentalism and the Native American Church. As was true for the generations of women and men from whom Lakes people have descended, keeping the integrity of their cultural ideas and practices – 'keeping the Lakes' way' – is dependent upon their application and interpretation of new and old ideas and practices to their current context.

Keeping the Lakes' Way: A Return to Refuge

The relationship between the Prophet Dance movement of the nineteenth century and the contemporary reburials at Vallican is indirect. The ideas and practices associated with the historical movement persist at Vallican in a discursive field, in a way of expressing concerns about the present, more often than as a direct application of specific historical activities. They are a pool of references which have filtered through generations and through various contemporary influences, a way of thinking, a world view which every individual interprets for herself. To be sure, these ideas may be seen among the Sinixt at Vallican in their 'constant concern for the dead,' which Spier (1935: 16) suggests was a basic motivating factor in the Prophet Dance movement. In addition to this, a considerable number of people at the site discuss ideas of prophecy and the coming destruction of the world as we know it, themes which are evident in the historical Prophet movement, environmentalism, and the Native American Church. The Lakes' remedy for such catastrophe is to lead a moral life, to resurrect the historical autonomy of their culture by building a new community where Lakes people can follow the righteous path down which their ancestors will lead them.

Now in middle age, Bob Campbell has told me that he was raised by 'medicine people' near Keller, Washington, on the Colville Reservation. Prophecy and telepathy, along with other spiritual activities like healing, were a daily part of their lives. They didn't need phones, he said to me, because the elders knew when visitors were going to arrive. They would just start preparing their place for company and soon after a family would appear. 'This kind of thing happens in this generation too,' he adds.

Four years after this conversation, Bob Campbell and Robert Watt advised me to come back to the West Kootenays at a certain time in 1998 because an old woman on the Colville Reservation had prophesied that a catastrophic event would occur on the West Coast; she had made many previous predictions in her life and all had come true, they said.

Robert Watt also made reference to prophecy when he told me that his people had 'dreamers' who foretold the coming of Europeans and the destruction they would bring with them. He says, 'It'll all come down eventually. My uncle said we'd be fighting for this – for everyone, not just our people.' Destruction, like prophecy, is a recurrent theme among the Sinixt at Vallican. 'We're in the end days,' says Robert Watt, and the signs are everywhere around us.

In the end days, everything that is sacred to aboriginal peoples will be attacked, and as far as the Sinixt are concerned, there is nothing more sacred than a graveyard like the one at Vallican. Charlie Quintasket (quoted in Wren 1989), a Sinixt elder and the brother of Christine Quintasket, says 'I've been thinking all my life about how we were dispossessed, displaced up there. It makes me realize one thing. The British ... called us savages, but they were the savages. I'd be ashamed to call myself a white man if I was going to desecrate a grave. That site is very sacred to us.' The desecration of graves is the height of immoral behaviour in the Sinixt's view. Yet such behaviour does not exist in isolation. Other forms of impropriety, such as logging and damming rivers, exist alongside disinterment. Destruction will be the end result of the current dominance of immoral worlds.

Many Lakes feel that to live ethically one must follow a moral code which maintains a reciprocal relationship between humans, the land, and the realm of spirits in which the ancestors dwell. Eva Orr calls this 'keeping the Lakes' way.' The ideal of keeping the Lakes' way requires that people not take for their own gain but instead give back by following a cultural ethic of egalitarianism, reciprocity, and peaceful living. Clearly, there are many contemporary and historic pressures that the Sinixt face which impinge on this idea of justice and morality. The repercussions are not a mere breach in ideology, but have caused real political, economic, and spiritual hardship for the Sinixt. Simply maintaining the camp at Vallican has gone from being what they initially saw as spiritual rectification to a legal and political battle with federal, provincial, and tribal governments. Undoubtedly, the Lakes' intense focus on death at Vallican is in part a recent response to losing control over their dead as well as their own political and cultural autonomy. However, as David Aberle (1959) suggests with his deprivation theory, pressures like these probably also fan the sparks of old world views.

Not unlike Kolaskin, the Sinixt emphasize the necessity of living a moral and righteous life in their difficult situation at Vallican in order to overcome the immorality of their opponents. In 1994 I met two young men, one of them the son of Annie Kruger, who are descendants of Sinixt people who had gone to live among the Okanagan at Penticton, British Columbia. They told me that when they first began to learn about the details of colonial history they became very angry and thought they should take some retaliative action. The youths went to their elders with a plan, but the elders responded by saying, 'You don't hit a mental.' That is, you do not harm a person who does not understand the significance of her actions. In effect, the elders were upholding their cultural ethic of pacifism despite the repercussions of the ignorant and destructive behaviour of the dominant society. In these youths' eyes, the elders advocated a moral response of restraint and negotiation rather than meeting violence with violence.

Here, morality becomes a defence. In fact, very similar to the doctrines of Kolaskin, environmentalists, and the Native American Church, the Lakes at Vallican view moral living as a salve against a coming apocalypse. Not only this, living a good life in spite of the world's chaos seems to heighten the Lakes' sense of separate ethnic identity, to set them apart from the majority. But their own isolated moral actions cannot cancel the adversity which they feel exists everywhere around them. Indeed, they feel the earth will not be able to bear the burden for much longer. Here, the Sinixt experience an intersection of moral and immoral worlds. Their own moral world is endangered by the weight of so many immoral ones, and the struggle to remain righteous in spite of threatening circumstances reinforces the Sinixt's sense of cultural identity and purpose.

In the chapter describing the history of the Lakes diaspora, I outlined some of the historical pressures which the Sinixt have endured. These include epidemics, a decreasing population, the encroachment and violence of settlers, miners, and governments, and the alienation from historic territory, among other events. The Sinixt have become a marginalized people, not only in the non-native societies of Canada and the United States, but also on the Colville Reservation, where, partly due to ethnic rivalries, there has been considerable political upheaval since it was first established in 1872. The Sinixt have always been a minority group there and have been particularly vulnerable since much of their traditional territory along the Columbia River in Washington State was taken out of the reservation in 1891 for the use of non-native immigrants (Ross 1968: 63).

Historic problems such as these are not events which the Sinixt have forgotten; rather, they see such history as the root of many present-day predicaments. To be sure, one important current dilemma, the Canadian government's lack of recognition of the Sinixt, is a product of the difficult historic conditions which forced them to move into their territory south of the international border. The current situation of pending deportation orders, court battles, and harassment by immigration officials and police officers stems from the Sinixt's Canadian 'extinct' status, with which they were labelled in the 1950s. Historic distress creates distress today. In the view of many Lakes people at Vallican, bureaucratic blunders obscure truth and deter moral action, such as the reburial of ancestral remains at Vallican.

But the Lakes' concern about the destructive life ways of non-Sinixt goes beyond the immediate context of their ancestors' graves. Conversation at Vallican often turns to the immoral worlds which generally affront the Sinixt's idea of social and spiritual responsibility. For example, they talk of various industries destroying the forests and waterways, along with a sustainable hunting and fishing economy. This kind of economy, they feel, will prompt the crash of a capitalist world system which cannot go on exploiting people and the earth indefinitely. Furthermore, they discuss how Christianity has created a hell where no hell existed. 'This was a Paradise,' says Robert Watt, 'We had no hell, just a happy hunting ground. [The missionaries] made it hell for us ... When they landed here, they landed in heaven, and look what they did to it.' Robert Watt believes that Christianity teaches us to pray to priests rather than directly to the Great Spirit. 'That,' he feels, 'is as evil as you get.'

Along with Christianity, the Sinixt have had to uphold their spiritual life despite 'New Age' appropriation of aboriginal religions. The West Kootenays, especially the Slocan Valley and Nelson area, support vibrant New Age communities as well as hippie communes, draft dodgers, and 'back-to-the-landers.' Many self-proclaimed experts of numerous forms of spirituality find consumers for their wares in this region. Acting as a representative of his people, Robert Watt has asked several 'experts' who specialize in Indian rituals to desist. He informs both native and non-native merchants that they are in Sinixt territory and that charging money for aboriginal spiritual practices is immoral.

'Do you have to do that around here?' he asks them. 'To us it's our religion, it's our way. It's not for the public like some kind of zoo or something.' If people persist, he is willing to be firm, 'to be the bad guy about that.' To one spiritual merchant, an Ojibwa named Sun Bear, he posed the question: 'How much did your elders charge you to do a pipe ceremony?' By the time Sun Bear died, he was making two or three hundred dollars for these ceremonies in Europe. Brian, a non-Sinixt visitor to the

Vallican site, remarked sarcastically that he had 'a good gig.' Robert's response was 'Yeah, he'll have a good gig when he dies and meets his ancestors ... The guy was weird, man. That guy couldn't even fit in, old Sun Bear. The only place he could fit in is when no Indians are around.'

According to the Sinixt, a considerable number of aboriginal people are like Sun Bear. They have managed to get trapped in a web of immorality as a result of their acceptance of non-native bureaucratic and economic structures. As mentioned earlier, Lakes people have been caught between the competing interests of several Canadian tribal councils over the Slocan Valley.[12] Not being recognized by the Canadian government, they are of course outside of the land claims and treaty process, and they feel that those who are in it for money rather than the preservation of ancestral land are 'sell-outs.' Says Marilyn James, 'You can see it in their eyes – ka-ching, ka-ching – the dollar signs light up.' By contrast, she says, 'Our prime mandate is our burials – protecting and repatriating our dead.'

To add to their feeling of distance from these aboriginal organizations, Sinixt independence has been threatened by the fact that, purely for bureaucratic reasons, they have had to depend on tribal councils in Canada as well as the Confederated Tribes of the Colville Reservation for legal representation in the repatriation of ancestral remains. Marilyn James remarks that the Canadian government can ignore the Lakes because they have been designated extinct, while other aboriginal bands ignore the Lakes because they aren't 'a power-house nation with money on their minds.'

The bureaucracy of the Colville Reservation has not escaped such criticism. Says Bob Campbell (quoted in Walter 1991), the Colville Tribal Council 'will climb all over the bones of their ancestors for money. Those people don't care about the Arrow Lakes band. They're part of the white culture now, part of business and government.' As a result of embracing the economic and political ethics and structure of the dominant American society, the reservation's bureaucracy has accrued large debts and has become involved in dubious business endeavours, says Robert Watt. He believes that 'someday that reservation is going to be lost – people will suffer.'[13]

Sinixt people keenly feel the impact of all these immoral worlds. A Lakes elder who lives in Oliver, British Columbia, Jim Stelkia (quoted in Hamilton 1992), says, 'It's going to be hope or death. We can't live the way we are now. My people will be living zombies in another twenty years.' In hope of countering the negative pressures on their 'traditional and spiritual rights,' the Sinixt people began 'working together ... through a traditional method of representation in 1989. The main purpose for the renewal of our traditional circle was, and still is, to retrieve ancestral burial remains excavated from burial sites and to rebury them in their ancestral homeland.' The Sinixt see reburial primarily as a spiritual act; this is evident in their choice to hold the Winter Dance at the Vallican grave site in 1998. Yet they have acknowledged that, because of struggles over land, the protection of burial grounds 'inevitably becomes a political issue' (Watt 1993: 2–3). Indeed, Sinixt people now gather at Vallican in an official capacity. As Robert Watt says, they have renewed their 'traditional circle,' an autonomous form of Lakes self-governance. This circle meets at Vallican's Council Fire, a place which sits on the physical border separating the living space of Lakes people and the Vallican graves (Sinixt/Arrow Lakes Band 1996b). Yet most people who attend the Council Fire do not live permanently in the area.

In an effort to monitor the activity of various opponents, which include some Lakes people and a provincial government which wants 'to turn our village and graves into a tourist attraction, public park, and picnic area,' certain Sinixt elders requested that Robert Watt maintain a security camp at Vallican. Originally from Inchelium, Washington, on the Colville Reservation, he has lived there for most of the time since 1989 in a one-room 'caretaker's cabin,' and since late 1996 built with the help of friends a new kitchen cabin which has replaced the former outdoor kitchen. When he isn't fighting off deportation orders or trying to raise money for legal battles and local environmental concerns, he hunts, works on digs with a local archaeological consulting firm and at cutting trails in a nearby park, visits various sacred sites in the area, deals with the media, and watches over the graves.

Robert Watt had hoped that living at Vallican would allow him to escape the political and economic fray of the dominant society, but he has had no such luck. He realizes that he could be 'a little freer' and could make a better living if he went back to the Colville Reservation, yet his compulsion to follow his elders' wishes and to protect his ancestors takes precedence over convenience. Other Sinixt people come to Vallican to visit and to attend the Council Fire, staying in campers or in the few tipis which are located around the site, sometimes relieving Robert Watt of his duties so that he can speak publicly on his people's behalf, attend court hearings, or simply take a break.

Lakes people are not the only visitors to the Vallican camp. For one, I have made visits there since 1993. Other non-Sinixt locals similarly spend time with Lakes people at the camp, some having formed a group called the Coalition of the Supporters of the Sinixt, which helps raise funds for Robert Watt's court case and other expenses. Since 1989, Lakes people and neighbouring residents, including local Quakers and Doukhobors, have observed Thanksgiving together. The first dinner took place at the Vallican Whole, a nearby community hall, but since then the celebrations have been hosted at the Vallican camp. In 1998, about one hundred and fifty people attended. Each year, the Sinixt give gifts away to individuals who have helped them; they also raffle items to help raise funds for legal costs and camp expenses.

Not all of those who call upon the camp are locals, however. In 1991 and 1996, exiled Tibetan monks took time during a diplomatic world tour to visit the Vallican camp after they had heard of the Lakes' attempts to return to land from which their ancestors had been alienated. As well, a German film crew visited to make a documentary about their situation, and in 1997, five Indonesian environmentalists came to Vallican to share ideas about the problems of deforestation in their country and in Canada; they hoped to learn from the Lakes' own efforts to change logging practices in the West Kootenays. Furthermore, children from the Outma Squilxw Cultural School, run by the Penticton Band, came for a fieldtrip in 1996. Some of the children from this Okanagan band can trace their lineage to Sinixt people who fled the West Kootenays in the nineteenth century; these children came to the Slocan to learn more about their heritage.

The Sinixt have received many such visitors from all parts of the world, including Russia, Turkey, India, Tasmania, South Africa, Japan, and Colombia. Corporations have also become involved. Mountain Equipment Co-op and Patagonia clothing, for example, have sponsored a poster featuring a photograph of Robert Watt with an old-growth cedar tree, under which is a brief summary of the Sinixt's colonial history and the present state of logging in the Slocan Valley (Sinixt/Arrow Lakes Band 1996a; 1996b).[14] Clearly the Sinixt have been adept at educating and including both natives and non-natives in their efforts to reconcile the economic and political struggles they experience at the Vallican burial site.

In the words of Vanessa Holloman, this small encampment has become a 'Mecca' for the Arrow Lakes people and others. It has also become a place of refuge where Sinixt people come to 'get completely away from the modern world,' as Bob Campbell (quoted in Walter 1991) says. Vallican is a place of cultural importance, yet as symbolic as it is, the Sinixt's response to encroachment and immorality does not stop with a Council Fire and security camp at this village and burial site. Robert Watt said to me one evening, 'If it's all destroyed, our Great Spirit will find another place for us, a happy hunting ground. When they landed here, they landed in heaven and look what they did to it ... The destruction is for everyone, not just us.'

While the Sinixt assert a morality of reciprocity which they feel would benefit all, they recognize that they must find a refuge where they can live safely as a separate community when the world does come crashing down. Not unlike the Lakes people who hoped to avoid nineteenth-century immigrants by remaining in the mountainous regions of their northern territory, that place, they feel, must be in their ancestral homeland. Yet there are many obstacles to this desire of theirs, to build a new community. A central problem is that they have no access to land, partly because they have no legal aboriginal status in Canada. Even though Bob Campbell feels the land which local citizens own is rightfully the Lakes' by inheritance, they respect private property, he says; they recognize that people have to live together. Crown land is not theirs to take either, even though others, such as multinational forestry corporations, have been given the right to extract resources from it. 'People who don't even live here make a living off this land,' says Robert Watt, 'I'm *from* here. I should be able to come and stay. I can't buy land – anything I get I'll have to go to jail for.'

Bob Campbell has an idea of how to overcome this difficulty. Even though it has been partially flooded by the Hugh Keenleyside Dam, he has told me that the Sinixt hope to re-establish the now defunct Arrow Lakes Band Reserve at Oatscott, on the west side of the Arrow Lakes. Lakes people have not spent the same kind of time at Oatscott as they have at the Vallican village and burial grounds, but they hope to do so in the future. Until now, the Lakes' focus on Oatscott has been on the graves there.

As we have seen, burial grounds are a central component of a living community, but self-sustainability is also important to the Sinixt. Bob Campbell's idea of a new Oatscott community is modelled on his childhood experience of living off the land near Keller, Washington, about fifty years ago. Of that place, he remembers a self-sufficient community which worked together to grow large gardens, keep animals, and gather foods off of the land. The community had no electricity and stored their produce by canning, drying, and keeping root crops in insulated pits. They also cut ice from the rivers and packed it in sawdust for the iceboxes in summer. Everything they consumed came from the land, except salt and sugar, he says.

It is interesting to note that Canadian Indian Agent R.L.T. Galbraith (quoted in Bouchard and Kennedy 1985: 95) wrote at the beginning of the twentieth century that the people at Oatscott similarly 'extensively cultivated their gardens and planted many fruit trees.' Growing food like this, pursuing self-sufficiency, is a sovereign act, says Bob Campbell, and he feels such an independent and worthwhile living can be built again at Oatscott if they can regain the reservation. He also feels optimistic that the Sinixt language can be relearned from those few who speak it now.

Of course, the feasibility of re-establishing the reserve is dependent upon the Canadian government's recognition of the Sinixt as an existing aboriginal people of Canada, which at present it does not. If the government does reverse its position on this point, the idea of this community then becomes dependent on both Canada's and British Columbia's willingness to reallocate the Oatscott Reserve. There would likely be long political and legal negotiations before the Sinixt and the federal and provincial governments came to such an agreement, if they ever do. The Sinixt certainly do not have the upper hand in the situation. Bob Campbell realizes this, saying that 'there's no point unless the children are interested, otherwise you're just doing it for yourself. It's a lot of work to rebuild, and the dedicated ones are older.' It seems that the future of a separate Sinixt community, one which dwells in culturally significant land, lies in the vision of the children.

In effect, to establish an independent community at Oatscott is akin to rebuilding the paradise which the Lakes feel they lost with colonization. Such a desire is not unlike that of environmental movements, the Native American Church, and the nineteenth-century prophets: to shun immorality, to rise above the destruction it brings, and to re-create a righteous and viable existence despite the mayhem. Robert Watt has expressed to me on several occasions that the Sinixt homeland was a paradise before the Europeans came. This notion may not be mere nostalgia for a romanticized precolonial era, but the product of a long-held cultural view.

Francis Heron, a manager at Hudson Bay Company's Fort Colvile, remarked in 1829 that these people had no concept of heaven or hell, that the earth was considered to be the perfect dwelling place (Chance 1973: 74–5; cf. Elmendorf 1935–6 in Eldridge 1984: 8). Such an earthly paradise, as expressed by Bob Campbell in his pragmatic hope to create a working community, may not be a strictly unattainable utopia. Neither is it a desire to revert entirely to an idealized distant past. After all, precontact Sinixt 'were a different people,' as Eva Orr has said. Those Sinixt did not drive trucks, plant vegetables, attend the Native American Church, teach at colleges, or work with members of the Valhalla Wilderness Society like the Sinixt of today. They are aware that being Sinixt now does not rest in lifeways that were frozen upon contact with Europeans. Their desire to build a new community is driven not so much by a desire to go back in time as by the impulse of cultural ethics and a *connectedness with*, rather than a *return to*, the past. Bob Campbell (quoted in Baker 1989) says, 'We had freedom ... We had a living system.' In the Sinixt's view, such a living system, based in their moral principles of egalitarianism and reciprocity, is possible to re-create today.

A free and viable community does not discount modern politics, economics, or legal problems. In fact, Bob Campbell has a 'bad feeling' that he would be dealing with the office administration necessary to help a new community function smoothly. Despite the need for some form of bureaucratic structure, it seems that such a world would nevertheless be ideal because in it they feel they would not be controlled by the actions of others to the degree they are at present. In other words, they would have a measure of autonomy. Ideally, theirs would be a world where politics, economics, and spirituality are congruent with cultural morality. Perhaps such a desire – to build heaven on earth – comes in part from the many negative pressures which the Sinixt now face, but it arises from the social memory of shamanism, prophecy, destruction, and resurrection as well. To be sure, intentions to build such a community, a refuge from the inevitable chaos which they feel will result from both the dominant society's and 'sell-out' First Nations' impropriety, reveal the Sinixt's hope for resurrection – a resurrection of political and economic autonomy out of their already existing sense of cultural identity.

How does the desire to create an independent and moral ethnic community relate back to our central issue, the meanings and motivations of the reburials at Vallican? The moral world which the Sinixt seek in a new community begins with the moral act of reburial. Earlier I discussed how mortuary rites, as commemorative ceremonies, assert cultural identity. We have also seen that proper care and respect for the dead is central to the Sinixt's idea of the sacred. But being one of the few ways that the Sinixt feel they can keep a reciprocal relationship with the earth, burial is also an act of responsibility. That is, by giving up their bodies to the ground, they return something of what they have taken from the earth over the course of their lives. This is part of what Marilyn James calls a 'cultural law': through interment, the Sinixt help to maintain the balance of reciprocal relations between three important elements of their universe: land, people, and ancestral spirits. Reciprocity with the earth through the burial of the dead is the responsible action of people who keep a moral relationship with land and ancestors, the other agents in their universe.

Since burial has reciprocal significance for the Sinixt, the repatriation and reburial of exhumed remains is a kind of reconstitution of the moral intentions of the ancestors. Yet reburial is more than fulfilling the last wishes of generations past. Because burial is an important factor in keeping a balance of relationships between land, people, and spirits, the exhumation of buried remains breaks the cycle of a reciprocal universe, thus initiating a cycle of chaos. In effect, to put the exhumed ancestors back into the earth is to re-establish a reciprocal relationship between the land and the Sinixt of *all* times, to bring space and time together, reinforce the strength of ethnic longevity, and make the universe function properly once again. Returning the bodies to their proper place becomes a symbolic way of reordering a moral world, of piecing together the crumbling shards of a precarious existence and making logic out of chaos.

In other words, reburial is a symbolic salve for the distressing circumstances of living Sinixt. This is not so different from the intentions of prophets like Kolaskin, who hoped to make a liveable world by promoting righteous living. By association, the place of reburial becomes a symbol for living well and responsibly. Indeed, a chronotope like the Vallican burial ground becomes a symbol of hope for the Sinixt's efforts to re-create a healthy and practicable moral world.[15]

In a way, the act of reburial does allow the ancestors to rise from the dead, as predicted by some nineteenth-century prophets. Reburial is an act which strengthens and maintains a relationship between the living and the spirit world through the 'resurrected past,' as I earlier named it: a chronotopic layer which mends the bond frayed by time-distance and the events of colonial history. Previously, we learned from Robert Watt's comment about Sun Bear that those who sell spirituality will be accountable to the ancestors. 'He'll have a good gig when he dies and meets his ancestors,' he says. It seems that we, the living, exist in an ongoing relationship with those who have died. Having moral authority, the ancestors are a part of a working universe, part of a living community. We see this to be true when Eva Orr, for example, tells us that she has received directives from those ancestral spirits which the Sinixt have reburied. So too, Bob Campbell (quoted in Baker 1989) comments, 'For us Indian people,

we only have our ancestors to depend on. Spiritually, we're taught to follow our ancestors.' Those ancestors have a social role that is very much
alive.

The ancestors have a viable social and spiritual role in the Sinixt's
world, a *living* role, though perhaps not in the literal way of physical bodies rising from the graves. Exhumation of their bodies has prevented the
ancestors from fulfilling their proper reciprocal roles with living peoples
and with the land. They have been prevented 'from fulfilling a law,' as
Marilyn James says. Reburial rectifies this problem. Similar to the ideas of
the Prophet Dance and more recent influences, their resurrection by way
of their reburial contributes to setting the world in order. For the
exhumed ancestors to again take their ascribed place among the dead is
to reconstitute a balance of relations between the various worlds – land,
spirit, and people – which make up the Sinixt universe. In this way, they
are able to once again take up their active role. They do indeed rise to
help create an ideal Sinixt world.

In this act of reburial, the Sinixt at Vallican have helped their ancestors
fulfil their spiritual commitments of reciprocity by reuniting them with
their land and their descendants. But by placing ancestral remains into
the earth, the Sinixt also seed the land with their *own* presence, commit-
ting themselves and future generations to that land. This is a spiritual act,
to be sure, and a moral one, but it is political as well. Reburial deliberately
asserts their presence in this territory despite the dominant society's view
that they do not belong there. Indeed, reburial commemorates and
memorializes the longevity of their cultural inhabitation of that region.
Marshall Sahlins (1993: 4) agrees that such acts are 'More than an expression of "ethnic identity" ... [they incorporate] the people's attempt to
control their relationships with the dominant society, including control
of the technical and political means that up to now have been used to
victimize them.'

As we have seen in their hope to build a community of their own, the
act of reburial also foreshadows the Sinixt's intention to transform their
mere presence at the Vallican encampment to a life lived off the land,
a life of socioeconomic and cultural well-being which comes out of
renewed and rejuvenated relationships with their territory and with the
spiritual world in which their ancestors dwell. Thus, the reburial activities
at Vallican are more than an isolated response to the disturbance of a few
graves. They are acts of hope and desire, ones which have been motivated
by distressing historical and present day circumstances, as well as by the
social memory of territory and cultural ideas about prophecy, destruc-

tion, and resurrection. Reburial is an amulet in the continuing desire to 'keep the Lakes' way,' to maintain their continuous identity in space and time, and to shake off their status of invisibility by re-creating a moral world in a viable, self-governed community. Indeed, reburial provides a locus of resurrection and continuity, of emergence from a difficult era to prospects for new life.

chapter six

Afterthoughts on Here and Now

Some time has passed since I was that nine-year-old contemplating stones on the bank of the Columbia River. Since then, the West Kootenays have changed. Indeed, when Lakes people came to the Slocan in concern for their dead, all of us changed. Once invisible to us, the Lakes have recently challenged our understanding of history and our sense of selves. They have challenged our sense of time and space, our own chronotopes. As a result, we have had the chance to watch our history transform; it has telescoped, sending us into a greater time-depth, making us aware that there is something more between mountain-time, that epic past of geology which so fascinated me as a child, and the so-recent Silver Rush. To be sure, people-time has had a place in the West Kootenays for much longer than many of us previously acknowledged.

With the reburials at Vallican, the Sinixt diaspora may be approaching its end; some of us are now awakening to their recent emergence into a land that has been latent for nearly one hundred years. However, not all of us have taken on the challenge, allowed in our minds the Sinixt's transition from invisible to living. Many, like John Norris (1995) in his *Historic Nelson*, still believe the European prophecy which claims that time begins with the arrival of non-native immigrants and that any other way of living shall vanish in the face of unilineal evolutionary progress.

Anthropologists have sometimes allowed themselves to be trapped by this prophecy. As witnessed in some court decisions, such as the rulings on *Delgamuukw v. HRMTQ* (McEachern 1991; Supreme Court of Canada 1997), the land claims process requires aboriginal peoples to prove the antiquity of their identity if they are to gain any political credibility among the governments of nation-states. Such a process forces native peoples to demonstrate unequivocally that they have objective ethnic distinctiveness and exclusive historical claim to territory. Anthropologists and other scholars of Native Studies have been asked to take part in these debates. Inevitably, they are required to make great lists about language, economy, politics, philosophy, and territory, cultural attributes which are meant to prove – or disprove – the longevity of a people's ethnicity.

This preoccupation with longevity is key. In the land claims process, the idea of cultural continuity has been constructed as an icon of legitimate political identity even though, as we know, the idea of continuity is problematic. Often the debate over aboriginal political rights deteriorates to attempts at proving a group's 'authenticity' of culture. Such authenticity is claimed by emphasizing historical continuity, even changelessness, over change. So the debate goes: continuity supports authentic culture whereas change diminishes it. But how can this be if no culture is static? By these criteria, no culture would be 'authentic' or 'real.'

All living people are current people with current ideas and current practices. All living people interpret again and again what they know, imagine, and feel about the past and apply that knowledge to their lives here and now. They apply social memory to their current context through historical consciousness and practice to create a viable contemporary way of life, a contemporary identity. In this way, living peoples can never be replicas of the people from whom they have descended. Among all peoples everywhere, culture is current.

Certainly, there are scholars at work in North America today who attempt to debunk the image of Indians as caught in their own time-eddy. They critique the belief that living aboriginal peoples must be duplicates of their ancestors in order to qualify as *bona fide* Indians. However, others engage the adversarial debate as advocates: proaboriginal scholars tend to emphasize continuity of culture while progovernment scholars tend to emphasize rupture.[1] This kind of polarization fails entirely to grasp the dialectic of change and continuity; it is blind to the integration of these social processes and instead asserts their opposition.

Not merely an interesting theoretical problem, this static view of the historical process has real political repercussions. For example, in writing his 'Reasons for Judgment' on the *Delgamuukw* case, Chief Justice Allan McEachern (1991) of the British Columbia Supreme Court embraced a framework of unilineal evolution, the prophecy of the Vanishing Indian, claiming that the aboriginal rights of Gitksan and Wet'suwet'en peoples had been extinguished with the arrival of European immigrants. As is true for all writers, his conclusions had their foundation in his own cultural world view, but his reasons were also supported by the testimony of the Crown's anthropological expert witness,[2] who described changes among the Gitksan and Wet'suwet'en since the arrival of Europeans as proof that they no longer have cultures of their own. This kind of finding reveals not only a failure of the political and legal process in regards to settling long-standing disputes between aboriginal peoples and the governments of Canada, but also a complicity among some Native Studies scholars in relegating aboriginal peoples to an archaic past.

More than this, anthropologists' and lawyers' idea that we can prove identity by way of 'objective' cultural attributes is itself faulty. Chief Justice McEachern feels that society has failed aboriginal peoples by not assimilating them into the dominant economy. He believes issues of identity and a desire for autonomy would have gone away if we had made a better effort to drag native peoples up the evolutionary ladder, leaving their Indianness behind. Of course, this approach altogether misses the point of ethnic identity. As we learned in chapter 2, ethnic identity ultimately has little to do with behaviour, language, or any of the various other attributes we consider to be objective markers of culture. Rather, identity comes from the way people define themselves through social memory as it applies to life in the present. As Gastón Gordillo (1992: 68) notes among the Tobas and Pilagás of the Pilcomayo River of the Argentine Chaco, two peoples can share so-called objective cultural features which make them look very similar to outsiders and yet still have distinct ethnic and political identities.

How do courts and politicians deal with this, something as subtle and nebulous as a people's view of themselves? So far, they have had difficulty. For anthropologists, it should be a little easier, but when we take part in debates over the historical authenticity of cultural practices and identity, we are perpetuating the misconception that Indians are only Indians if they act like their seventeenth- or eighteenth- or nineteenth-century ancestors. No non-native culture is expected to prove its authenticity in a legal forum by these criteria. No non-native society is granted identity only if it remains frozen in time. Why then aboriginal peoples? By participating in a polarized debate about change and continuity rather than properly integrating the two concepts, anthropologists are in danger of transforming their work into a mere product of a political and legal process. So what, then, is the role of the anthropologist? The adversarial process itself is in need of change, and anthropologists could possibly take a guiding role to help disengage the competing prophecies of aboriginal peoples and non-native North Americans.

The difficulty of working on aboriginal issues goes further than anthropologists' direct role in land claims debates, however. I am not naïve to the political persuasions integral to the production of all scholarship. Indeed, as Foucault would argue, all power/knowledge is political. Yet, as many who work in the field today well know, North American Native Studies are particularly fraught with overt political tensions and sensitivities. This is nothing new for anthropologists. In fact, political conflict between aboriginal peoples and colonial governments has occurred for longer than anthropology has existed as a discipline. One early North American ethnographer, James Mooney (1896), was very much involved in the strained relations between natives and non-natives during his research for 'The Ghost Dance Religion and the Sioux Outbreak of 1890' and other studies. So too, anthropologists like Verne Ray and James Teit were instrumental in explaining the history of Plateau peoples to U.S. and Canadian governments. As we earlier learned, James Teit worked as an advocate for the Sinixt man Alexander Christie when problems arose over the prospects for a reserve which he and his family had hoped to establish at the confluence of the Columbia and Kootenay Rivers.

Advocacy like Teit's has clearly been a part of anthropological scholarship in North America since the beginning. But these anthropologists were not shy about getting beyond advocacy and writing the world as they saw it. They attempted to set out the complexities of the societies in which they worked. Today, however, there is a greater feeling of constraint in the field, both for anthropologists and for the North American peoples from whom they learn. The difference comes from the heightening uneasiness in negotiations between First Nations and nation-states. Such an anxious political climate proffers wariness. Aboriginal peoples feel more and more threatened by the political implications of what scholars have to say about them, and scholars, in turn, feel more and more concerned about how their own scholarship might be used in the political arena.

Plainly, there is much at stake for all, and anthropologists often find themselves caught in the middle of opposing factions. As a result, we have been forced into a situation of fearful caution, taking elaborate care about what we write and how we write it. We are sometimes too careful, to the point of self-censorship. Surely, when scholars begin to fear that any statement they make could have severe political repercussions, their academic discipline becomes threatened with paralysis.

Whether native or non-native, anthropologists working in North America need to step back a little. We do not serve best as professional advocates, but rather as independent scholars. While we may be pulled by both sides in an adversarial debate, our best contribution can only come from cultivated disinterest. This may sound hopelessly old-fashioned. I am quite aware that none of us is objective in the way scholars from previous generations thought they were. Undoubtedly all knowledge has its position of bias. But there are degrees. Ultimately, the *démodé* motivation, 'contribution to knowledge,' may be the foundation of clearest integrity. Whether we can achieve any such distance in this political climate is a legitimate question. Even so, we must endeavour to step back and recount. While none of us is unbiased, any political conclusions to which we arrive must have their basis first in thorough, dispassionate research. Actively initiating our work as advocates could undermine our discipline's integrity and competence. It could cause further deterioration of an already bleak situation.

Partly in response to these political tensions with which anthropologists must currently grapple, the Sinixt Interior Salish have chosen this time to shed their status as an invisible people. They have drawn together from the peripheries of their historical territory, from reservations and towns around Washington State and British Columbia, converging on the site of Vallican in the Slocan Valley. The disinterment of ancestral remains in their territory has been an affront to their sense of morality, spirituality, and cultural independence, enough so that they have been willing to make their presence known to the dominant society in Canada. In fact, after a long diaspora, some of them have chosen to take up refuge in their northern territories, as did the Lakes people of generations past when non-native immigrants first came to the Plateau in the nineteenth century.

Sinixt people based at Vallican have had some success in repatriating and reburying the exhumed bodies of their ancestors. Whether they will also be successful in their plans to build an autonomous community is difficult to say. Given their 'extinct' status in Canada and the incohesiveness of the ethnographic and documentary evidence upon which governments depend so greatly to make decisions about territorial rights, they will undoubtedly have an uphill battle.

Despite the poorly established written record, however, this people keenly remembers the difficult relationship it has had with European Americans and Canadians over the past two centuries. With the immigration and bureaucratic problems they experience at present, it seems that this relationship has not become much easier with time. Their lives are still full of distress, just as they were in the early years of their diaspora.

Yet the Sinixt's feelings of historical connection with their ancestors and land, their relationship with space and time, has been strong enough to withstand the many political, legal, and economic obstacles which they face in order to maintain a world of reciprocal relations. Nevertheless, it is no easy task to proclaim one's existence to an incredulous world, to uproot its tenacious prophecies of the Vanishing Race.

All of us experience the dynamic tension between change and continuity in our identity. As we have seen in the multiple time layers in the Vallican chronotope, this tension is expressed with particular eloquence among the Sinixt Interior Salish. Allowing for the sublime intricacy in her cultural identity, the Lakes elder Eva Orr sees her people as both changing and continuous. She recognizes that the ancestors who have been exhumed are time-distant from the living Sinixt who so carefully rebury them today. Even so, she asserts that she and other contemporary members of her community 'keep the Lakes' way.' Eva Orr (quoted in Walter 1991) said at a reburial ceremony, 'Today, we're here to put these people back where they belong. We can't do anything else for them but put them back. We can't do anything from our day. They were a different people.'

Those ancestors were a different people. They did not live as the Lakes live today. But Eva Orr and other Sinixt of the present are nevertheless able to keep the way of the past. This is not a contradiction, but rather an evocative dialectic, full of the tensions of ever-moving cultural identity. Distance from the ancestors' epic past is reconciled with social memory and historical consciousness, with the connectedness between living and time-distant people.

Eva Orr's words poignantly express the to and fro-ness, the manifold dynamics of culture. But if culture is so dynamic, what then is actually being kept by Lakes people? Is it material culture and objective attributes, as the courts would believe? Is it duplicated thoughts, thinking and behaving in replication of mothers and grandmothers and great grandmothers? No. While contemporary ways of being have their basis in the ways of persons past, these things alone cannot make us who we are. True, concepts and practices can be tenacious, but above all else, it is the feeling of connectedness, the idea of a shared identity between past and present that is kept by living peoples who remember and commemorate their history. At the root, it is our idea of ourselves here and now that remains. It is our consciousness of our identity that has such power. For Eva Orr and the people of her community, to keep the Lakes' way is to know, live, and feel the power of that identity which connects them to all the layers of an intricate cultural past.

Selected Spelling Variations of 'Sinixt'

SPELLING	YEAR OF ORIGINAL REFERENCE	AUTHOR AND CITATION
Spellings as Rendered by Lakes People		
Snaitcekst	After his birth in the 1870s	Aeneas Seymour (Lakin 1976)
S-nai-tcekstet	1914	Alexander Christie (1914)
Si-na-aich-kis-tu, Sinschirst	Before her death in 1936	Christine Quintasket (Mourning Dove 1990)
Sinaistxt	1989	Sinixt/Arrow Lakes Band (1989a)
Historical Spellings		
Chatth-noo-nick [?]	c. 1814	Aaron Arrowsmith (1814), cartographer
Sinachicks	1824	George Simpson (1931), Hudson's Bay Company (HBC)
Sinatcheggs	1825	Alexander Ross (1855), HBC Fort Okanogan
Sinaetcht	1830	John Work, HBC Fort Colvile*
Sin Natch Eggs	1859	John Arrowsmith (1859), cartographer

SPELLING	YEAR OF ORIGINAL REFERENCE	AUTHOR AND CITATION
Sanihk	1858	John Sullivan, Palliser Expedition (Graham 1945: 122)
Sinyakwateen	1861	North American Boundary Commission (c. 1861)
Sinuitskistux	c. 1861	Charles Wilson (1866), North American Boundary Commission
Snichick	c. 1866–70	Jason O. Allard, HBC Fort Shepherd (1926)
Snaiclist	1871	Pierre-Jean De Smet (1905), Jesuit missionary
Snaicisti, Snaesesti	1879	Alexander Diomedi (1978), Jesuit missionary
Snaichist	1882	Giuseppi Caruana, Jesuit missionary*
Snaichisti, Snaichist	1893	St Francis Regis Mission Records*

Ethnographic Spellings

Sinahoiluk	1864	William F. Tolmie*
S-na-a-chikst	1892	George Dawson (1892)
Senijextee	1896	James Mooney*
Snaai'tckstg	1900	Franz Boas*
Sinuaítskstuk	1911	Edward Curtis*
Snai'.tcɛkstɛx, Snrai'tcɛkstɛx, Senijextee, Snai'tcɛkst	c. 1910–13	James Teit (1910–13, 1930)
Sina'itskstx	1935	William Elmendorf (1935–6)
Sna'itckstk^u	1936	Verne Ray (1936b)

SPELLING	YEAR OF ORIGINAL REFERENCE	AUTHOR AND CITATION
Sinaiksti	1973	David Chance (1973)
sngaytskstx	c. 1978	Randy Bouchard and Dorothy Kennedy (1985)

*Cited in Bouchard and Kennedy (1984: 80, 103, 119, 120; 1985: 6).

Selected Historical Sinixt Village and Resource Sites

*Site Names Listed by Ray and Teit**

SITE NAME	LOCATION
Sxone'tk^u (Teit)	Columbia River below Marcus, Wash.
npepkolá't'skin (Ray)	Winter and spring village two miles down the Columbia River from Marcus, Wash.
kɩxkɩ'us (Ray)	Large winter village one mile down the Columbia River from Marcus, Wash.
nt'sɪlt'sɪli'tk^u (Ray) NisEltsElē'tuk (Teit)	Village at or near Marcus, Wash.
átstləktst'cɪn (Ray)	Large village with some year-round occupancy across the Columbia River from Marcus, Wash.
sɪntkɪlxuwe'ltən (Ray)	Winter hunting camp across the Columbia River from Bossburg, Wash.
tɬtitko's (Ray)	Spring root-digging camp between Bossburg and Northport, Wash.
stce'xələk^u (Ray) Stce'xEllk^u (Teit)	Village on the Columbia River below Northport, Wash.
ntsətserri'sem (Ray) NtsEtsErri'sEm (Teit)	Village near Northport, Wash.

*Ray (1936b: 124–8) and Teit (1930: 209–11)

SITE NAME	LOCATION
sɩnqi′lt (Ray)	Village at Northport, Wash.
sn'ȧkewi′lten (Ray)	Camp near Northport, Wash.
unnamed (Teit)	Village at the former site of Hudson's Bay Company's Fort Shepherd, on the west bank of the Columbia River just north of the international boundary
Nkolē′latk^u (Teit)	Lower Pend Oreille River
nquli′la' (Ray) Nkoli′la (Teit)	Year-round village one mile up the Columbia River from the mouth of the Pend Oreille River
tcѡlxi·′t'sȧ (Ray) TcEaulExxi′xtsa (Teit)	Hunting camp at Trail, BC
snskəkəle′um (Ray) SnskEkEle′um (Teit)	Camp at a creek close to Trail, BC, noted for service berries
KEluwi′sst (Teit)	Camp at Rossland, BC, noted for berries
kupi′tɬks (Ray) QEpi′tɬes (Teit)	Important meeting place, gravesite, and village, as well as a root-digging and hunting camp on the north side of the confluence of the Columbia and Kootenay Rivers, at Brilliant, BC (called kp′ítl'els by Bouchard and Kennedy 1985: 112)
Ntoxē′^{u}tk^o (Teit)	Columbia River from the Arrow Lakes to Marcus, Wash.
Ti′k^{u}t (Teit)	Arrow Lakes area
sm·a′ip' (Ray)	Camp at south end of Lower Arrow Lake
məmatsi′ntɩn (Ray)	Village on Lower Arrow Lake noted for spring mountain goat hunting, exact location uncertain
plu′me' (Ray)	Hunting and fishing camp at Deer Park on Lower Arrow Lake
xaie′kən (Ray) Xaiē′kEn (Teit)	Site at a creek below Burton, BC, noted for kokanee salmon
snexai′tsətsəm (Ray) Snexai′tskEtsEm (Teit)	Site across Lower Arrow Lake from Burton, BC, noted for huckleberries (near the former Arrow Lakes Indian Reserve, or Oatscott Reserve)

SITE NAME	LOCATION
nəmi·'məltəm (Ray) Nɛmīʹmɛltɛm (Teit)	Village on Whatshan (formerly Caribou) Lake west of the Arrow Lakes, noted for hunting caribou
tciʹuken (Ray) Tciʹukɛn (Teit)	Site south of Nakusp, BC, noted for caribou hunting
neqoʹsp (Ray) Neqoʹsp (Teit)	Site at Nakusp, BC
kuʹsx̱anaʹks (Ray) Kuʹsx̱ɛnaʹks (Teit)	Site at Kuskanax Creek, north of Nakusp, BC
kospiʹtsa (Ray) Kospiʹtsa (Teit)	Site at Arrowhead, BC, noted for salmon fishing and root digging
skəx̱iʹkəntən (Ray) Skɛx̱iʹkɛntɛn (Teit)	Large winter village and trading site across the Columbia River from Revelstoke, BC, augmented in winter and summer by temporary trappers, hunters, berry-pickers, and fishers from downriver
nk'umaʹpuluks (Ray) Nkɛmaʹpɛlɛks (Teit)	Important meeting place and hunting, berrying, root-digging, and fishing village on uppermost end of Upper Arrow Lake at Comaplix
sınpətłʹme.ʹp (Ray)	Camp on upper Trout Lake, beginning of the portage to Upper Arrow Lake
siaʹuks qa·liʹsu (Ray) Kaliʹso (Teit)	Hunting and fishing camp on lower Trout Lake
Słokeʹn (Teit)	Slocan Valley generally, including the river and lake, noted for salmon fisheries which allowed for well-populated villages
sketuʹkəlôx (Ray) Skɛtuʹkɛlôx̱ (Teit)	Village on Slocan River
nkweioʹxtən (Ray) Nkweioʹxtɛn (Teit)	Village up the Slocan River from sketuʹkəlôx/SkɛtuʹkɛlôX
ka·ntca·ʹk (Ray) Kãʹntcãʹk (Teit)	Village on Slocan River just below Slocan Lake
sihwi·ʹləx (Ray) Sihwīʹlex̱ (Teit)	Village on lower end of Slocan Lake

SITE NAME	LOCATION
takələ̣x̌aitcəkst (Ray) TakɛlɛX̌aitcɛkst (Teit)	Village midway up Slocan Lake, near New Denver, BC
snkəmi′p (Ray) Snkɛmi′p (Teit)	Village at upper end of Slocan Lake
Nta′lltɛx̌i′tk° (Teit)	Kootenay River downstream from Kootenay Lake
Ntsa′kuɫawi′ɫxᵘ (Teit)	Bonnington Falls on the Kootenay River upstream from the mouth of the Slocan River, noted for salmon fisheries
nttkuli′tkᵘ (Ray) Sntɛkɛli′t.kᵘ (Teit)	Fishing, hunting, and berrying village one mile up the Kootenay River from the mouth of the Slocan River, noted for the salmon fishery nearby at Bonnington Falls
nx̣a·x̣a′tsən (Ray)	Fishing and hunting site on the Kootenay River across from Nelson, BC
k′iyá′mlupᵘ (Ray) Kaia′mɛlɛp (Teit)	Village at Nelson, BC
yakskukəni″ (Ray)	Fishing, root-digging, and hunting site on the Kootenay River six or seven miles east of Nelson, BC
ktca′ukuɫ (Ray)	Late spring camp at Balfour, BC
na·x̣spoá′lk′en (Ray)	Temporary camp on the west shore of upper Kootenay Lake (exact location uncertain)
stɯxtɫu′stən (Ray)	Year-round village at Malo, Wash.
skwá′rəxən (Ray)	Village at Addy, Wash.

James Teit (1930: 210) mentions that 'there were a number of smaller villages or camps, all more or less permanent.' He did not list fully the villages in Washington State, although he notes that there were about eight main villages there, three of which I list above. He also notes that there were Lakes people living on the Lower Kettle River and at Christina Lake, BC.

For a review of the historical and ethnographic literature describing Sinixt place names, see Bouchard and Kennedy (1984; 1985).

Notes

Chapter Two: Presence

1 Teit (1910–13).
2 Although it demands proof of exclusive occupation of land to establish exclusive aboriginal title over a territory, the recent Supreme Court of Canada (1997) decision on *Delgamuukw* also recognizes that some territories were used jointly and makes allowances for site-specific rights and for shared exclusivity in land claims. These provisions may help alleviate a little of the tension between First Nations with overlapping claims to land.
3 The Lakes do not have the same degree of anonymity in the United States as they do in Canada. This is likely because they have been more visible to the dominant society there, being residents of the Reservation of the Colville Confederated Tribes and nearby communities in Washington State.
4 I have chosen to use words like 'aboriginal' and 'native' without capitals. I realize that many authors prefer to capitalize as a gesture of respect. However, I consider these homogenizing categories to be colonial constructs with no identifying features; they are more akin to words like 'people' or 'group.' I choose rather to capitalize terms identifying specific ethnicity, such as 'Sinixt' and 'Interior Salish,' except in cases where capitalization is well entrenched, such as in the term 'Indian.' For similar reasons, I choose to use the lower case for 'western' peoples and upper case for terms like 'Canadians.'
5 The term 'Sa-al-tkw't' is also used as a synonym for Sinixt. But for one exception, I have not heard Sinixt people refer to themselves thus. My only other contact with this term has been through two documents, a wilderness map (Valhalla Society 1993) and a written statement made by Robert Watt (1993).
6 Ray spells their name 'sna'itckst".' James Teit (1930: 199) believes their name,

which he spells 'Snai'tcɛkst,' derives from the word *ai'tcɛkst*, meaning *Salvelinus namaycush* or lake trout (Scott and Crossman 1973: 227). Bouchard and Kennedy (1985: 6, 99) agree with this etymology, although they disagree on the species of fish, claiming that the name 'sngaytskstx' translates as 'Dolly Varden people' from *gaytskst*, the Sinixt term for Dolly Varden char or *Salvelinus malma*, which is plentiful in the waters of the Arrow, Slocan, and Kootenay Lakes and their associated river systems.

7 'Colville' is not an aboriginal term. Hudson's Bay Company Governor George Simpson (1947 [1825]: 48) named the fort at Kettle Falls for his employee, Andrew Colvile. Note that I reserve the original spelling 'Colvile' for the HBC fort. Subsequent applications of the name, such as for the Washington State reservation and the U.S. Army fort of that name, adopted the spelling 'Colville.'

8 I use the spelling 'Skoyelpi' as rendered by a Jesuit missionary in the mid-nineteenth century (De Smet 1905).

9 According to Ruby and Brown (1986: 42), 'The Confederated Tribes of the Colville Reservation, Washington, are composed primarily of descendants of the following Salish and Shahaptian-speaking peoples: Colville [Skoyelpi], Entiat, Methow, Nespelem, Nez Percé, Sinkaietk (Southern Okanagon), Palouse, Sanpoil, Senijextee [Sinixt], Sinkiuse, and Wenatchee.' Sinixt people at Vallican say that there are fourteen different cultural groups and that the reservation is divided into districts which tend to be separated along ethnic lines.

10 As mentioned above, Ray (1936b: 111, n. 19) has noted that residents of various ethnicities on the Colville Reservation sometimes call themselves 'Colvilles.' Perhaps it is due to this that Sinixt-Skoyelpi author Christine Quintasket (Mourning Dove 1990) occasionally calls Sinixt peoples 'Colvilles,' such as when she misidentifies two Lakes chiefs, Andrew Aropaghan and James Bernard (Mourning Dove 1990: 181). James Bernard, a Lakes chief in the Kelly Hill area for over thirty years, was one of anthropologist Verne Ray's main informants during his fieldwork among the Sinixt. Ray (1936b: 99; 1975: 133, 143–4), as well as ethnographers Bouchard and Kennedy (1985: 67–70), lists both him and Aropaghan (variously spelled) as successors to the famous Lakes leader Grégoire.

11 Important to note, before he ever entered into Sinixt territory in 1811, David Thompson called the 'Flatbows' or Lower Kutenai people the 'Lake' for their association with the southern part of Kootenay Lake. Reading Thompson's *Columbia Journals* can therefore be perplexing, especially since the volume's editor provides no clarification of this unusual usage (Belyea 1994). Certain historians, such as Clara Graham (1945: 28–31), sometimes fall into the trap by taking Thompson's 'Lake' category at face value, and thus mistake the

Lower Kutenai Flatbows for the Sinixt Interior Salish in descriptions of early-
nineteenth-century life in the region. Thompson's reference to a Kutenai-
speaking Lake people appears to be unique. Ross Cox (1957 [1831]: 264), an
early fur trader in the region, makes it clear that non-natives could easily
distinguish between Salish and Kutenai languages, so they themselves would
not have had trouble differentiating between the two versions of 'Lake' peoples when they encountered them. Other than Thompson's early use of the
name, the terms Lake, Lakes, or Arrow Lakes people refer to Interior Salish
speakers.

12 All of Bouchard and Kennedy's (1984; 1985; 1997) aboriginal language spellings use this system. Other linguistic renderings simultaneously exist. Verne
Ray (1936b: 120, n. 38), for example, uses the system as outlined by the American Anthropological Association's 1916 report 'Phonetic Transcription of
Indian Languages.' James Teit, on the other hand, crafted his own linguistic
system, according to his editor, Franz Boas (1930: 25–6).

13 The authors of the RCAP documents (1996) note that linguistic classification
has political undertones. The Commission says, 'the fact that some Aboriginal
groups use distinct ethnic labels often leads to erroneous identification of
their dialect as a distinct language.' Fair enough, but RCAP does not take the
next step and acknowledge that the bestowal of linguistic classification is itself
political. Wilson Duff (1969: 15) admits that linguistic 'division is somewhat
arbitrary and inconsistent' and largely 'descriptive' rather than indicative of
'functioning social or political units.' Of the Columbia Plateau, historian
David Chance (1973: 98) has noted that the non-native oversimplification of
ethnicities began early in the nineteenth century; for convenience's sake, fur
traders started categorizing indigenous peoples by larger linguistic groups
rather than by locally recognized political units. Given that names of language
families are thus decided arbitrarily, choosing one ethnic name like Okanagan
over others for a larger classificatory label is a political act whether we intend
it to be or not. To be sure, large linguistic classifications have frequently
become 'common sense' political classifications which imply ethnic homogeneity. Not being a linguist myself, I cannot comment on the extent to which
the Sinixt language differs from related 'Okanagan' languages. This is not an
important issue in regards to identity, however. As I commented earlier, cultural traits like language do not necessarily define ethnicity. The Royal Commission on Aboriginal Peoples agrees with this. Yet many people continue to
equate distinct ethnicity with linguistic diversity. Selecting the name 'Okanagan' or 'Okanagan-Colville' over others as a linguistic class serves to obscure
the identity of non-Okanagan ethnic groups which are linguistically related.

14 Towards the north of Sinixt territory, Revelstoke, BC, has forty inches of pre-

cipitation per annum as compared to eight at Yakima, Washington, in the
southern Columbia Plateau (Ray 1936b: 105). Turnbull (1977: 96) designates
Lakes territory an 'Interior Wet Belt.' See also Mohs (1982b: 9–14, 21–4) for
an overview of climate, geomorphology, and biogeoclimatic zones in the area.

15 Kent (1980) believes that the ideal of pacifism in the Plateau is contentious.
See also Chatters (1989) for archaeological evidence suggesting that warfare
was more common in the Columbia Basin than previously thought. Christopher Miller (1985) believes warfare escalated as a result of the increase in
disease as well as social, economic, and climatic stresses during the period
leading up to the arrival of European immigrants. Ray (1975: 149) later noted
that the Sinixt were less committed to pacifism than were the Sanpoil or
Skoyelpi, possibly because they experienced encroachment by other culture
groups in recent times. However, Ruby and Brown (1986: 188) claim that
Sinixt chiefs, including the nineteenth-century chief Grégoire, were
renowned for their peacemaking abilities.

16 Ray (1939: 149) adheres to diffusionary concepts of cultural 'centres' and
'peripheries,' allowing for substantial internal differentiation, even drawing
several cultural subcategories within the Plateau region, one of which he
reserves for the Sinixt. He places the Plateau centre among the Sanpoil,
Skoyelpi, Southern Okanogan, Lower Spokane, and Columbia. Such diffusionary frameworks are questionable because they suggest that the so-called
centre is not influenced by the periphery. Perhaps some cultures do have
more dominance in a region, but Ray's choice of the Sanpoil et al. is also dis-
putable because these are the peoples with whom he had done most of his
fieldwork. True, Ray (1936b: 117) does claim to have at least visited 'every
group in the [Columbia] Basin.' Nevertheless, one wonders to what conclusions he might have arrived if he had focused his energies on other peoples in
the region. Even so, Ray did recognize how other culture areas, such as the
Northwest Coast and the Plains, affected and were affected by the Plateau.
Therefore, he was aware of the potential for give and take between culture
groups and that no group ever exerts absolute cultural dominance. In short,
Ray attempted to work with the intricacy he encountered in the field and
allowed it to enter into his theoretical formulations, a feat not easily achieved
especially when working with such a large geographical area. Ray's early
efforts must be applauded for their subtlety and fluidity. Interestingly, Ray's
complex approach has not always been heeded by those who came afterward.
Ideas about a homogenous, bounded Plateau culture area still appear to exist,
as in Christopher Miller's (1985: 10) suggestion that sharp divisions developed
between cultural units around seven hundred years ago.

Despite Ray's recognition of diversity within the culture area, the homoge-

nizing effect of the sagebrush-and-horses stereotype of the Plateau has nevertheless served to obscure the cultural individuality of local ethnic groups. For
the Sinixt Interior Salish, this problem has been magnified due to the scarcity
of ethnographic documentation and to the fact that this people began to
reside more frequently during the nineteenth century among other Interior
Salish speakers in the south of their territory, particularly the Skoyelpi and
Sanpoil. This recent intensified contact with neighbours may have accelerated
the sharing of culture traits, thus making our understanding of the historical
differences between the Sinixt and other peoples even more ambiguous.
Hence, while Ray (1936b: 108; 1939: 147) observes the distinctiveness of the
Sinixt, later in his comparative analysis he qualifies this remark, contending
that they are rather closely 'affiliated south in most aspects of culture.' Important to note, Ray asserts a southerly cultural focus without fully considering
the Lakes' recent history. He therefore assumes that the similarities which
Sinixt people hold with their southern neighbours have always existed.

Chance (1973: 5) also notices this problem with Plateau scholarship, con-
curring that upper Columbia ethnographers 'attempt to portray the Indian
cultures as they were before contact' instead of properly acknowledging historical forces such as 'the cultural impact of the [Hudson's Bay] Company,'
for example. True, much of the ethnographic and historical literature depicts
the Sinixt in the southern portion of their territory where they were in direct
contact with the supposed centre of Plateau culture. Undoubtedly the Lakes
have been influenced by their neighbours to the south, yet there is little question that this kind of contact precipitates the *sharing* of cultural attributes
between cultural parties rather than the unmitigated predominance of one
over another. Certainly the Lakes have had some cultural impact on their cultural neighbours, just as those neighbours have had a cultural influence on
them.

17 The degree of awareness of the Sinixt among West Kootenay residents may
have since changed as a result of the Lakes' attempts to meet and educate
their neighbours. The local press coverage of events at the Vallican encampment and burial ground may also have had some consequence on non-native
understanding of this people, although the few newspaper articles which have
been published are themselves frequently misleading, vague, or wrong. For
instance, the October 1997 newspaper coverage of a Castlegar 'Inter-tribal
Elders' Gathering' never distinguishes between the historical residents of the
Arrow Lakes and the organizers of the event, the Shuswap Tribal Council, the
Okanagan Tribal Council, and the Ktunaxa (Kutenai)/Kinbasket Tribal Council (Morran 1997a; Kerkhoff 1997a; 1997b). Another example of such omission is an article on local treaty negotiations which discusses the Westbank

Indian Band's (Okanagan) and the Ktunaxa/Kinbasket Tribal Council's over-lap of claims to the West Kootenays, without ever making reference to the his-torical occupation of the area by the Sinixt (Morran 1997b).

18 Bouchard and Kennedy are coauthors with Nancy J. Turner (1980) of *Ethno-botany of the Okanagan-Colville Indians of British Columbia and Washington*. In this book, they include a small amount of information on the Lakes.

19 It is unclear where Duff (1969: 15, 32–3) obtains his information on the Sinixt. He cites Verne Ray, but comes to quite different conclusions about their ethnic identity. He notes that the 'Arrow Lakes band' is considered 'extinct in Canada.' Duff's reference to the 1916 Indian Reserve Commission may explain the erroneous data, since this governmental body had a poor understanding of Lakes identity and history. See chapter 3 for a thorough dis-cussion of the British Columbia and Canadian governments' general confu-sion regarding the people of the Arrow Lakes and Columbia River valley.

20 Chief Grégoire is cited variously. For example, in 1840, Jesuit Modeste Demers entered his name as Grégoire Kessouilih (Catholic Church Records 1972: 61). Indian Commissioner R.L.T. Galbraith (1914) anglicized his name to Gregory for the 1914 Royal Commission on Indian Affairs. James Teit (1930: 270) offered phonetic versions: *Kerkwá* and *Kɛsawī'lɛx*. Bouchard and Kennedy (1985: 69) list other spellings including Gre-Gore, Greg-whah, and Gregora. This chief was already politically active upon the arrival of the Jesuits in 1838 and remained chief until the mid-1870s. For a more complete list of Sinixt chief name references beginning in 1830, see Bouchard and Kennedy (1985: 69–70).

21 For a more detailed account of Sinixt seasonal rounds, see Elmendorf (1935–6) and Bouchard and Kennedy (1985).

22 Christine Quintasket's cultural identity is a little unclear. She and her family are registered as Lakes people on the Colville Reservation, but she came from Lakes, Skoyelpi, and Okanagan descent. Her maternal grandfather was a Lakes man from the Trout Lake area in British Columbia. Christine's father was named Joseph Quintasket, or Skiyu, of Kelly Hill (J. Miller 1989: 162–3). Christine Quintasket's brother, Charlie, was one of Bouchard and Kennedy's Lakes informants. The two share a father, but not the same mother. I do not have a complete genealogy, but presumably Charlie Quintasket is from a sec-ond marriage because his sister's mother died in 1902, and he was born in 1909 (Bouchard and Kennedy 1984: 399; Mourning Dove 1990: 10). Charlie Quintasket is one of the Sinixt elders who was present at the Vallican site dur-ing the protest of 1989.

23 For more favourable views of James Teit, see Sprague (1991) and Wickwire (1993).

24 See Appendix 2 for a selected list of Sinixt village sites, as recorded by James
    Teit (1930) and Verne Ray (1936b).

Chapter Three: The Latent Land

1 Quoted in Rodlie (1993).
2 For an interesting discussion and critique of the use of the concept of
   'diaspora' in the social sciences, see James Clifford's essay 'Diasporas' in
   Routes: Travel and Translation in the Late Twentieth Century (1997).
3 Robert Watt's case was heard by the Federal Court of Appeal in Vancouver,
   BC, 16–18 November 1998. At the time of press, the decision had not yet been
   handed down.
4 As mentioned in the previous chapter, some scholars like Ray (1975: 127,
   129a) actually place the Lakes' southern boundary right at Kettle Falls.
5 Epidemics continued to ravage aboriginal communities right into the
   twentieth century. From the Kelly Hill, Washington, area of Lakes territory,
   Christine Quintasket has commented that during an influenza epidemic a
   little after the turn of the century the aboriginal peoples received better
   treatment south of the international boundary than north of it. She writes
   that:
   > while we are proud of America's part in the Red Cross, thankful for what it
   > has done for the [aboriginal peoples], there is something lacking in its true
   > efficiency, in all that it is supposed to stand for. No aid had been offered the
   > stricken Indians across the Canadian border. Relief is sent to foreign lands,
   > not even denighed [denied] the baby murdering, women mutilating Hun,
   > but none has been forthcoming for the dying, simple minded natives at our
   > very door on the North ... Whole families have been, and are afflicted, in
   > many cases not one is left to provide firewood for warming the fevered suf-
   > ferers. Oftimes corpses have rotted in the room where the sick lay moaning
   > in delirium – dying with the piteous cry for water scarce articulated by
   > baked and parched lips. I would that there were more white men and white
   > women like those of Marcus [then site of the largest Lakes village in Wash-
   > ington], the little hamlet on the banks of deep rolling Swanetka [the
   > Columbia River]. (Mourning Dove 1990: 192)
6 Also spelled Melchior, Mikichlore, Mechior, and Meltour (Bouchard and
   Kennedy 1985: 69–70), this individual was likely a military leader for the Lakes
   from the 1870s to the 1880s. He does not appear to have been a central political leader, as were Grégoire and Aropaghan.
7 James Teit (1930: 209, 210) notes the Revelstoke and Slocan villages independently of Ray, spelling them Skᴇx̣i'kᴇniᴇn and Kā́ntcā́k. Elmendorf (1935–6)

also records the long-time usage of the Upper Arrow Lake settlement as an
important wintering site.

8 See Arthur J. Ray's *Indians in the Fur Trade* (1974) for an overview of how the
fur trade and North American aboriginal economies were initially compatible.

9 Fort Colvile was considered the best location for the Hudson's Bay Company's
operations in the Columbia Basin. It had good arable land and was an important, central meeting place for peoples of various ethnicities. The site is now
flooded by the Franklin Roosevelt reservoir. Fort of the Lakes was also called
McKay House, after its manager, John McKay. According to the Jesuits of the
Québec Mission (1955: 7–9), *la maison des lacs* was under construction in
October 1838. Fathers Demers and Blanchet considered the place 'wretched,'
largely because one of the *bateaux* in their group capsized in the *dalles des morts*
(Death Rapids), resulting in the drowning of twelve passengers, many of
whom were children of fur traders. I have seen only one reference to Fort Fosthall. Kate Johnson (1951: 81, 94) describes ruined foundations visible at the
mouth of Fosthall Creek on Upper Arrow Lake until the 1890s. Johnson's Fort
Fosthall may have actually been the Jesuits' mission outpost, St Peter's Station,
which appears very close to this site on Pierre-Jean De Smet's c. 1842–8 map of
the region (Peterson and Peers 1993: 118–19). Alternately, it may have been
located alongside St Peter's to take advantage of the religious gathering place,
although there is no mention of this in De Smet's (1905) letters. Burns's
(1966: 254) description of a 'Fort Forty-Nine' located just north of the international line in 1858 was probably Fort Shepherd. This fort was sometimes called
Fort Pend Oreille as well since the site was on the Columbia across from the
mouth of the Pend Oreille River. Fort Shepherd (sometimes mistakenly
spelled Sheppard) was established in 1856 as a replacement for Fort Colvile to
avoid U.S. customs tariffs and hostilities between aboriginal peoples and the
U.S. Army. Named for a Hudson's Bay Company governor, John Shepherd,
Fort Shepherd was never as successful as its forerunner, the model Fort
Colvile. Fort Shepherd was permanently closed in 1870 (Graham 1945: 102–3;
Hudson's Bay Company Archives 1939). A thorough perusal of documents at
the Hudson's Bay Company Archives in Winnipeg may help clarify the ambiguous roles the minor forts played in the Arrow Lakes region. In addition, any
journals, records, and letters left behind by fur traders would likely add to the
historical information currently available on the Sinixt. See Map 3 for historical locations of the HBC forts.

10 According to John Alan Ross (1968: 48), a Presbyterian missionary named
Samuel Parker arrived into Oregon Territory in 1835. Reverend Parker visited
aboriginal peoples at Fort Colvile in 1836. Oregon Territory, as the Columbia-
Fraser Plateau was then called, included what are now British Columbia, Wash-

ington State, and Oregon. Until the Oregon Treaty of 1846 which established the international boundary between the United States and British North America, the area was claimed by both American and British non-natives.

11 Grégoire's Lakes wife also received baptism on August 18, 1840, and took the Christian name Marie. The two were then married by Roman Catholic custom (Catholic Church Records 1972: 61). De Smet (1905: 549) is mistaken when he assumes Grégoire was baptized in 1838 by Father Blanchet along with the Sinixt children at Fort of the Lakes. The thirteen Lakes baptized at Fort of the Lakes in October 1838 were considered by the Jesuits to be children of 'infidels.' Using their baptismal names, they were: Louis and Baptiste, sons of SchoornlesKekil and an unnamed Lakes woman; Josephte, daughter of Kackeloone and an unnamed Lakes woman; Charlotte, daughter of Moleneck and an unnamed Lakes woman; Claude, son of Kalnitcha and an unnamed Lakes woman; Marie, Louise, and Jean Baptiste, children of Nouilkz and Sinsinte; Marguerite, Josephte, and Isabelle, daughters of Plitchouegge (a chief) and Kwildimalkss; and Pierre and Paul, sons of Tchiloomtchachame and Houloulmatts (Catholic Church Records 1972: 13–14). The large 1845 baptism at Kettle Falls is described by De Smet (1905: 480–2) in his *Life, Letters, and Travels.*

12 See Map 3 for the historical location of St Peter's Station and other early Jesuit missions. See also De Smet's colourful 'Map of Northern Rocky Mountains and Plateau,' c. 1842–8, in Peterson and Peers (1993: 118–19). After its founding in about 1845, St Peter's Station was first administered by Father Hoeken (De Smet 1905: 482).

13 Many Plateau peoples received baptism from the Jesuits, but this does not mean that they forsook their 'traditional' spirituality. The Jesuits were apparently aware of the complex integration of multiple religious perspectives in the Plateau, including Catholicism and local spirituality (J. Ross 1968: 51). Whitehead (1988: 15) notes that 'the nineteenth-century Jesuits held a far more liberal attitude towards religious practice than the ... Oblates' who came into the region later. Hence, while the Jesuits hoped to Christianize through fairly drastic means such as the reduction, they did not feel the need to obliterate all aspects of indigenous spirituality. Burns (1966: 49) comments that many Plateau peoples enjoyed the ceremonial aspects of Catholicism, but were not too keen on the concept of outright 'conversion.' At Toronto's 1996 International Festival of Authors, a contemporary Spokane writer named Sherman Alexie (1996) made similar assertions about the compatibility of Catholicism and Interior Salish spirituality, although he also acknowledged the Jesuits' destructive political and economical impact on his people. In my fieldwork at Vallican, I heard no such empathy for the ways of Catholic missionaries or their religion. Such complex negotiations and adaptations of vari-

ous cultural influences – this play between change and continuity – will be discussed further in later chapters.

14 In 1853, a bill was passed separating U.S. Oregon Territory into two: the northern portion being Washington Territory, the southern retaining the original name, Oregon. Beginning in the southern Plateau, Isaac Ingals Stevens, the first Governor of Washington Territory, immediately sought treaties to wrest lands from aboriginal title (Reichwein 1990: 278). His goal was not only to offer land to pioneers of European descent, but also to put through a northern transcontinental railroad (C. Miller 1985: 110).

15 A thorough study of the complex intertribal relations during the Plateau Indian Wars is beyond the scope of this work. Confederations between groups were continually forming and dissolving, depending on both immediate objectives and long-standing associations. Refer to Garth (1964), Ray (1960), Reichwein (1990), and J. Ross (1968) for greater detail on this period and later.

16 Some of my Lakes informants have told me that Sinixt people fought with the war party of Hin-mah-too-yah-lat-kekht, or Chief Joseph, in the Nez Percé War of 1877. It is important to note here that scholars in Canada sometimes forget the impact of American military operations and settlement on aboriginal peoples who live north of what is now the international boundary. We have an obligation to acknowledge our blind spot and incorporate this crucial political history of First Nations in Canada: our understanding of them should not dissolve at the border. For greater detail on the Plateau Indian Wars, see the large American literature on the subject, including Beal (1971), Burns (1966), Gidley (1981), Glassley (1953), Haines (1991), and Victor (1891).

17 Writes Burns (1966: 26), 'Among settlers, trappers, and miners there were perceptive individuals who appreciated Indian virtues, and there were brutes who instinctively harmed any Indian. A man might be friendly with the local Indians or afraid or wary or truculent or contemptuous.' Violent or not, the new immigrants' primary goal was to elbow a way onto the land, reason enough for the Plateau communities to take on a defensive position.

Richard Fry, an early prospector in the West Kootenays, is a good example of such variation of response in a single immigrant. Fry fought against Plateau peoples in the Cayuse War, then around the time of the Colvile goldstrike married a Sinixt woman, Justine Soqu-stike-en, at St Paul's Mission. Even though her husband had previously fought against aboriginal peoples, Justine brought Richard Fry into her social world, although not always without tension. Richard Fry's brother Alfred was killed in a dispute with native peoples at the Pend Oreille River in the early 1860s; Richard was subsequently threatened and, as a result, the couple left the village there. The two made a living in the Slocan, the upper Pend Oreille, and on Kootenay Lake by combining her usual seasonal rounds with gold panning, ferrying, and mercantilism (Affleck 1976b: 161; 1976c: 155; 1978: 16; Graham 1971: 80–2; see also Norris 1995 for a semifictitious version of the Frys' story). Cindy Fry, the great granddaughter of Justine Soqu-stike-en and Richard Fry, is one the Lakes people who has frequented the Vallican site in recent years.

18 Causing some difficulty in defining the northerly extent of American jurisdiction, the exact position of the boundary was not clear to locals until surveyors from the North American Boundary Commission came through in 1861 (Bouchard and Kennedy 1985: 16; Wilson 1970 [1861]).

19 In 1861, Grégoire was still the main chief of the Sinixt and would then have been about sixty years old. Hence, Wilson's (1970 [1861]: 111) 'chief of the Lake Indians' who 'remembers the first whites coming into the country' is almost certainly Grégoire. Former Hudson's Bay Company employee Jason Allard (1926) remembers that in about 1866 Grégoire 'was a great friend of the whites and was frequently a guest at the officers' tables at [the HBC's] Fort Colville and Fort Sheppard [sic].'

20 For further detail on the Colville Reservation, and especially the intensification of nationalism among individual ethnic groups, see Reichwein (1990), J. Ross (1968), and Gidley (1979).

21 The colony of British Columbia joined the Dominion of Canada in 1871, becoming a province before the establishment of the Colville Reservation in 1872. In 1865–6, after the Palliser Expedition and the North American Boundary Commission had travelled through, another colonial survey was made of the West Kootenays. However, its reports seem to have been overlooked by the new provincial government. In 1882, British Columbia officials considered the West Kootenays terra incognita and commissioned another survey (Affleck 1976b: 3–4).

22 A private contractor hoped to construct a road between Northport, Washington, and Rossland, but could not get permission to cross the Colville Reservation. The American interests in the Rossland mines contributed to the U.S. government's decision to revoke the northern portion of the Colville Reservation in 1891 so that the overland route could be constructed (Graham 1963: 213). Rossland, unlike other mining sites in the West Kootenays, was primarily noted for its gold. Although it was to be considered the centre of mining in Canada by 1898, Rossland was also of great importance to the American economy. Americans had invested heavily in all of the mining endeavours in the West Kootenays and the subsequent profits served to finance the building of major U.S. urban centres, such as Spokane, Washington (Graham 1963).

23 See for example Fisher (1977) and Tennant (1990).

24 Upon its inception, the Arrow Lakes Indian Reserve's population was twenty-two, although a 1903 census counted twenty-six people. The numbers declined thereafter. Formerly called Christie's Landing by settlers (possibly after the Lakes family called Christian or Christie), Oatscott was the name Major William Lascelles gave to this point of land which he pre-empted close to the Arrow Lakes Indian Reserve around 1903. He named it for two members of the Scott Polar Expedition of 1912 (K. Johnson 1951: 112–13, 124; Gordon 1963).

25 For example, Fire Valley or Inonoaklin Creek, to the south of Oatscott, was the main trail over the Monashee mountains, west to the Okanagan territory. It is now the route of a minor highway. The town of Edgewood was established at the head of this trail in the late nineteenth century. Up to then, this site and the surrounding area had been intensively used by aboriginal peoples (Turnbull 1977; Bouchard and Kennedy 1985: 95). Some distance to the north of Oatscott, a large red ochre deposit existed a short way up Pingston Creek Valley (K. Johnson 1951: 90), and was undoubtedly a very important economic trading site for Lakes people.

26 Alexander Christie is called Alexander Christian in some documents, as in Megraw (1915a) and Webber (1975). Some of the descendants of this man, the Boyd family, now live at Inchelium, Washington, on the Colville Reservation. Jim Boyd, formerly married to Robert Watt's sister, has visited the Vallican site and gave a concert at the Vallican Whole community centre to raise funds for the 1990 campaign to repatriate ancestral remains from the Royal British Columbia Museum in Victoria.

27 The displacement of aboriginal peoples by settlers was, of course, a common occurrence during this era. Notably, Galbraith himself had contributed to a similarly difficult circumstance near Cranbrook, British Columbia. Galbraith pre-empted eighteen thousand acres on Joseph's Prairie and subsequently sold it in 1885 to Colonel James Baker, legislative representative for the East Kootenays from 1886 to 1898. Backed up by the North West Mounted Police, Baker fenced the entire parcel of land and thus displaced the resident Kutenai group under Chief Isadore, despite their protest (Graham 1945: 161–2, 182–3).

28 Also known as Antoine Christian.

29 On 2 March 1911, Alexander Christie found his sister Mary dead on a river bank not far from kp'ítl'els. He went to the police to report that he had seen the footprints of a man in the snow around Mary's body and that she was partially undressed. The police officer who investigated claimed not to see any tracks and the coroner concluded that Mary Christie had stripped to cool herself from a fever, collapsed from the illness, fell over a cliff, and subsequently

died of exposure. In the view of Alexander Christie and his family, however, the circumstances remained dubious and this anxiety may have intensified their concerns about their security, as well as that of their land and graves (*Nelson Daily News* 1911a; 1911b).

30 Baptiste Christian's 'Colville' wife, Sophie, was actually Lakes. According to Bouchard and Kennedy (1984: 279, 282), the couple went south to a Lakes village called sn7i7zxína7 on the Columbia River south of the boundary.

31 At Vallican, the story goes that Alexander Christie was killed trying to protect his home at the mouth of the Kootenay, and that his wife and three children fled, probably to the Marcus area. Marilyn James points to miners as the culprits, although the murder was never solved.

32 The McKenna-McBride Commission of 1916 forged an agreement between British Columbia and Canada stating that 'in the event of any Indian tribe or band in British Columbia at some future time becoming extinct, then any lands within the territorial boundaries of the Province which have been conveyed to the Dominion ... for such tribe or band, and not sold ... shall be conveyed to the Province' (British Columbia 1916: 10–11).

Chapter Four: Competing Prophecies

1 Quoted in Hamilton (1992).

2 Quoted in Walter (1991).

3 Leslie Spier (1935: 5) coined the term 'Prophet Dance.' It refers to movements which Spier felt were essentially similar, but which had been given various names in the ethnographic literature, such as Ghost Dance, Dream Dance, and Praying Dance.

4 See a recent publication by Armin W. Geertz (1994), *The Invention of Prophecy*, which shows how both academics and Hopi peoples 'construct' prophetic movements and meaning for various ends, including political ones.

5 See Spier, Suttles, and Herskovits's (1959) vigorous (if not scathing) rebuttal of David Aberle's (rather gentle) article (1959) on deprivation theory.

6 Fogelson (1985: 79–81) has attempted to make his readers understand the social meaning of loss by offering Shuswap oral histories of the epidemics. He writes that 'it is not easy to envision the impact of population decimation by numbers alone. We can intellectually grasp the structural and functional implication of drastically reduced populations, but it is more difficult to come to a symbolic and emotional understanding of such events from the perspective of another culture.' Elsewhere, he says that 'we have too few accounts of the native affective reactions and cognitive rationalizations of these catastrophic die-offs' (Fogelson 1989: 139).

7 'Delgamuukw' is a misspelling of the Gitksan chief name Delgam Uukw. See
   Gisday Wa and Delgam Uukw's publication (1987), *The Spirit in the Land: the
   Opening Statement of the Gitksan and Wet'suwet'en Hereditary Chiefs in the Supreme
   Court of British Columbia.*

8 I cannot here delve into the complex social and ethnohistorical theory which
   criticizes positivist document-centred historiography. However, it is worth saying that the predominance of the latter methodology has been a real detri-
   ment to aboriginal peoples' political and legal battles. Referring to *Apsassin v.
   the Queen*, Gerry Attachie (quoted in Ridington 1990: 203–4), chief of the Doig
   River Band in northeastern BC, put the dilemma succinctly. He says, 'I talk to
   some of the elders and they told me that, "We always going to be small ...
   'cause Government they have power in a piece of paper." That's how we lost
   first round in this case. They believe the papers more than the elders' testimony. It's, it's pretty sad, you know.'

   Fogelson (1989: 142) has remarked that even after writing became common
   to North American peoples, some shunned documentation of their cultures
   and histories. I have found this to be true of the Sinixt in regards to their
   mythology. Such resistance may be motivated by an intention to maintain oral
   customs as well as to deliberately adopt 'a low-profile invisibility as a defensive
   strategy to avoid possible discrimination, persecution, conscription, and perceived threats to their autonomy.' Despite these efforts, neither documentation nor the avoidance of it has provided much protection for the legal rights
   of Indians.

9 See also Joseph Epes Brown (1982), Vecsey and Venables (1980), and Barre
   Toelken (1976) as just a few more examples of academics who depict North
   American aboriginal peoples as a homogenous entity. For refutation and critical analysis of such stereotypes, see Daniel Francis's *The Imaginary Indian: The
   Image of the Indian in Canadian Culture* (1992) and Robert Berkhofer's now classic treatise *The White Man's Indian: Images of the American Indian from Columbus
   to the Present* (1978).

10 In the summer of 1995, O.J. Simpson was tried in Los Angeles, California, for
   the murder of his ex-wife Nicole Brown Simpson and her friend Ronald Gold-
   man. The mass media and much of the public were fixated on the trial, some
   U.S. television stations broadcasting the lengthy court proceedings live for
   weeks on end.

11 If we are to agree with Whorf's hypothesis, one wonders how the decline of
   some aboriginal languages might affect cultural views of time. It would be
   interesting to see if the cultural view persisted among individuals who did not
   learn their native language.

12 The theory of Gupta and Ferguson (1992) depends on the work of Anderson

(1983), which discusses the idea of communities as 'imagined' by displaced and colonized peoples. By imagined, these scholars certainly do not mean *imaginary* community (that is, fictitious), but rather community that has been *idealized as unified* even though it has been, in actuality, dispersed due to various historical circumstances.

Chapter Five: Emergence

1 Quoted in Hamilton (1992).
2 Quoted in Walter (1991).
3 For details on the villages noted by Teit (1930) and Ray (1936b), see Appendix 2.
4 For other archaeological studies on the Vallican area, see British Columbia Heritage Conservation Branch (1982) and Williams (1982).
5 Also known as Lavina Celestes.
6 Other environmental groups which have worked with the Sinixt are the Western Canada Wilderness Committee and Canada's Future Forest Alliance (1997). Close relationships like these between environmental groups and aboriginal peoples are not uncommon in North America. The non-native support group of the Innu people of Labrador, for example, was founded by the Canadian Environmental Defence Fund. The Friends of the Innu work to change or stop the mining industry and NATO military air training, asserting that their practices cause environmental damage which disrupts the Innu's hunting and gathering economy (Hildebrand and MacLachlan 1997).
7 For more information on the Ghost Dance at Wounded Knee, see James Mooney's 'The Ghost Dance Religion and the Sioux Outbreak of 1890' (1896) and Dee Brown's *Bury My Heart at Wounded Knee* (1971).
8 In a more personal circuitous route, while participating in a Native American Church ritual on the Colville Reservation, Bob Campbell felt he was directed by a vision to 'keep the Lakes' way,' that is, to embrace forms of ritual life more particular to his own ethnicity. He has since left the NAC.
9 Christine Quintasket's spiritual training in the early part of this century contradicts William Elmendorf's (1935–6) assertion that females did not take part in vision quests. Elmendorf's informant may have been limited in her knowledge of non-Christian aspects of Sinixt spirituality because his discussion of such matters is brief.
10 Ideas of resurrection also appear in Sinixt mythology. For example, stories tell how the trickster figure Coyote returns to life with the help of Fox after having been killed by an opponent (Bouchard and Kennedy 1984: 325–6; 1985: 104;

Teit 1930: 211). Evidently, the concept of resurrection is not uncommon, manifesting itself in a variety of venues in Sinixt culture.

11 See Barbara Tedlock's article (1983), 'A Phenomenological Approach to Religious Change in Highland Guatemala,' for a Mayan example of outward adoption of Catholicism for the sake of inward preservation of indigenous beliefs.

12 In a presentation to a representative of the United Nations, Marilyn James and Robert Watt (1994: 6) stated: 'Neither our ancestors nor the members of the Sinixt Nation have ever relinquished our inherent rights to any individual, any government, or any other organization, *including* other native tribes or native nations.' In Marilyn James's opinion, the Kutenai, Shuswap, and Okanagan tribal councils know that the Sinixt have rightful historical claim to these lands. However, they are also aware that the Sinixt are officially extinct according to the Canadian government and cannot make legal claims. Marilyn James feels that these tribal councils have taken advantage of the Sinixt's weak legal and political position and have thus expanded the boundaries of their traditional homelands. As of 1998, Sinixt representatives were negotiating with surrounding First Nations in an effort to be officially recognized by them, and were beginning to have favourable responses.

13 Since the time of my initial fieldwork at Vallican, the Colville Tribal Council has taken some interest in Robert Watt's immigration case and has offered to assist in the financing of his legal proceedings. Because of their similar concern in securing crossboundary rights, Colville, Kutenai, and Okanagan tribal councils have become official intervenors in the federal appeal case, which was heard in Vancouver by a panel of three judges on 16–18 November 1998. The judgment had not been released by the time of press.

14 This poster is entitled *Guardians of the Rainforest: Ancient Legacy, Perpetual Growth, Sacred Responsibility: The Sinixt Aboriginal People Come Home.* The text and photograph of Robert Watt actually use the romanticized motif of an Indian communing with nature to the Sinixt's own benefit. Besides attempting to raise awareness of the Sinixt's legal predicament in Canada, the producers of the poster also hope to raise funds for Robert Watt's deportation case and for efforts opposing destructive forestry practices in the West Kootenays (Sinixt/Arrow Lakes Band 1996a; 1996b; Burgoon 1997).

15 See Keith Basso (1984) for a superb account of how, among the Navajo, landscape is similarly fraught with moral codes.

Chapter Six: Afterthoughts on Here and Now

1 For a discussion of this kind of polarized debate, see my article 'The Manipula-

tion of Culture and History: A Critique of Two Expert Witnesses,' which compares and contrasts the opposing academic discourse of two Native Studies scholars in a legal case concerning the rights of Heiltsuk people to herring roe fisheries on the central British Columbia coast (Pryce 1992).

2 The Crown's expert witness in this case, Sheila Robinson, was educated as a cultural geographer; Chief Justice Allan McEachern nevertheless accepted her testimony as anthropological evidence.

References

Unattributed quotations come from fieldnotes taken between December 1993 and May 1998.

Aberle, David F. 1959. 'The Prophet Dance and Reactions to White Contact.' *Southwestern Journal of Anthropology* 15: 74–88.

– 1966. *The Peyote Religion among the Navajo*. Viking Fund Publications in Anthropology, no. 42. New York: Wenner-Gren Foundation for Anthropological Research.

Affleck, Edward L., ed. 1976a. *Columbia River Chronicles: A History of the Kootenay District in the Nineteenth Century.* The Kootenays in Retrospect Series, vol. 1. Vancouver: Alexander Nicolls.

– 1976b. *Kootenay Pathfinders: Settlement in the Kootenay District, 1885–1920.* The Kootenays in Retrospect Series, vol. 2. Vancouver: Alexander Nicolls.

– 1976c. *Kootenay Yesterdays.* The Kootenays in Retrospect Series, vol. 3. Vancouver: Alexander Nicolls.

– 1978. *Kootenay Lake Chronicles.* The Kootenays in Retrospect Series, vol. 4. Vancouver: Alexander Nicolls.

Alexie, Sherman. 1996. *Reservation Blues.* New York: Warner.

Allard, Jason O. 1926. 'Adventures of Jason Allard as Commanding Officer in Trading Post just Sixty Years Ago.' *Vancouver Province.* 19 September.

Anastasio, Angelo. 1974. *Ethnohistory of the Spokan Indians.* Petitioners Exhibit 180. Indian Claims Commission Docket 47. New York: Garland Press.

Anderson, Benedict. 1983. *Imagined Communities.* London: Verso.

Arrowsmith, Aaron. 1814. *A Map Exhibiting all the New Discoveries in the Interior Parts of North America.* 1785. Additions to 1814. National Archives of Canada, Ottawa.

Arrowsmith, John. 1859. *A Map Showing Portions of British Columbia and Vancouver*

Island with Portions of the United States and Hudson's Bay Territories. Hudson's Bay Company Archives, Winnipeg.

Baker, Bonnie. 1989. 'Indians Claim Ancestors at Vallican.' *Nelson Daily News,* June.

Bakhtin, Mikhail M. 1981. 'Forms of Time and of the Chronotope in the Novel: Notes toward a Historical Poetics.' In Michael Holquist, ed., *The Dialogic Imagination,* 84–258. Austin: University of Texas Press.

Barkley, Bill. 1990. Letter from Bill Barkley, Director of Royal British Columbia Museum, to members of the Sinixt/Arrow Lakes Band. 1 February.

Barth, Frederik. 1969. *Ethnic Groups and Boundaries: The Social Organization of Cultural Difference.* Boston: Little and Brown.

Basso, Keith H. 1984. '"Stalking with Stories": Names, Places, and Moral Narratives among the Western Apache.' In Edward M. Bruner, ed., *Text, Play, and Story: The Construction and Reconstruction of Self and Society,* 19–55. 1983 Proceedings of the American Ethnological Society. Washington, DC: American Ethnological Society.

Beal, Merrill. 1971. *'I Will Fight No More Forever': Chief Joseph and the Nez Perce War.* Seattle: University of Washington Press.

Belyea, Barbara, ed. 1994. Introduction. In David Thompson, *Columbia Journals,* ix–xxiv. Montreal and Kingston: McGill-Queen's University Press.

Bergeron, J.G.H. 1915. Letter from J.G.H. Bergeron, Privy Council, to Secretary of State. Victoria. 25 March.

Berkhofer, Robert F., Jr. 1978. *The White Man's Indian: Images of the American Indian from Columbus to the Present.* New York: Vintage Books.

Bloch, Maurice. n.d. 'Time, Narratives, and the Multiplicity of Representations of the Past.' Unpublished manuscript.

Bloodworth, Jessie A. 1959. 'Human Resources Survey of the Colville Confederated Tribe.' Unpublished report prepared for the Bureau of Indian Affairs Portland Area Office, Colville Agency, Washington.

Boas, Franz, ed. 1930. Preface. In James Teit, 'The Salishan Tribes of the Western Plateau.' *Forty-Fifth Annual Report of the Bureau of American Ethnology,* 25–6.

Bouchard, Randy, and Dorothy Kennedy. 1984. 'Indian Land Use and Occupancy in the Franklin D. Roosevelt Lake Area of Washington State.' Unpublished manuscript prepared for the Colville Confederated Tribes and the United States Bureau of Reclamation.

– 1985. 'Lakes Indian Ethnography and History.' Unpublished manuscript prepared for the BC Heritage Conservation Branch, Victoria.

– 1997. 'Ethnography and Ethnohistory of the Keenleyside Power Plant Project Study Area.' Unpublished manuscript prepared for the Columbia Power Corporation, Victoria.

Boyd, Robert. 1994. 'The Pacific Northwest Measles Epidemic of 1847–1848.' *Oregon Historical Quarterly* 95(1): 6–47.

British Columbia. 1872. *Map of British Columbia, being a Geographical Division of the Indians of the Province according to their Nationality or Dialect.* Victoria: Office of Superintendent of Indian Affairs.

– 1916. *Report of the Royal Commission on Indian Affairs for the Province of British Columbia.* Vol. 2. Victoria: Acme Press.

British Columbia Heritage Conservation Branch. 1982. 'Vallican Archaeologcial Site DjQ j 1, Vallican, B.C.' Unpublished manuscript.

Brown, Dee. 1971. *Bury My Heart at Wounded Knee: An Indian History of the American West.* New York: Holt, Rinehart and Winston.

Brown, Joseph Epes. 1982. 'Time and Process.' In *The Spiritual Legacy of the American Indian,* 115–21. New York: Crossroad.

Burgoon, Marilyn. 1997. Letter from Marilyn Burgoon of the Coalition of Supporters of the Sinixt to Paula Pryce. Winlaw, BC. January.

Burnett, Peter H. 1904. 'Recollections and Opinions of an Old Pioneer.' *Oregon Historical Quarterly* 5(1): 64–99.

Burns, Robert Ignatius. 1966. *The Jesuits and the Indian Wars of the Northwest.* New Haven: Yale University Press.

Canada's Future Forest Alliance. 1997. *British Columbia: A Major Factor in the Canadian Brazil of the North.* Newsletter of Canada's Future Forest Alliance. New Denver, BC. April.

Catholic Church Records. 1972. *Catholic Church Records of the Pacific Northwest: Vancouver.* Vol. 1. Translated by Mikell De Lores Wormell Warner. Annotated by Harriet Duncan Munnick. St Paul's, Oreg.: French Prairie Press.

Casey, Edward S. 1987. *Remembering: A Phenomenological Study.* Bloomington: Indiana University Press.

Chance, David H. 1973. *Influences of the Hudson's Bay Company on the Native Cultures of the Colvile District.* Northwest Anthropological Research Notes. Memoir no. 2. vol. 7(1), pt 2. Moscow, Idaho.

Chatters, James C. 1989. 'Pacifism and the Organization of Conflict on the Plateau of Northwestern America.' In D. Tkaczuk and B. Vivian, eds., *Cultures in Conflict: Current Archaeological Perspectives,* 241–52. Proceedings of the Twentieth Annual Conference of the Archaeological Association of the University of Calgary. Calgary: University of Calgary Archaeological Association.

Christie, Alexander 1914. 'Statement of Alexander Christie or Christian of Mouth of Kootenay River, B.C., to the Royal Commissioner of Indian Reserves.' 25 June.

– 1915. Letter from Alec Christie or Christian to Indian Agent Megraw. Bossburg, Wash. 25 June.

Christie, Antoine. 1912. Letter from Antoine Christie or Christian to Indian
    Affairs. Castlegar, BC. 9 May.
Clifford, James 1997. *Routes: Travel and Translation in the Late Twentieth Century.*
    Cambridge: Harvard University Press.
Colville Confederated Tribes. 1990. Memorandum from Cultural Resource Com-
    mittee to Colville Business Council. 17 September.
Connerton, Paul. 1989. *How Societies Remember.* Cambridge: Cambridge University
    Press.
Cox, Ross. 1957 [1831]. *The Columbia River, or Scenes and Adventures during a Resi-
    dence of Six Years on the Western Side of the Rocky Mountains among Various Tribes of
    Indians hitherto Unknown.* Edited by Edgar I. Stewart and Jane R. Stewart. Nor-
    man: University of Oklahoma Press.
Dawson, George M. 1892. 'Notes on the Shuswap People of British Columbia.'
    Proceedings and Transactions of the Royal Society of Canada for the Year 1891, 9: 3–44.
    Montreal.
de Aguayo, Anna. 1987. 'On Power and Prophecy: A Nineteenth Century Prophet
    Movement Amongst the Carrier Indians of Bulkley River, British Columbia,
    Canada.' Unpublished manuscript.
De Smet, Pierre-Jean. 1905. *Life, Letters and Travels of Father Pierre-Jean De Smet, S.J.,
    1801–1873.* Edited by H.M. Chittenden and A.T. Richardson. Vols. 1–4. New
    York: Francis P. Harper.
– 1993. [c. 1842–8]. 'Map of Northern Rocky Mountains and Plateau.' In Jacque-
    line Peterson and Laura Peers, *Sacred Encounters: Father De Smet and the Indians of
    Rocky Mountain West,* 118–19. The De Smet Project, Washington State Univer-
    sity. Norman: University of Oklahoma Press.
Diomedi, Alexander. 1978. *Sketches of Indian Life in the Pacific Northwest.* Edited by
    Edward J. Kowrach. Fairfield, Wash.: Ye Galleon Press.
Dubois, Cora. 1938. *The Feather Cult of the Middle Columbia.* General Series in
    Anthropology, no. 7. Menasha, Wis.: George Banta.
Duff, Wilson. 1969. *The Indian History of British Columbia: The Impact of the White
    Man.* Anthropology in British Columbia Memoir no. 5. vol. 1. Victoria: Royal
    British Columbia Museum.
Dyen, I. 1962. 'The Lexicostatistically Determined Relationships of a Language
    Group.' *International Journal of American Linguistics* 28: 153–61.
Eldridge, Morley. 1984. 'Vallican Archaeological Site (DjQ j 1): A Synthesis and
    Management Report.' Unpublished non-permit report prepared for the BC
    Heritage Conservation Branch, Victoria.
Eliade, Mircea. 1954. *The Myth of the Eternal Return or, Cosmos and History.* Bollingen
    Series 46. Princeton: Princeton University Press.
Elmendorf, William W. 1935–6. 'Lakes Ethnographic Fieldnotes.' Unpublished
    manuscript.

Fentress, James, and Chris Wickham. 1992. *Social Memory.* Oxford: Blackwell.

Fisher, Robin. 1977. *Contact and Conflict: Indian-European Relations in British Columbia, 1774–1890.* Vancouver: University of British Columbia Press.

Fogelson, Raymond D. 1985. 'Night Thoughts on Native American Social History.' *The Impact of Indian History on the Teaching of United States History: Chicago Conference,* 67–89. Occasional Papers in Curriculum Series, no. 3. D'Arcy McNickle Center for the History of the American Indian. Chicago: Newberry Library.

– 1989. 'The Ethnohistory of Events and Nonevents.' *Ethnohistory* 36(2): 133–47.

Francis, Daniel. 1992. *The Imaginary Indian: The Image of the Indian in Canadian Culture.* Vancouver: Arsenal Pulp Press.

Frank, Andre Gunder, and Barry K. Gills, eds. 1993. *The World System: Five Hundred Years or Five Thousand.* New York: Routledge.

Galbraith, John S. 1957. *The Hudson's Bay Company as an Imperial Factor: 1821–1869.* Toronto: University of Toronto Press.

Galbraith, R.L.T. 1914. 'Examination of Indian Agent Galbraith before the Royal Commission on Indian Affairs for the Province of British Columbia.' Victoria. 28 October.

Galois, R.M. 1996. 'Measles, 1847–1850: The First Modern Epidemic in British Columbia.' *BC Studies* 109: 31–43.

Garth, Thomas R. 1964. 'Early Nineteenth Century Tribal Relations in the Columbia Plateau.' *Southwestern Journal of Anthropology* 20(1): 43–57.

Geertz, Armin W. 1994. *The Invention of Prophecy: Continuity and Meaning in Hopi Indian Religion.* Berkeley: University of California Press.

Gidley, M. 1979. *With One Sky above Us: Life on an Indian Reservation at the Turn of the Century.* Windward: Webb and Bower.

– 1981. *Kopet: A Documentary Narrative of Chief Joseph's Last Years.* Seattle: University of Washington Press.

Gisday Wa, and Delgam Uukw. 1987. *The Spirit in the Land: the Opening Statement of the Gitksan and Wet'suwet'en Hereditary Chiefs in the Supreme Court of British Columbia, May 11, 1987.* Gabriola, BC: Reflections.

Glassley, Ray H. 1953. *Pacific Northwest Indian Wars.* Portland: Binfords and Mort.

Gordillo, Gastón. 1992. 'Cazadores – Recolectores y Cosecheros: Subordinación al Capital y Reproducción Social entre los Tobas del Oeste de Formosa.' In H. Trinchero, D. Piccinini, and G. Gordillo, *Capitalismo y Grupos Indígenas en el Chaco Centro-occidental,* 13–191. Buenos Aires: CEAL.

– 1997. Personal communication.

Gordon, J.H. 1963. Letter from J.H. Gordon, Acting Director of the Department of Citizenship and Immigration, Indian Affairs Branch, to Mr Herbert W. Herridge, M.P. 19 November.

Graham, Clara. 1945. *Fur and Gold in the Kootenays.* Vancouver: Wrigley.

– 1963. *This Was the Kootenay.* Vancouver: Evergreen Press.

– 1971. *Kootenay Mosaic.* Vancouver: Evergreen Press.

Gunn, Celia M. 1989. Letter from Celia M. Gunn, Coordinator of Vallican Archaeological Park Society, to Mario George, member of the Osoyoos Indian Band
Specific Land Claims Committee. 5 September.

Gunn, Celia M., and Laurie Morgan. 1989. Letter from Celia M. Gunn and Laurie
Morgan, representatives of the Vallican Archaeological Park Society, to Alan
Hoover, Chief of Anthropological Collections, Royal British Columbia
Museum. 26 November.

Gunn, N. 1969. *The Silver Darlings.* London: Faber and Faber.

Gupta, Akhil, and James Ferguson. 1992. 'Beyond "Culture": Space, Identity, and
the Politics of Difference.' *Cultural Anthropology* 7(1): 6–23.

Haines, Aubrey L. 1991. *An Elusive Victory: The Battle of Big Hole.* West Glacier,
Mont.: Glacier Natural History Association.

Hamilton, Suzy. 1992. 'Sinixt Hope to Rebury Remains.' *Vancouver Province,* 17 May.

Herskovits, Melville J. 1938. *Acculturation: The Study of Culture Contact.* New York:
J.J. Augustin.

Hewitt, Cliff. 1989. Letter from Cliff Hewitt, Manager of British Columbia Heritage Trust, to Yvonne Swan. 20 November.

Highwater, Jamake. 1981. *The Primal Mind: Vision and Reality in Indian America.*
New York: Harper and Row.

Hildebrand, Dale, and Shona MacLachlan, eds. 1997. *Friends of the Innu Newsletter*
1(1). Canadian Environmental Defence Fund.

Hirst, Abraham. 1914. Letter from Abraham Hirst, Justice of the Peace, to Indian
Affairs. Syringa Creek, BC. 6 June.

Hogan, Mike. 1991. 'Arrow Lakes Repatriate Their Ancestors.' *Grand Forks Gazette,*
9 October.

Hubert, Jane. 1989. 'A Proper Place for the Dead: A Critical Review of the
"Reburial" Issue.' *Journal of Indigenous Studies* 1(1): 27–62.

Hudson's Bay Company Archives. 1939. 'Fort Shepherd.' Unpublished manuscript.

Imhoff, Sharlene. 1993a. 'No Longer on the Shelf: Comments by St. Mary's Band
Chief Sophie Pierre on the Past, the Future, and the Suffering in Between.'
Castlegar Sun, 24 November.

– 1993b. 'Ktunaxa Chief Fighting Back.' *Trail Times,* 9 December.

James, Marilyn, and Robert Watt. 1994. *Presentation to Dr. Miguel Alfonso Martinez,
United Nations Special Rapporteur for the U.N. Study on Treaties and Agreements with
Indigenous Peoples.* Seattle: Daybreak Star Cultural Centre.

Johnson, Kate. 1951. *Pioneer Days of Nakusp and the Arrow Lakes.* Nakusp, BC.

Johnson, Olga W. 1969. *Flathead and Kootenay: The Rivers, the Tribes, and the Regional Traders.* Glendale, Calif.: Arthur H. Clark.

Jorgenson, Joseph G. 1969. *Salish Language and Culture: A Statistical Analysis of Internal Relationships, History, and Evolution.* Bloomington: Indiana University Press.

Kehoe, Alice Beck. 1981. *North American Indians: A Comprehensive Account.* Englewood Cliffs, NJ: Prentice-Hall.

– 1989. *The Ghost Dance: Ethnohistory and Revitalization.* Toronto: Holt, Rinehart and Winston.

Kent, Susan. 1980. 'Pacifism – A Myth of the Plateau.' *Northwest Anthropological Research Notes* 14(2): 125–34.

Kerkhoff, Karen. 1997a. 'Renewing Links to the Past.' *Castlegar Sun,* 22 October.

– 1997b. 'Storyteller Urges Tribes to Say No to Exploitation.' *Castlegar Sun,* 22 October.

Kroeber, Alfred L. 1963 [1939]. *Cultural and Natural Areas of Native North America.* Berkeley: University of California Press.

Lake, Randall A. 1991. 'Between Myth and History: Enacting Time in Native American Protest Rhetoric.' *The Quarterly Journal of Speech* 77(2): 123–51.

Lakin, Ruth. 1976. *Kettle River Country: Early Days along the Kettle River.* Orient, Wash.: Statesman-Examiner.

Linton, Ralph. 1943. 'Nativistic Movements.' *American Anthropologist* 45: 230–40.

McDougall, John. 1910. Letter from John McDougall, Superintendent General of Indian Affairs. Ottawa. 8 January.

McEachern, Allan. 1991. 'Reasons for Judgment.' *Delgamuukw v. HRMTQ.* Smithers: British Columbia Supreme Court. Registry No. 0843.

McMillan, Alan D. 1988. *Native Peoples and Cultures of Canada: An Anthropological Overview.* Vancouver: Douglas and McIntyre.

Martin, Calvin, ed. 1987. *The American Indian and the Problem of History.* New York: Oxford University Press.

Megraw, A. 1915a. Letter from A. Megraw, Inspector of Indian Agencies, to Alec Christian. Vernon, BC. 14 June.

– 1915b. Letter from A. Megraw, Inspector of Indian Agencies, to Assistant Deputy and Secretary, Department of Indian Affairs, Ottawa. Vernon, BC. 24 July.

Miller, Christopher L. 1985. *Prophetic Worlds: Indians and Whites on the Columbia Plateau.* New Brunswick, NJ: Rutgers University Press.

Miller, Jay. 1989. 'Mourning Dove: The Author as Cultural Mediator.' In James A. Clifton, ed. *Being and Becoming Indian: Biographical Studies of North American Frontiers,* 160–82. Chicago: Dorsey Press.

Mohs, Gordon W. 1982a. 'Archaeological Investigations at the Vallican Site (DjQ j 1), Slocan Valley, Southeastern British Columbia.' Unpublished manuscript.

– 1982b. 'Prehistoric Settlement Patterns in the Columbia/Lakes Region of Southeastern British Columbia and Northeastern Washington.' Unpublished manuscript.

– 1983. 'Recent Archaeological Investigations at the Vallican Site (DjQj 1), Slocan Valley, Southeastern British Columbia.' Unpublished manuscript presented at the 36th Annual Northwest Anthropological Conference. Boise State University. Boise, Idaho.

– 1988. Letter from Gordon W. Mohs to Rick Foulger, President, Vallican Archaeological Park Society. 31 October.

Momaday, N. Scott. 1976. 'Native American Attitudes to the Environment.' In W.H. Capps, ed., *Seeing with a Native Eye*, 79–85. New York: Harper and Row.

Mooney, James. 1896. 'The Ghost Dance Religion and the Sioux Outbreak of 1890.' *Bureau of American Ethnology Annual Report* 14: 641–1110.

– 1928. *The Aboriginal Population of America North of Mexico.* Smithsonian Miscellaneous Collections. 80: 7.

Moore, R.I. 1992. Editor's Preface. In James Fentress and Chris Wickham, *Social Memory*, vii–viii. Oxford: Blackwell.

Morran, John. 1997a. 'Awakening the Land.' *Castlegar Sun*, 1 October.

– 1997b. 'Treaty Negotiations Move Slowly Past Midway Point.' *Castlegar Sun*, 5 November.

Morris, Pam, ed. 1994. *The Bakhtin Reader: Selected Writings by Bakhtin, Medvedev, and Voloshinov.* London: Edward Arnold.

Mourning Dove (Christine Quintasket). 1990. *Mourning Dove: A Salishan Autobiography.* Edited by Jay Miller. Lincoln: University of Nebraska Press.

Nelson Daily News. 1911a. 'May Be Case of Foul Play: Body of Indian Woman Found near Castlegar, Circumstances Are Mysterious.' 3 March.

– 1911b. 'Exposure Was Cause of Death: Indian Woman Died from Cold, following Fall Down Cliff – No Evidence of Violence.' 4 March.

Norman, Ron. 1995a. 'First Nation Includes Castlegar Airport in Land Claim.' *Castlegar Sun*, 14 June.

– 1995b. 'Castlegar Area Listed on First Nations' Map.' *Castlegar Sun*, 21 June.

– 1995c. 'Native Front.' *Castlegar Sun*, 21 June.

Norris, John. 1995. *Historic Nelson: The Early Years.* Lantsville, BC: Oolichan Books.

North American Boundary Commission. c. 1861. 'Sinyakwateen Depot.' North American Boundary Commission. Unpublished photograph. National Archives of Canada, Ottawa.

Nuttall, Mark. 1992. *Arctic Homeland: Kinship, Community, and Development in Northwest Greenland.* London: Belhaven Press and Scott Polar Research Institute, University of Cambridge.

Overholt, Thomas W. 1974. 'The Ghost Dance of 1890 and the Nature of the Prophetic Process.' *Ethnohistory* 21(1): 37–63.

Parker, Arthur. 1913. *The Code of Handsome Lake, the Seneca Prophet*. New York State Museum Bulletin No. 163. Albany: New York State Museum.

Pearce, R.H. 1953. *The Savages of America: A Study of the Indian and the Idea of Civilization*. Baltimore: Johns Hopkins University Press.

Peterson, Jacqueline, and Laura Peers. 1993. *Sacred Encounters: Father De Smet and the Indians of Rocky Mountain West*. The De Smet Project, Washington State University. Norman: University of Oklahoma Press.

Pierre, Sophie. 1990. Letter from Sophie Pierre, Area Coordinator of the Kootenay Indian Area Council, to Bob Campbell. 29 May.

Pryce, Paula. 1992. 'The Manipulation of Culture and History: A Critique of Two Expert Witnesses.' *Native Studies Review* 8(1): 35–46.

Québec Mission. 1955. *Notices and Voyages of the Famed Québec Mission to the Pacific Northwest: 1838–1847*. Portland: Oregon Historical Society.

Ray, Arthur J. 1974. *Indians in the Fur Trade*. Toronto: University of Toronto Press.

Ray, Verne F. 1933. *The Sanpoil and Nespelem: Salishan Peoples of Northeastern Washington*. University of Washington Publications in Anthropology, vol. 5. Seattle: University of Washington Press.

– 1936a. 'The Kolaskin Cult: A Prophet Movement of 1870 in Northeastern Washington.' *American Anthropologist* 38: 67–75.

– 1936b. 'Native Villages and Groupings of the Columbia Basin.' *Pacific Northwest Quarterly* 27(2): 99–152.

– 1937. 'The Bluejay Character in the Plateau Spirit Dance.' *American Anthropologist* 39: 593–601.

– 1939. *Cultural Relations in the Plateau of Northwestern America*. Publications of the Frederick Webb Hodge Anniversary Publication Fund, vol. 3. Los Angeles: The Southwest Museum Administrator of the Fund.

– 1960. 'The Columbia Indian Confederacy: a League of Central Plateau Tribes.' In Stanley Diamond, ed., *Culture and History: Essays in Honor of Paul Radin*, 771–89. New York: Columbia University Press.

– 1975. 'Aboriginal Economy and Polity of the Lakes (Senijextee) Indians.' In *Final Report Colville Interpretive Theme*. Vol. 2, 127–63. Unpublished manuscript for the Colville Confederated Tribes. Nespelem, Wash. Adapted from an original manuscript prepared in 1947 from fieldnotes taken in 1931 and 1944.

Reed, Madame Justice B. 1994. 'Reasons for Order.' *Robert Watt v. E. Liebelt and The Minister of Citizenship and Immigration*. Federal Court of Canada. No. IMM-6881-93. 21 July.

Reichwein, Jeffrey C. 1990. *The Emergence of Native American Nationalism in the Columbia Plateau.* New York: Garland.

Ridington, Robin. 1990. 'Cultures in Conflict: The Problems of Discourse.' In *Little Bit Know Something: Stories in a Language of Anthropology,* 186–205. Vancouver: Douglas and McIntyre.

Rodlie, Lana. 1993. 'Forum.' *Environmentally Speaking.* Lethbridge. 30 July.

Romero, Francis Louis. 1990. Unpublished document declaring hereditary lineage of the Sinixt chieftainship of Francis Louis Romero. Victoria. 25 September.

Ross, Alexander. 1855. *The Fur Hunters of the Far West.* Vol. 2. London: Smith, Elder, and Company.

– 1966 [1849]. *Adventures of the First Settlers on the Columbia River.* Ann Arbor: University Microfilms.

Ross, John Allan. 1968. 'Political Conflict on the Colville Reservation.' *Northwest Anthropological Research Notes* 2(1): 29–91.

Royal British Columbia Museum. 1990. 'Transfer of Title between Royal British Columbia Museum and the descendants of the Arrow Lakes people representing the Okanagan Tribal Council.' Victoria. 25 September.

Royal Commission on Aboriginal Peoples. 1996. 'The State of Languages.' *Gathering Strength.* Vol. 3. Ottawa: Royal Commission on Aboriginal Peoples.

Ruby, Robert H., and John A. Brown. 1986. *A Guide to the Indian Tribes of the Pacific Northwest.* Norman: University of Oklahoma Press.

– 1989. *Dreamer-Prophets of the Columbia Plateau: Smohalla and Skolaskin.* Norman: University of Oklahoma Press.

Sahlins, Marshall. 1981. *Historical Metaphors and Mythical Realities: Structure in the Early History of the Sandwich Islands Kingdom.* Association for Social Anthropology in Oceania. Special Publication No. 1. Ann Arbor: University of Michigan Press.

– 1993. 'Goodbye to *Tristes Tropes*: Ethnography in the Context of Modern World History.' *Journal of Modern History* 65(1): 1–25.

Schama, Simon. 1995. *Landscape and Memory.* Toronto: Random House.

Scott, Leslie M. 1928. 'Indian Diseases as Aids to Pacific Northwest Settlement.' *Oregon Historical Quarterly* 29: 144–61.

Scott, W.B., and E.J. Crossman. 1973. *Freshwater Fishes of Canada.* Bulletin 184. Ottawa: Fisheries Research Board of Canada.

Sherbinin, J.W. 1912. Letter from J.W. Sherbinin, Doukhobor Society, to R.L.T. Galbraith, Indian Agent. 7 September.

Simpson, George. 1931. *Fur Trade and Empire: George Simpson's Journal.* Edited by Frederick Merk. Cambridge: Harvard University Press.

– 1947 [1825]. *Part of the Dispatch from George Simpson, Esq. Governor of Ruperts Land*

to the Governor and Committee of the Hudson's Bay Company London. Edited by
E.E. Rich. London: Hudson's Bay Company Record Society.

Sinixt/Arrow Lakes Band. 1989a. 'Arrow Lakes Indian Band Meeting Minutes.'
Keller, Wash. 16 June.

– 1989b. Press Release. 19 September.

– 1996a. *Guardians of the Rainforest: Ancient Legacy, Perpetual Growth, Sacred Responsibility: The Sinixt Aboriginal People Come Home.* Poster sponsored by Mountain
Equipment Co-op, Patagonia, and Alton Jones. Photograph by Garth Lenz.

– 1996b. 'The Vallican Camp of the Sinixt/Arrow Lakes Peoples.' Unpublished
manuscript.

– n.d. 'Sinixt Cultural Zones.' Unpublished manuscript.

Slotkin, J.S. 1975. *The Peyote Religion: A Study in Indian–White Relations.* New York:
Octagon Books.

Smith, Paul Chaat. 1994. 'Home of the Brave.' *C Magazine* (Summer): 31–42.

Smyth, Fred J. 1938. *Tales of the Kootenays.* Cranbrook: Courier.

Spier, Leslie. 1935. *The Prophet Dance of the Northwest and Its Derivatives: The Source of
the Ghost Dance.* General Series in Anthropology, no. 1. Menasha, Wis.: George
Banta.

– 1936. *Tribal Distribution in Washington.* General Series in Anthropology, no. 3.
Menasha, Wis.: George Banta.

Spier, Leslie, Wayne Suttles, and Melville J. Herskovits. 1959. 'Comment on
Aberle's Thesis of Deprivation.' *Southwestern Journal of Anthropology* 15: 84–8.

Sprague, Roderick. 1991. 'A Bibliography of James A. Teit.' *Northwest Anthropological Research Notes* 25(1): 103–15.

Stewart, Omer C. 1987. *Peyote Religion: A History.* Norman: University of Oklahoma
Press.

Strong, William D. 1945. 'The Occurrence and Wider Implications of a "Ghost
Cult" on the Columbia River Suggested by Carvings in Wood, Bone, and Stone.'
American Anthropologist 47(2): 244–61.

Supreme Court of Canada. 1997. 'Reasons for Judgment.' *Delgamuukw v. HMTQ.*
Ottawa: Supreme Court of Canada. Registry File No. 23799. 11 December.

Suttles, Wayne. 1957. 'The Plateau Prophet Dance among the Coast Salish.' *Southwestern Journal of Anthropology* 13: 352–96.

Swan, Yvonne. 1989. Letter to the editor. *Nelson Daily News.* 7 September.

Tedlock, Barbara. 1983. 'A Phenomenological Approach to Religious Change in
Highland Guatemala.' In Carl Kendall, John Hawkins, and Laurel Bossen, eds.,
Heritage of Conquest: Thirty Years Later, 235–46. Albuquerque: University of New
Mexico Press.

Teit, James. 1909a. 'Lakes Ethnographic Fieldnotes and Letters to Franz Boas, May
20, 1909 and July 17, 1909.' Provincial Archives of British Columbia, Victoria.

- 1909b. *The Shuswap*. American Museum of Natural History Memoirs, no. 4, Part 7.
- 1910–13. 'Notes to Maps of the Pacific Northwest.' Unpublished manuscript.
- 1912. Letter from James Teit to Secretary General of Indian Affairs. 16 May.
- 1930. 'The Salishan Tribes of the Western Plateaus.' Edited by Franz Boas. *Forty-Fifth Annual Report of the Bureau of American Ethnology*, 25–396.

Tennant, Paul. 1990. *Aboriginal Peoples and Politics: The Indian Land Question in British Columbia, 1849–1989*. Vancouver: University of British Columbia Press.

Thompson, David. 1971. *Travels in Western North America, 1784–1812*. Edited by Victor G. Hopwood. Toronto: Macmillan.

- 1994 [c. 1810]. *Columbia Journals*. Edited by Barbara Belyea. Montreal and Kingston: McGill-Queen's University Press.

Thompson, E.P. 1967. 'Time, Work-Discipline, and Industrial Capitalism.' *Past and Present* 38: 56–97.

Toelken, Barre. 1976. 'Seeing with a Native Eye: How Many Sheep Will It Hold?' In W.H. Capps, ed., *Seeing with a Native Eye*, 9–24. New York: Harper and Row.

Turnbull, Christopher J. 1977. *Archaeology and Ethnohistory in the Arrow Lakes, Southeastern British Columbia*. National Museum of Man Series. Archaeological Survey of Canada Paper No. 65. Ottawa: National Museums of Canada.

Turner, Nancy J., Randy Bouchard, and Dorothy Kennedy. 1980. *Ethnobotany of the Okanagan-Colville Indians of British Columbia and Washington*. Occasional Papers of the British Columbia Provincial Museum, no. 21. Victoria: British Columbia Provincial Museum.

Turney-High, Harry Holbert. 1941. *Ethnography of the Kutenai*. Memoirs of the American Anthropological Association, no. 56. Menasha, Wis.

Valhalla Society. 1993. *Visitor Guide to the White Grizzly (Pic-ha-kee-lowna) Wilderness*. New Denver, BC.

Valhalla Wilderness Society and Slocan Valley Watershed Alliance. 1996. *Our Forest, Our Home*. Newsletter of the Valhalla Wilderness Society and the Slocan Valley Watershed Alliance. Edited by Anne Sherrod. New Denver, BC.

Vecsey, Christopher and Robert W. Venables, eds. 1980. *American Indian Environments: Ecological Issues in Native American History*. Syracuse: Syracuse University Press.

Victor, Frances Fuller. 1891. *The Early Indian Wars of Oregon*. Salem, Oreg.: F.C. Baker.

Vizenor, Gerald. 1986. 'Bone Courts: The Rights and Narrative Representation of Tribal Bones.' *American Indian Quarterly* 10(4): 319–31.

Walker, Deward E., Jr. 1969. 'New Light on the Prophet Dance Controversy.' *Ethnohistory* 16: 245–55.

Wallace, Anthony F.C. 1956. 'Revitalization Movements.' *American Anthropologist* 58: 264–81.

Walter, Jess. 1991. 'Tribe Buries Bones, but not Its Past.' *Spokesman-Review and Spokane Chronicle.* 22 September.

Watson, James L., and Evelyn S. Rawski, eds. 1988. *Death Ritual in Late Imperial and Modern China.* Berkeley: University of California Press.

Watt, Robert. 1993. 'Testimonial given by Robert Watt, Sinixt/Arrow Lakes Nation also known as the Sa-al-tkw't.' Presented at International Testimonials on the Violations of Indigenous Sovereignty Rights. Albuquerque, NMex. 9 December.

Webber, Harold. 1975. *People and Places.* Castlegar: Cotinneh Books.

Weir, D.A. 1973. Letter from D.A. Weir, District Superintendent of Economic Development, Kootenay-Okanagan District, to D.G. Marshall. Vernon, BC. 10 December.

Whitehead, Margaret, ed. 1988. *They Call Me Father: Memoirs of Father Nicolas Coccola.* Vancouver: University of British Columbia Press.

Whorf, Benjamin Lee. 1983 [1941]. 'The Relation of Habitual Thought and Behavior to Language.' In Leslie Spier, A. Irving Hallowell, and Stanley S. Newman, eds. *Language, Culture, and Personality: Essays in Memory of Edward Sapir,* 75–93. Westport: Greenwood Press.

Wickwire, Wendy. 1993. 'Women in Ethnography: The Research of James A. Teit.' *Ethnohistory* 40(4): 539–62.

Williams, Jean H. 1982. 'Faunal Remains from the Vallican Site (DjQj 1) in Southeastern British Columbia.' Unpublished manuscript.

Wilson, Charles. 1866. 'Report on the Indian Tribes inhabiting the Country in the Vicinity of the Forty-ninth Parallel of North Latitude.' *Transactions of the Ethnological Society of London.* Vol. 4, 275–332. London: John Murray.

– 1970. *Mapping the Frontier: Charles Wilson's Diary of the Survey of the 49th Parallel, 1858–1862, while Secretary of the British Boundary Commission.* Edited by George F.G. Stanley. Toronto: Macmillan.

Wren, Patricia. 1989. 'Indians Vow Fight to Halt Bulldozers at Ancestral Site.' *Wenatchee World.* 1 September.

Index

Aberle, David, 74, 75–6, 130, 169n5
'aboriginal,' 157n4
advocacy, 142–6
agency, 81, 84
agriculture: American facilitation of,
53; Jesuit facilitation of, 46; necessity of, 53; resistance to, 126; Sinixt,
47, 53, 63, 66, 136–7
Alexie, Sherman, 165–6n13
Allard, Jason O., 24, 167n19
Anastasio, Angelo, 18
ancestors: and relationship with living,
11, 109, 113–14, 115–16, 117, 121,
122, 129, 133, 139–40
ancestral remains: exhumation, 4, 6,
101, 115–16; jurisdiction of, and
autonomy, 101, 102, 130; protection, 9, 134, 147; repatriation, 6,
100–2, 106, 115, 133, 146, 168n26;
symbolism of, 106. *See also* reburial;
world renewal
Anderson, Benedict, 170–1n12
anthropological gaze, 83–4
anthropology: and international border, 166n16; and politics, 145–6;
and problems of advocacy, 142–6,
172–3n1

antihistoricism, 9, 14, 20, 21, 74,
75, 83, 85–6, 89, 143–4, 160–1n16.
See also 'invented traditions';
Social Darwinism; unilineal evolu-
tionism
Apsassin v. HRMTQ, 170n8
archaeology, 116; as cultural verifica-
tion, 112; of kp'ítl'els, 65; limits of
data, 12–13; and Prophet Dance, 74;
of Vallican site, 99–100, 171n4; of
West Kootenays, 99
Army, United States, 40, 48, 50, 51,
164n9
Aropaghan, Chief Andrew, 17, 102,
125, 158n10, 163n6
Arrow Lakes, 16, 33–4, 55; Lower, 99;
social memory of, 111; Upper, 47,
52, 163–4n7, 164n9
Arrow Lakes Band, 6, 22, 101. *See also*
Sinixt Interior Salish
Arrow Lakes Historical Society, 100
Arrow Lakes Indian Reserve, 62–4,
68; desired reallocation of, 136–7;
population of, 168n24; Sinixt attitudes towards, 63; and subsistence,
137
Arrowsmith, Aaron, 17, 34